'WOAD TO THIS'
& THE CLOTH TRADE OF FROME

Carolyn Griffiths

ISBN 978-0-9930605-5-7

Design and Technical Support by Jon Stean
Typeset In Caslon Bd BT, Park Avenue BT and Calibri

Caslon Typeface designed by William Caslon (c. 1692 - 1766)

Published by the Frome Society for Local Study
For a full list of FSLS Publications please visit www.fsls.org.uk

Pre-press support provided by Darren Haine - Unity Printworks, Frome
Printed for Think Digital Books by Harrier LLC

CONTENTS

PREFACE

Writing a book was not on my list and there was no obligation, but what do you do when you find three mid 18th and early 19th century workbooks of natural dyed wool and cloth samples? These documents were the livelihood of artisan craftsmen who worked in Frome more than 250 years ago, in the town where I now live. Their dye techniques which have long since disappeared from commercial practice evolved from practical experimentation and were in use for thousands of years before the development of synthetic dyes with which we are so familiar today. Processes that first relied on successful harvests then entirely on the senses of touch, smell, look and feel learned from apprenticeships and years of experience. How remarkable then, to find six more workbooks from the same town delivered to Chancery as part of an 18th century settlement of a legacy. Books held in the archives that were unopened, protecting colours that have remained so beautiful and vibrant after hundreds of years.

The purpose of the book is one which I hope portrays the social and industrial history of the day to day working lives of ordinary people in the cloth trade. It is about the town, the workers, the dyers and the making of cloth with an emphasis on Frome's dye books of the 1700s presented in full page photographs. A book to dip into and enjoy over a cup of tea or to sit and read sections that appeal. To see the photographs of the old documents with the spelling of words that was inconsistent until standardisation in the 1800s. The letters sent to and from clothiers that are frank and full of candour, and the workhouse accounts and bankruptcy papers that portrays the destitution endured by those fallen on hard times. All of this and more are part of an industrial heritage of the cloth trade that deserves to be shared.

The archives and Frome Museum reference library hold many other documents that could add further information to this research. A review of the Quarter Sessions Cloth Inspector's Accounts for the amount of cloth produced in the area, or perhaps a comparative study of the different dye methods from the workbooks. For those who choose to try practical experimentation of the recipes, there are several books that could be consulted which provide up to date transcriptions that comply with the current health and safety standards.

ACKNOWLEDGEMENTS

I have enjoyed many research days at the county and national archives and at the local Frome museum and library. I would like to extend my thanks and appreciation to the staff who were so helpful and interested in the project. In particular Anne Buchanan and Mary Henderson at Bath Central Library and Dan Brown of Bath in Time who were as enthusiastic about the collection as I was. The assistance and copy editing by Alastair MacLeay from the Frome Society for Local Study and the encouragement from Michael McGarvie FSA. Jennie O'Kane, Diane Rouse and Brian Marshall at the Frome Museum for their generous help to find documents and artefacts. Others who also deserve mentioning include the Somerset Heritage Trust, Jane de Gruchy, archivist at Somerset Archives and Local Studies, Somerset Archaeological and Natural History Society; The Hampshire Records Office; Claire Skinner, archivist at the Wiltshire and Swindon Archives; Elizabeth Owen, the curator of the John Bright Collection, a Heritage Lottery funded project; and Hannah Dunmow, The Clothworkers' Company archivist. Finally a special thank you to Ken Rogers, author and retired archivist from Wiltshire Archives.

I am also extremely grateful for all the support provided by Jon Stean and Darren Haine, I could not have produced this book without their patient assistance and invaluable technical knowledge. www.woadtothis.com

This book is dedicated to Mick Pound, a dear friend who died too soon. He always offered the right measure of encouragement and humour 'Is there a volume two in the pipeline?' NO

CHAPTER 1

'WOAD TO THIS'

'...I was much struck in the summer before the harvest, when I rode frequently to promote the recovery of my health, at seeing such abundant provision for the wants of man in almost every field, the wheat, the barley & the oats, the potatoes, the turnips & the beans, the grass and clover, the garden produce, the wood and teasels for manufacture and the cattle upon a thousand hills. I had too often passed these bounties unnoticed!'

Diary of Thomas Bunn of Frome - 1836

'*Woad to this*' is such a curious phrase and the first line of an 18th century dye recipe book.[1] What is it, what does it mean and where does it come from? I live in the market town of Frome in Somerset and wander almost daily into the town centre walking past the Blue House, an alms house for elderly residents. An imposing building, its name adopted from the days when a Blue School was first built on the site in the 18th century and which did not close until 1921. It was originally built in the mid 1400s

1.1 Watercolour of Woad by Anne Mieke Lumsden

and endowed as an alms house by the Leversedge family then Lords of the Manor. It was rebuilt for the third time in the 1720s as a building which was occupied by fourteen poor elderly women and a blue school for twenty two boys. I was intrigued to read that in 1674, the rent from a tenement in Goose Street, Beckington was used to purchase gowns once in every three years for the alms house ladies[2] and that later a new blue gown was provided every two years[3]. The boys were clothed in the distinctive uniform of charity schools, a dark blue knee length frock coat over breeches probably tailored from cloth produced in the town.

1.2 Blue House - Frome

The indigo blue, which today is synonymous with the colour of our jeans, was produced in medieval Europe and earlier by fermenting macerated leaves of woad, *Isatis Tinctoria.* This was followed by a fermentation in the vats to convert the precursors of indigo to a soluble blue dye. *'Woad to this'* was the dyer's process by which they obtained a standard blue shade. It was the start of a fascinating project to search for answers, but instead raised far more questions. My research was broad, and the market town of Frome offered an abundance of primary sources in many archives for cloth production and commercial dyeing of wool in England. The blue dye, extracted from woad, was carted to the town as early as the 14th century and by the late Middle Ages was traded along with wool and cloth and it was still grown in the 19th century in nearby villages. The book sets out to weave across hundreds of years of the cloth and dyeing trades. First,

1.3 Charity School
WF Knapton

by describing the plant and its cultivation, then diving into the 1700s to share the everyday working documents that still survive and reveal how these occupations existed relatively unchanged until the arrival of the 19th century industrialisation. Apart from a few samples of woad dyed cloth from the 1600s, the 18th century dye receipts and letter books were the closest I came to understanding the working process of dyeing; it then made sense to return to the intertwining strands of the textile commerce from the distant past.

1.4 Woad Flower

Woad, *'Isatis Tinctoria.'* is a biennial plant of the brassicaceae family from which a blue dye can be extracted. Although indigo is not present in the plant itself it contains precursor substances in the leaves which can be dissolved in alkaline solution and reduced by fermentation to extract blue pigment which reverts to an insoluble blue in contact with oxygen. In its first year the plant produces a rosette of a mid-green oblong leaves 6 to 10 inches long with pale mid-veins. The following year it sends up a single, smooth main stem up to 5 ft tall with alternately arranged arrow shaped leaves along its length. The top then divides into numerous branches with clusters of bright yellow flowers, each one with an equal number of sepals and petals.

1.5 Woad Seed

Depending on when it is planted, it flowers between May and July. In the right soil conditions the plant is a vigorous grower, which is self-pollinating and has a long tap root. The developing lime green seeds hang down in arches from the slender flower stalks and turn bluish-black when ripe. The pendulous single seed pods about a half an inch in length are wedge shaped. When ripe, the unopened pods drop to the ground where the seed can be dispersed by the wind. The rosette of leaves

1.6 Rosette of Woad Leaves

of the first year's growth is collected for blue dyeing. It needs to be harvested promptly as it is loved by the cabbage white butterfly and the caterpillars can decimate the leaves in a few days just leaving the bare skeleton.

Woad, originated in the Middle East, while the introduction of farming brought about its migration to Europe where it was grown in some areas of Britain, including Somerset. Historically the origin for the name woad is unclear. Pliny, the Roman naturalist, referred to it as *'Glastum'*, possibly the origin of the name Glastonbury. *'Vitrum'* was its Latin name meaning both woad and glass and in Gaelic and Welsh it was called *'glas'* meaning grey-green or blue.

Dioscorides, a Greek pharmacologist and botanist in the 1st century, gave it the name *Isatis Tinctoria* which is used today. Several herbals list it for its dye and medicinal properties, one of which mentions its use '*...to stop the running out of bloude and upon fretting ulcers and rotten sores.*[4]' The herbalist, William Turner published *'Libellus de re Herbaria'* in 1538 which included a description of wild and cultivated woad and the origin of the name as Isatis or Glastum, a herb which dyers of wool use and which is commonly called *'Wad'*. As dean of Wells cathedral in 1551, he created an apothecary garden, which has been restored, where he grew medicinal and dye plants including woad and madder. Derivatives include *'goud'*, *'ode'*, and *'wad'*, however wad can also mean 'little wood' so perhaps the name Wadman could be either a man of the woods or a woad merchant. There is a traditional belief that the deep blue was used as a war-paint or tattoo by the ancient Britons to frighten their enemies. Its early use has been corroborated by excavations of the iron age settlement at Dragonby, North Lincolnshire[5], which revealed traces of woad plant matter and spindle whorls in a pit, suggesting dyeing and textile manufacture. At Beverley in Yorkshire an excavation of Viking artefacts also suggests evidence of woad dyeing along with a vessel that may have been used as a vat. While it is unconfirmed, there are several localities where it is said to be wild, one is around Guildford, another on the banks of the Severn at Tewkesbury, and a third around Cranborne Chase where in the 1590s a Salisbury clothier, George Bedford, was growing more than 100 acres.[6] Woad continued to be grown commercially for the preparation of indigo vats in Wisbech, Lincolnshire until the 1930s as it was considered the most durable colour for police uniforms.

Profitable agricultural production has always been a farming necessity and whenever economic circumstances have changed, farmers have sought to diversify their crops. Over the centuries, woad was grown intermittently as a commercial crop in England. It was heavily dependent on a temporary workforce of unskilled, itinerant workers and at harvest time it supplemented the earnings of the poorly paid cloth workers. Families earned more for a few weeks labouring in the fields than they could spinning; in turn, this created a shortage of yarn for the weavers. The crop was not generally recorded in farming almanacs because of the itinerant work force involved in its production, but an account of 1625 covering forty one acres at Milcote in Warwickshire, shows that 150 to 250 people were employed daily between May and September weeding and picking the ripe leaves.[7] Along with spinning, some parish overseers saw it as very suitable work for the poor.

Historically, the changes from arable to pasture, the quality of the dye, the prospective financial gain, and the availability of a reliable foreign supply all influenced the decision to plant woad. Information on how to grow alternative crops was widespread in the 17th century and as printed books on agriculture became available, gentlemen farmers viewed crops such as madder, woad and saffron as profitable investments. Migrant woad men contracted with the landowners for several acres of land for a period of up to three years where they set up temporary woad mills to

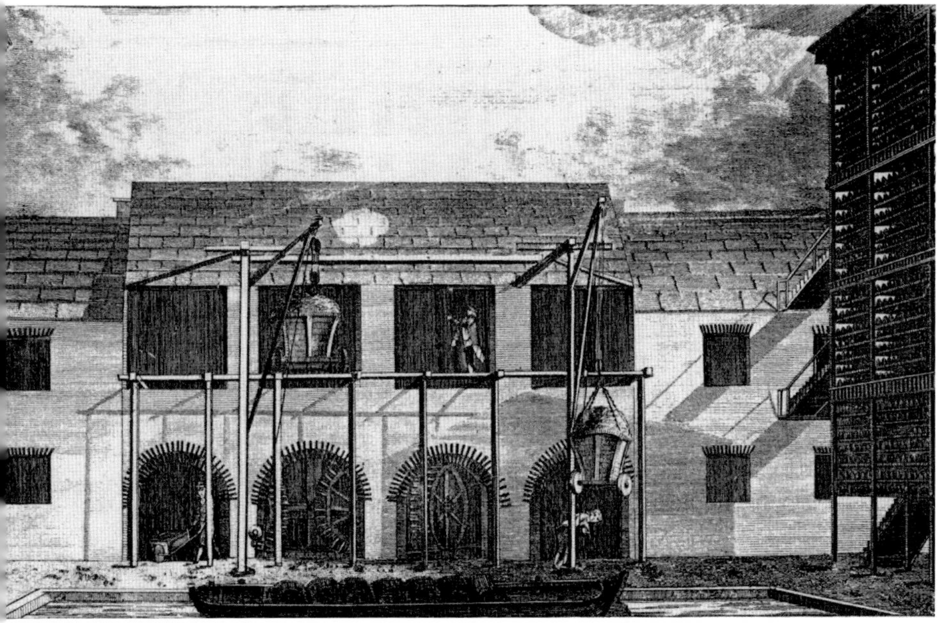

1.7 Lincolnshire Woad Buildings with Woad Apparatus - early 19th century

process the leaves. They constructed open sided drying sheds and once the land was depleted they moved to another location. By the 18th century, in the cloth producing areas of the country, woad was a potential mainstream crop, worked as part of a twelve year rotation although, in practice, the itinerant woad men continued their contractual work. An acre of land could produce a ton of woad and in a good season nearly a ton and a half.[8] Occasionally it was recorded as a tithed crop, but it seldom appears in farming records in the South West. There are some data for 1585; an enquiry reported that 605 acres of woad were grown in Somerset, 575 in Wiltshire and 1039 in Dorset.[9]

Imagine a world without blue. White for purity, black for mourning and red representing Christ's blood, dominated the early medieval period and it was not until the 12th century that the colour blue gained its popularity.[10] Crimson and scarlet red dyes were very expensive and a good strong black was difficult to achieve unless the cloth had been coloured with a base of woad dye when it was said to be *'woaded.'* Most of the population wore clothes woven from the natural colour of wool which offers grey whites through to dark browns and some were dyed red with madder. As blue became fashionable, documents suggest that the growing and processing of woad remained much the same until its use was phased out following the introduction of synthetic indigo in 1878. However, from the 1580s the purpose it served in the dyeing process changed, it was no longer used as a colourant, but as an aid to fermentation when combined with the indigo pigment extracted from the Asian plant, *Indigofera*

Tinctoria. Today, sodium dithionite has transformed how indigo is extracted from woad for small scale dyeing although traditional fermentation methods are still used.

The woad crop is described in an early 11th century transcription

> *'...In harvest one may reap; in August, September and October one may mow, set woad with a dibble, and gather home many crops.... in spring one should, if the weather permit, set madder, sow flax and woad seed.[11]'*

In the middle of the 13th century, instructions were written by Adam de Damerham a Benedictine monk of Glastonbury Abbey.

> *'In the month of March, take thy sede, and sowe it in goude londe well raked, and clene and wan it is grown eight inches longe, than reap it and grind it fine, and make a ball hereof, as much as a ferthing luv, and let them dry apon a hurdle in the sun, and then grind them again finely into powder, and then sifte it through a small ryddyrue, and the grit thereof grind it again and sift it agen as ye dyde a fore, and then lay the powder upon a fair paved floor about half fote thick, and then upon it cast water and turn and wende it with a shovel til it not be wet but not be dry but be mixed to, and then lay it up to a heap, as ye would malt till it take heat, as hot as you may suffer your hand therein. And then lay it abroad, and let the heyte pass away thereof, an lay it together again to a heap till it be as hot as it was, and then everyday do in the same wyle till it will take no more heat, and then it must be led abroad again upon a fair paved floor, and dry it with turning with*

1.8 *Indigofera Tinctoria*

1.9 *Isatis Tinctoria*

a shovel every day, till it be dry and then it is full made to go to the wodevat, and to be good blue.[12]'

An old 18th century recipe states the woad balls were of a size of a 'ferthing luv' which it has been suggested was probably a 'farthing loaf ' in a Somerset accent.[13]

Britain's climate is very damp, and like other crops, woad could be unreliable as the leaves ground in the mill to a paste had to be dried quickly to prevent them from becoming flyblown and mouldy as this could destroy an entire harvest. Documents mention that woad was grown extensively in Somerset on land owned by the abbeys of Muchelney and Glastonbury.[14] In the 18th century '...*Great quantities of the herb called woad, the ancient glastum once peculiar to the county, are raised here, in Keynsham, for the purpose of dyeing.*[15]' Both Glastonbury and Keynsham abbeys are less than twenty miles from Frome and until the dissolution, the monks were at the forefront of many agricultural and technological innovations. Travel and foreign ideas have always encouraged discussion, and the similar climate, soils and crops of the Low Countries and Northern France could have fostered trials on English land owned by the church and the manorial estates. The working knowledge would have spread to local farmers and dyers. Adam de Damerham may have stayed in Mells, the liberty owned by the Benedictine monks, on his journeys to and from Glastonbury, and shared his knowledge of the complex process with people in the local area.

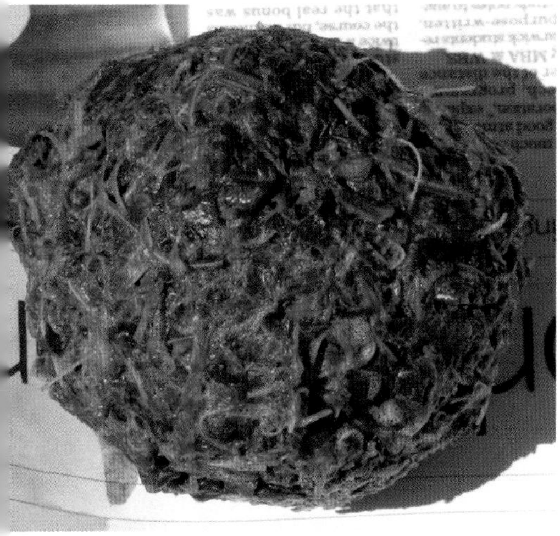

1.10 Woad Ball from Fresh Leaves

England enjoyed a flourishing demand for dyed cloth, and anecdotally woad may have been grown extensively in the early Middle Ages. By the mid 14th century, labour became scarce and expensive following the heavy death toll of the plague and land for crops, which required considerable manual labour, was turned over to pasture. Scattered outbreaks of the disease continued throughout the centuries and the knowledge to grow the crop may have been lost. However, the demand for the blue dye increased and woad was imported.

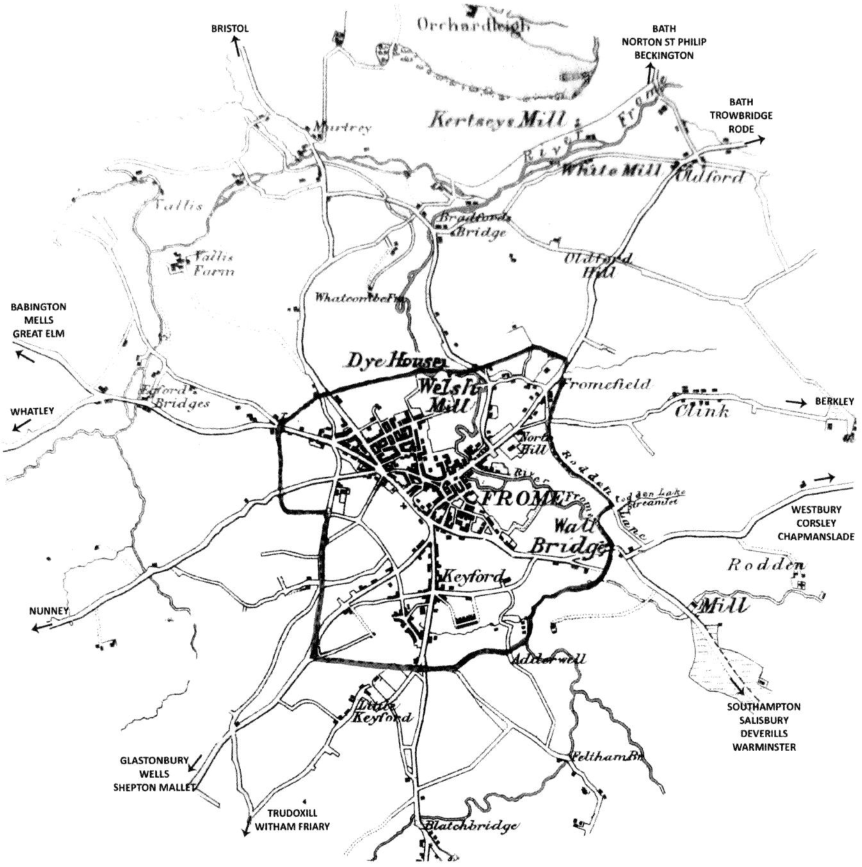

1.11 Based on 1868 Map of Frome

Woad was cultivated as a commercial crop in several countries, in particular Germany and France. It was imported to England in vast quantities between the 13th and the mid 16th century and it was also traded by Italy, Spain, Portugal and later from the Azores by John Smythe, a Bristol merchant. Price inflation and war frequently disrupted foreign imports and by the 1540s the limited availability of dyestuffs, linens and canvas created an opportunity for the domestic cultivation of madder, woad, flax, hemp and oil. The first recorded commercial venture of growing woad in England was in 1542 when two separate licenses were issued to lease ground and employ local labour. One was a partnership between two gentlemen from Wiltshire and one from Dorset to cultivate the crop in Lymington near Southampton.[16] The printing press helped to broadcast scientific and agricultural knowledge as written information became widely obtainable and skilled immigrant workers supplied the practical experience to grow and process the crops.

It was around this time that Portuguese merchants trading with India introduced indigo also called 'ynde' or 'anil'. A memorandum dated 27th April 1577 sent by the dyers of the City of London requested permission to use the newly imported indigo in addition to woad in the

1.12 Indigo Blocks

common woad vats to produce a cheaper more *'oryent'* blue, and have a perfect and durable colour of blue, azure and watchet.[17]

The gentry continued to show a renewed interest in agriculture for their home farms, which they had previously leased to tenants for the production of wool. They implemented initiatives to increase basic food crops, and were cultivating more adventurous ones with a view to profit. Encouraged by government policies, and their coffers fortified by royal grants of land and licenses that promised personal gain, they formed partnerships with the merchants to experiment with novel industrial crops like madder, carrots, pumpkins, fennel and fruit.

For some, profit was more important than food. During the last decades of the 16th century, successful crops such as woad were grown to the exclusion of grain causing the government considerable concern. There was also an increasing alarm at the amount of starch from food grain that was used for the extravagant lace ruffs.

'...A Brief Description on the True and Perfitt Makinge of Woade, with a Declaration of the Apte Ground and Soyle for that Purposse'[18] was presented to the king's council giving an account of cultivating woad in 1586. The amount of woad grown in England in the same year can be estimated for twelve southern counties as 4,910 acres, which yielded about six hundred tons of dye. This at a time when the total amount imported was about twenty thousand tons, English woad contributed to less than three percent of the market.[19] Perhaps in response, the following proclamation to regulate the woad industry was issued:

> *'...No manner of person shall directly or indirectly after the publication hereof, breake up, or cause to be broken up, any manner of grounde of what nature soever it be, for the use or purpose to sowe or plant woade in, neyther that any person doe continue any grounds already broken up for that purpose to the use of woade, lying within foure myles of any market towne, or other*

towne occupying the common trade of clothing, or any citie within this Realme, or within eight miles of any house of her Majesties reserved for her accesse...[20]'

A revision in 1587 '*...every woad farmer was required to pay 20s per annum to the queen for the right to cultivate this plant. No grower might plant more than 20 acres in one year nor might more than forty to sixty acres be cultivated in any one parish. Woad moreover was not to be cultivated in any locality where there was a risk of depriving the poor of their accustomed work, or of its damaging fruitful ground.[21]'*

The policy was cancelled two years later except for the restriction of the distance from the royal residences, as the smell of the fermentation process was so offensive.

By the end of the century, there was an even greater demand for a domestic supply of blue dye as the exports of the new coloured cloths replaced the white cloth trade. This was taken up by many counties in the Southwest, as gentlemen farmers enthusiastically cultivated woad attracted by ever higher prices. There is a reference to woad growing for several years near Cranborne Chase and in Collingbourne Ducis,[22] both within a day's ride from Frome. One entrepreneur, George Bedford, was a Salisbury clothier whose inventory included

'*...Woade already grayned and in balls, 18 tonnes worth £400, lease for land and 'an olde woade house and fower woad mylles worth £10 whereof two are at Martin and two are at Blagdon...[23]'*

His business partner Henry Sherfield was a lawyer, whose letters and account books from the late 16th to the early 17th centuries provide considerable information on woad growing in the area. Together, they financed and negotiated short term leases from local farmers for two or three years and subcontracted work, via the church overseers, to the parish poor, to prepare the ground, harvest and process the leaves which were then sold directly to the dyers. Henry Sherfield's first wife was Rebecca, whose father Christopher Baily was a clothier from Southwick, about seven miles from Frome. She had previously been married to Henry Long a clothier of Whaddon and when George Bedford died in

1.13 1626 Letter to Henry Sherfield from Henry Cabbell
Sample of Woad Dyed Yarn and Cloth

1607, Henry married his widow, Maria whose family were also in the cloth trade.

Henry Sherfield was engaged in the growing of woad for more than 20 years. According to his letters, he was invited several times to visit clothiers in Beckington. In February 1626, he received a letter from Henry Cabbell, a Salisbury dyer, who was processing his crop.

'...I have sett your woad, it is very fyne woad to work but the value is nott to be sett of it by ease.[24]*'*

Henry Cabbell, who may have been related to the Cabells of Frome, had planted the woad but could not assess the value of the crop.

Two interesting notes on woad confirm the lack of confidence in early scientific knowledge. A book titled 'The Theater of Plants' published in 1640 by John Parkinson

'...Some have sowen it in our owne land, but they have founde it to be the cause of the destruction of their bees.[25]*'*

This was refuted by Nicholas Culpeper in 1653

'...They say it possesseth the bees with a flux, but that I can hardly believe, unless bees be contrary to all other creatures.[26]*'*

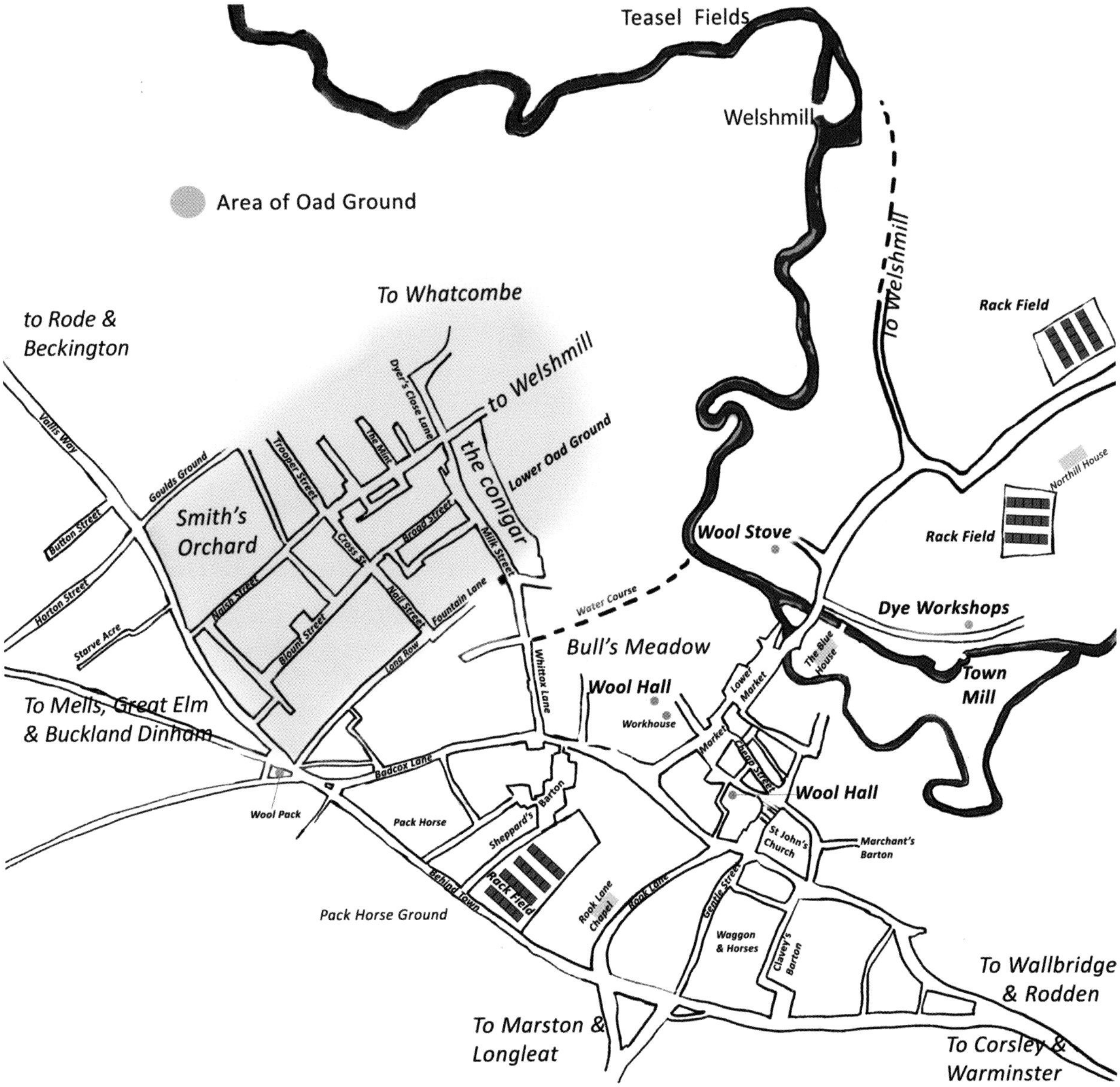

1.14 Frome Cloth Industry from 18th and 19th Century Maps

Frome field names in the 17th century indicated that woad had been cultivated locally. The land of the Manor of St Katherine consisted of an area known as Woadground later corrupted to Oad Ground. This lay behind the Conigre and West End sweeping uphill over what were to become Milk and Trinity Streets across flat land to Vallis Way. Woad Close is mentioned in 1677 when Richard Style paid his church rates and as far as the churchwardens were concerned, New Close was synonymous with Oad Ground.[27] Oad End hence West End[28] where now stands West End House was renamed by the late Mr Cruttwell from

Wode Hill House. This area may have included Lower Oad Ground[29] which led down to Low Water and Whatcombe via Dyer's Close Lane.

There do not appear to be any direct references to woad in the archives but experience had shown that the crop was used to break up grass before planting corn so it may have only been cultivated for a few years. Its evocative association in people's memory with the workers whose hands were stained blue by its preparation, or its rotten smell when it was left to ferment in the field for several weeks may have given the area the name which has remained unchanged for so long. Houses were built on the land around 1685 and by 1727 there were sixty houses rated in Oadground[30] which suggested that woad was grown before then.

In Frome, woad may have been cultivated as early as 1253 when the chantry of St Catherine's was endowed with land given by the Branch family[31] and Adam de Damerham was journeying to and from Glastonbury. It may have lapsed for a period after the devastation of the plague and not planted until 1538 when the land was acquired by the Thynnes after the dissolution of the monasteries. It seems more plausible that it was grown in the 1580s as a novel and lucrative industrial crop. The scale of woad cultivation in England was quickly seen to have a negative impact on the fertility of the soil and fears that 'vital grain supplies were threatened by the craze for woad growing' prompted Elizabeth I to restrict woad agriculture around the market towns. A slow transition from mainstream to alternative agriculture took place from the 1580s to 1650s and a new flexibility was introduced to land use. It became more common place to lay down old plough land to leys for up to twelve years before ploughing again so unusual crops like woad were gradually introduced into conventional rotations.[32]

In the late 16th and early 17th centuries, large tracts of former church land were sold to several clothiers. John Sheppard acquired the area between Catherine Hill and Rook Lane which was formerly a chantry and later became Sheppards Barton, Wine and High Streets. Land was bought by the Whitchurch and Baily families who were linen drapers and merchants. Richard West, a yeoman, later sold part of what is now the Trinity area to John Yerbury a clothier from Atworth. It was around this time, as the commercial coloured cloth manufacture expanded, that the dyeing trade of Frome started to thrive. As businessmen, the merchants, clothiers and dyers may have discussed the merits of cultivating woad and it may have proven financially advantageous to grow the crop on Oad Ground in the early 17th century as parts of the Woad Acts were rescinded or were perhaps ignored. Letters written in 1614 by Thomas Bower and James Ley of Beckington[33] to Henry Sherfield seem to indicate that he owned land in the area and as he was a keen grower of woad, he encouraged its cultivation. As houses were built on Oad Ground, the growing of woad may have moved to Mells and Rode.

A good read for landholders in the mid 1700s was

> *'A new treatise of Husbandry, gardening and other curious matters relating to Country Affairs. Containing, a Plain and Practical Method of Improving all Sorts of Meadow, Pasture and Arable Land and making them produce greater Crops of all Kinds, and at much less than the present Expence.' Samuel Trowell, Gent; Printed for James Hodges, at the Looking-Glass on London Bridge. 1739.[34]'*

which included the following passage:

> *Section III 'Weld or Would, Woad or Wade, Madder, Saffron etc.*
>
> *The best land for it, with the usage of it, and advantages thereby. Woad is a valuable commodity, and is the real foundation and solidity of many colours: a woaded colour is free from staining, and excellent for holding its colour; nay, any dark or sad colour must be woaded, to fix its colour; It was one of greatest profit to the Masters, of any fruit the land did bear. It hath flat long leaves, the stalk is small and tender, the leaves are of a bluish green colour, the seed is like an ash-key or seed, but not so long, with little blackish tongues; the root is white and simple: it is a very good seed to grow, and thrives well, and beareth a yellow flower on rich land, that is dry and warm, or a little sandy; though the manure helps it, if very rich, to bring forth a better crop; sixteen bushels an acre put on the land when the seed is sown; tis better on the hills side, where lands are good pasture, for the bottoms will not do; but the choicest is your home, coarse or lesser grounds, lying near a town... tis taken by the operator for so many years, to work the land, as shall be agreed for.*
>
> *The charge of making this woad is great, though it pays well at the*

end. It must be well ploughed; if the ground is hilly, they must be cast; they generally plough outward, or cast all their lands at the first ploughing, and after harrow it well, then sow it with about four bushels of the seed; and after the well harrowing, pick it clean of clots, turf and stones; when the woad begins to grow, weed it well; then as soon as the leaf is ready to cut, and having all hands and things necessary, which may be sooner or later as the season is; your mill being prepared with a double wheel, and the tooth or ribs, that cut the woad are placed from one side to the other, very thick wrought, sharp and keen at the edge; as soon as the woad is cut, and comes out of the field, it is to be put into the mill and ground, one kilnfull after another, as fast as may be; the juice of the leaf must be preserved in it, and not lost by any means; When ground, tis to be made in round balls, about the bigness of a common ball, and laid one by one to dry; and as soon as dried, then put them together, and others put in their places to dry.

The time of sowing is the beginning of March; and, from the beginning of cutting the crop, lasts till Autumn; then the season will not ripen it as before; and then the mill is at leisure to grind it all over again; then you may make it stronger or weaker as you please; for from this mixing of the woad makes the difference between woad and woad, that the dyers will hardly buy any parcel, till they have tried it in colouring, for there are three or four sorts of woad proceeding from each time of cutting; tis ripe in June; sometimes two cuttings and so on every month, while the season lasts; Often in making up they put two or three times cuttings together, but the first cutting is the best, which is called the Virgin woad; It has bore many prices, from £6 a ton to twenty or thirty pounds a ton. And doth generally pay the master well after all his care, trouble and expence'.

Woad was cultivated for hundreds of years. The dye was known in Frome by the 14th century as there are existing records, but it is only possible to speculate when it might have been cultivated on Oad Ground. In the 18th and 19th centuries it was cultivated around Mells, Rode and probably Frome as it was mentioned in the letters of John Olive, a local dyer, and by Thomas Bunn in his diary. A field called 'Blue Ball' ground in Nunney was leased by John Newport.[35] Several indentures exist for leasing the land near the mill at Rode Bridge between 1755 and 1784 which confirm that at least 21 acres were sown with woad.

The first of two leases between James Frampton and Thomas Whitaker, dyer and clothier of North Bradley, for 21 years is dated 1755; it describes the land, but the crop is not specified. The second lease between James and Thomas, dated 25th March, 1777 for seven years, mentions the same boundaries:

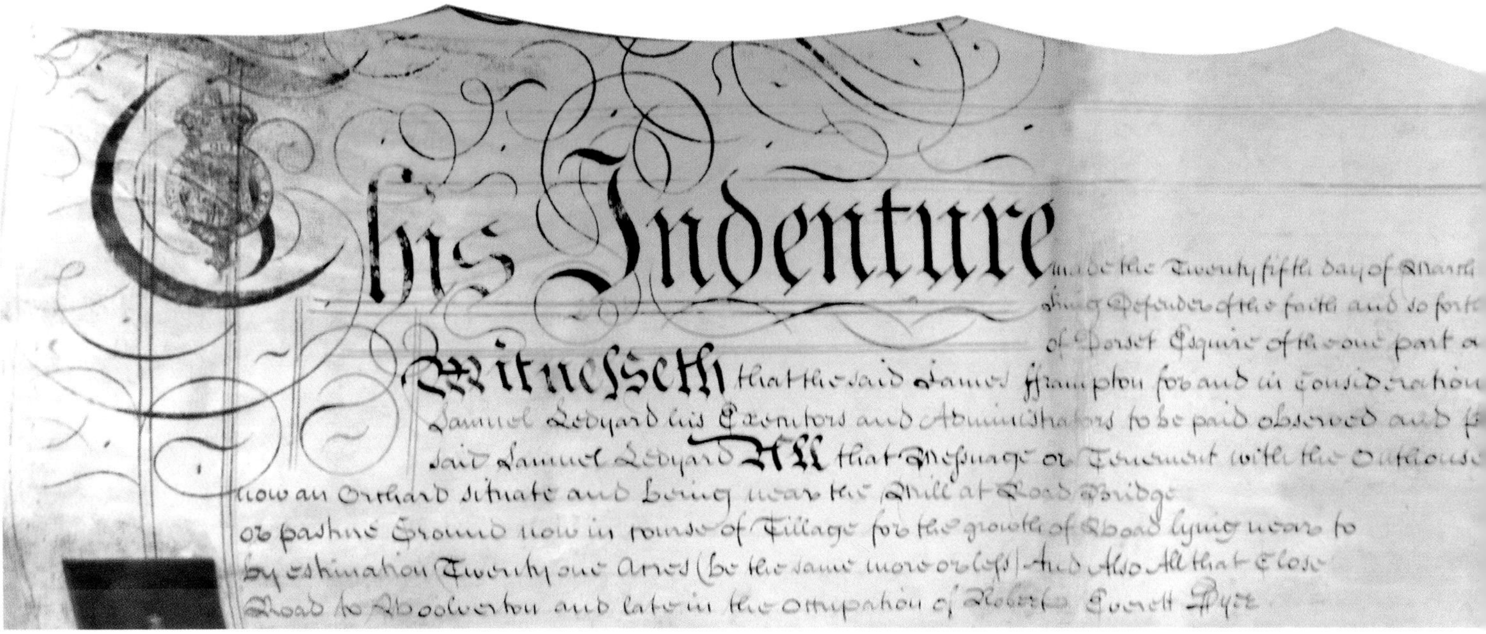

1.15 Indenture for Growing Woad at Rode

> *'...and one close of meadow containing by estimation ten acres, being near the Mill at Rode Bridge now in the occupation of Thomas Whitaker... and also those several closes of meadow or pasture ground now in the course of tillage for the growth of wood lying near to the said last mentioned close and commonly called Road Mill Grounds containing by estimation twenty one acres. ...at all times during the said term granted, preserve and keep the said three closes of woad ground sufficiently and properly manured and in the same course of good tillage as they are now for the growth of wood.*[36]*'*

The final lease for seven years dated 25th March 1784 is between James and a new lessee, Samuel Ledyard of Rode, dyer and clothier states that

> *'...the Mill at Rode Bridge, late in the occupation of Robert Everett, dyer, as tenant, and also all those closes, meadows or pasture ground now in the course of tillage for the growth of woad commonly called Road Mill Ground ... and will at the end of the said term leave the said closes in the same good condition as they now are without impoverishing or injuring the same in any manner whatsoever...*[37]*'*

A paper on the Agriculture of Somerset was written in 1795 by John Billingsley, who remarked that it was cultivated about 40 years earlier by one Harvey, more generally known as the *'Woad-Man'*, at a farm near Mells where there was also a woad mill. He may have been one of the itinerant woad farmers who contracted with the church overseers for the parish poor to work the fields on his behalf.

In his classic book, *'Agriculture in the County of Somerset '* published three years later, John Billingsley describes woad as an important article of cultivation:

> *'...Raised principally in the neighbourhood of Keynsham its quality is much esteemed. It requires careful management, but flourishes in soft deep fat loam. The green crops are cut by hand by women and children carted home and thrown into a mill, where the leaves are cut and bruised to a pulp by a heavy iron ribbed roller. It is then laid in small heaps, pressed close and smooth.*
>
> *After lying about a fortnight in this state, the heaps are broken up and formed by the hand into oval balls which are then dried on hurdles exposed to the sun. They turn dark brown on the outside and thus they are sold to the dyer. The crop is generally a profitable one, near ½ ton per acre. The nett profit of course must be governed by the goodness and price of the article. But it seems on average to be so lucrative a culture that the few farmers who can raise it ever discontinue the practice.'*

There was considerable interest to cultivate woad during the Napoleonic wars when the continental blockade increased the price of indigo. John Olive a local dyer wrote two letters, held in the Somerset Heritage Centre archives, to Mr John Wheadon, a dyer from Chard.

> *Frome, 16th December 1802 'Sir, In answer to your letter of the 11th instant respecting the preparing your land for woad....I will send you a double quantity of seed...3 bushells per acre will be sufficient. Enclosed is our standard colour fixed at 16d per lb of Spanish wool...*[38]*'*

The letters suggest that John Olive specialised in the dyeing of blue wool for the production of military uniforms.

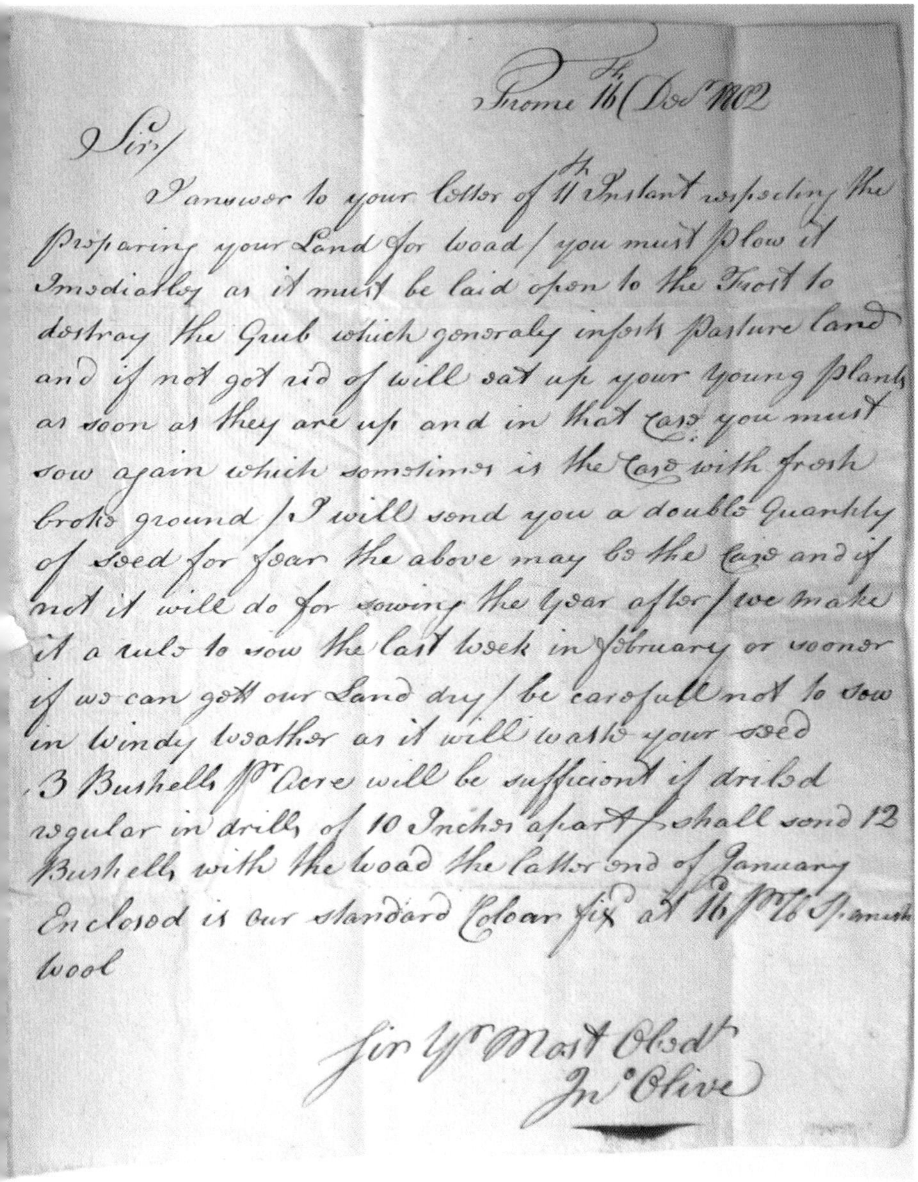
Frome 16th Decr 1802
Sir/
I answer to your Letter of 11th Instant respecting the
preparing your Land for Woad / you must plow it
Imediatley as it must be laid open to the Frost to
destroy the Grub which generaly infests Pasture land
and if not got rid of will eat up your Young Plants
as soon as they are up and in that Case you must
sow again which somtimes is the Case with fresh
broke ground /. I will send you a double Quantity
of Seed for fear the above may be the Case and if
not it will do for sowing the Year after / we make
it a rule to sow the last week in February or sooner
if we can gett our Land dry / be carefull not to sow
in Windy weather as it will wash your seed
. 3 Bushells per Acre will be sufficient if drilled
regular in drills of 10 Inches apart / shall send 12
Bushells with the Woad the latter end of January
Enclosed is our standard Colour fix at 16/ per lb Spanish
wool

Sir Yr Most Obedt
Jno Olive

1,16 Planting Woad

Finally, Mr John Parrish of nearby Shawford was paid a small sum for his article on woad in 1809.

'...I have the honour to be a member of the Bath and West of England Agricultural Society, where many noble and exalted characters unite their talents to promote the public benefit. And to one of its earliest and most respectable members I presume to address this information.'

In a letter addressed to the President

'Woad is a plant which, combined with indigo, gives the best and most permanent blue dye hitherto discovered. It is of great importance to our commerce, as well as to agriculture, therefore I conceive that in rendering its cultivation and preparation better known and understood, it may be greatly beneficial to the nation.

I have been many years a considerable consumer of woad, and have cultivated it with much success. I shall endeavour to give instructions for carrying on each process, and leave those who shall undertake it to proceed as they think best. This plant is cultivated in different parts of England for the use of dyers. Sow the seeds in March if the season invite, and the soil be in condition to receive it: but it requires a deep loamy soil and is better still with a clay bottom, such as is not subject to become dry too quickly. These plants are frequently destroyed in the germination by flies, or animalculæ, and by grubs, snails, &c. In order to preserve them, I have steeped the seeds with good success in lime and soot, until they begin to vegetate. Further, it is vain to expect a good crop of woad, of a good quality, from poor and shallow land.

The difference of produce and its value is so great, that no one of any experience will waste his labour and attention on such lands upon so uncertain a produce. In wet seasons, woad from poor land is of very little value. I once had occasion to purchase at such a time, and found that there was no possibility of regulating my vats in their fermentation; and I was under the necessity of making every possible effort to obtain some that was the produce of a more congenial season. I succeeded at last. At this time several dyers experienced much difficulty, and one of eminence in the blue trade suffered so much by woad of his own growth, that he declared his resolution to decline the trade altogether. I had from the same defect purchased such other woad as would do, and informed him where he could get it, he succeeded as usual. His own he disposed of to a dry salter, who sold it again somewhere in the country; and it occasioned such a cause of complaint, as I believe rendered the claim of payment to be given up, or partly so; of this I am not certain having only from report. I mention this in order to give those who wish to become growers of woad, such information as may properly direct them.

The leaves of woad on good land in a good season grow very large and long, and when they are ripe shew near their end a brownish spot inclining to purple towards its centre, while other parts of the leaves appear green, but just beginning to turn a more yellowish shade; and then they must be gathered, or they will be injured. Woad is to be gathered from twice to four and even five times in the season. The land, after woad, is always clean, and the nature of the soil appears to be greatly changed in favour of the wheat crop; Considerable fortunes have been acquired by the culture of woad.'

Mr John Parrish[39]

[1] Bath Reference Library Special Collections; Dyebook of Wallbridge Mill
[2] Blue House Appeal 1993 and History and Description of the public charities in the Town of Frome Notes from Crocker's Historical Account of the same Charities
[3] McGarvie, M 2013: 85
[4] Plowright, C 1903: 100
[5] North Lincolnshire Museum Services
[6] Bettey, JH 1978: 112-117
[7] Thirsk, J 1997: 37
[8] Billingsley, J 1794:
[9] Bettey JH 2005: 276 - 290
[10] Pastoureau, M. 2001: 50
[11] Hurry, JB 1930: 54
[12] Hearne, T 1722: LXXXVII
[13] Edmonds, J 2006: 17
[14] Hearne, T 1722: LXVIII
[15] Rack & Collinson Vol II 1791: 400
[16] Thirsk, J 1997: 82
[17] Edmonds, J 1998: 38
[18] Lansdowne MS No 121 Victoria History of Somerset 1911 ii, p421
[19] Edmonds, J 1998:19
[20] Blake, R 1585: -
[21] Hurry, J 1930: 63
[22] Kerridge, E 2005: 218 & Thirsk, J. 1985: 541
[23] JL Jervoise Papers HRO 44M69/D12/4/36
[24] HRO 44M69/L30/76
[25] Hurry, J 1939: 242
[26] Culpeper, N 1653: 193
[27] McGarvie, M 2003:94
[28] Belham, P 1973: 63
[29] Leech, R 1981: 3-4
[30] McGarvie, M 2003: 95
[31] Belham, P 1973: 54
[32] Thirsk, J 1997: 19-20
[33] HRO 44MM69/L40/36 & 24
[34] Trowell, S 1739: 33
[35] SHC DD\BR\IS/1
[36] SHC DD\X\WS/5
[37] SHC DD\X\WS/5
[38] SHC DD\SAS/C909
[39] Bath & West Society Archives

CHAPTER 2

WOAD & INDIGO DYEING

'Wanted: Sober, steady man who understands the management of blue vats and superintendence of a small dyehouse for dyeing wool – Apply Sheppards of Frome'

Bath Chronicle, Sept 24th 1795

From an early period people sought different ways of making and fixing colour to adorn themselves, their clothing, and their dwellings. Berries, leaves, ash and soils can all stain and scratching a surface leaves coloured marks. One of the earliest uses of colour in this country was red ochre found on the remains of the 'Red Lady of Paviland', which has been dated to 24,000 BC. Although true red, green and blue dyes were not discovered until much later, try rubbing a woad leaf, as it starts to feel wet it leaves no colour, but as you continue rolling the leaf between

2.1 Woad Dye Vat - Indigo Changing from Yellow to Blue on Exposure to Oxygen

your fingers it gradually changes till a dark blue stain appears. This does not wash off with soap and warm water but wears away with time.

Long before the chemistry was understood, the methods for producing dyes evolved empirically by trial and error. Crushing, fermenting, heating and combining berries, leaves and bark or mixing pastes with mineral and metal salts, all produce colours for weaving, embroidery, writing, illumination and body art. Some dyes work well with protein fibres like wool or silk and others have an affinity with the cellulose fibres of linen, hemp and cotton. Historically alchemists and dyers experimented to combine compounds and develop the rules to make dyes light fast and durable. Colourful substances which at first looked promising may have simply been discarded when experimentation with the known methods was unsuccessful. Most of these procedures were complex and the reputation and wealth of a business depended on individual skill, experience and knowledge. Recipes were kept secret, passed only from master to sons and trusted apprentices, but notes written in code attest to deceit and industrial espionage in spite of the threat of severe punishment or even death.

From the Middle Ages, along with the fulling mills for scouring and milling cloth, commercial dyeing must have evolved quickly. Well equipped workshops were an economic necessity for dyeing hundred-weights of wool and cloth and dye stuffs were imported in large quantities from overseas merchants. Large scale dyeing did not use just the harvests of fields and hedgerows to produce colour in a natural and idyllic sort of way. It was considered one of the dirty, hazardous, and stinking trades and, like the tallow and tanning works it was relegated to the periphery of towns. Harmful solutions of arsenic, urine, copper, and lead were used to cleanse, dye and finish wool and cloth, all of which were simply disposed of on the ground or in the river courses raising numerous complaints by those living nearby and working further down the stream.

Dyed cloth was for society's elite, its colour introduced to textiles by *'dyeing in the wool'* and blending the colours before spinning the yarn, by dyeing skeins for patterns in borders or for weaving whole lengths of cloth. The material itself, once woven white, was also *'dyed in the piece'*.

There are many examples in museum collections of ancient textile fragments with coloured details.

During the Anglo-Saxon period luxury materials were imported but the coarser wool and linen cloth could be dyed from plants grown locally, woad for blue, weld for yellow and madder for shades of red. These dyes could be combined to produce compound colours of greens, blacks and purples. For most however, clothing was the natural sheep colour or bleached by the sun to make it whiter. In the late Middle Ages work clothing of '*sheepes colloure*' is listed in several wills, and coloured aprons may have designated trades such as butchers, tanners and dyers.

After the Norman conquest threads of wool and silk were dyed for use in Opus Anglicanum, the finest English medieval embroidery of couched gold threads for ecclesiastical vestments. The cloth for the Othery cope[1] made in the 15th century was dyed with woad and over-dyed with lichen to create a purple velvet ground with floral embellishments of pomegranates and lilies. The Virgin Mary and figures of angels couched in gold thread adorn the cloth. Commissioning tapestries and ecclesiastical vestments bestowed important status on the owners who extravagantly displayed their wealth and power. Their wills bequeathed these luxuries to the church to ensure prayers would be said for the salvation of their souls and those of their families. During conservation work, the true colours of threads and cloth can sometimes be seen on the reverse or in the seams where they are not exposed to light. One property of natural indigo is that it does not penetrate the core of the fibres like other dyes but bonds to the surface where it remains very fast to light which makes it easy to identify. Today, some old tapestries suffer from a blue disease, where the colours have faded leaving a dominant blue hue as only the indigo ground

2.2 15th Century Othery Cope - on display at Glastonbury Abbey

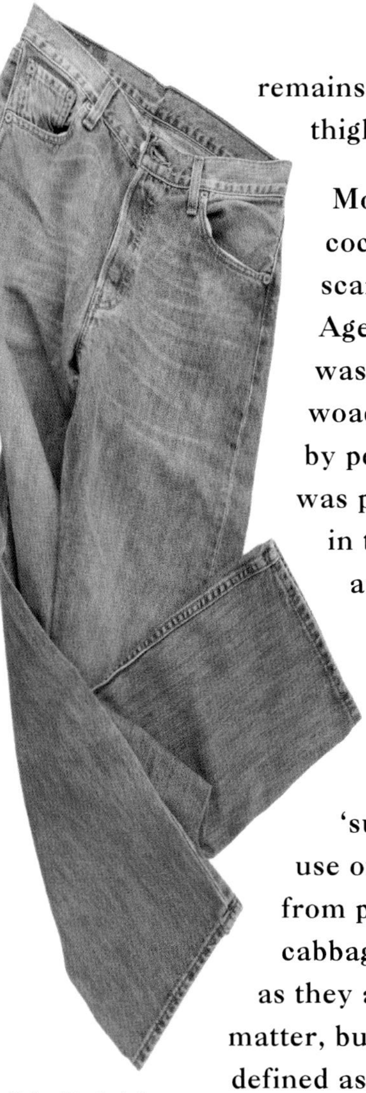

remains. However, over time, indigo rubs off with wear, like the thigh area of a well worn and loved pair of old blue jeans.

Most Dyestuffs are of vegetable origin except for cochineal, lac and kermes, which are scale insects that give scarlet, purple and crimson. During the English Middle Ages, madder which produces shades of orange red and rust was the predominant dye for clothing. The yellow from woadwaxen, which grew wild, was often gathered and sold by peasants to supplement meagre earnings. Blue from woad was possibly not used as extensively, although it was grown in this country, it was difficult to extract from the plant and may not have been easily available until it was imported in large quantities from France in the 14th century. Its very early appearance worldwide is intriguing as it is such a complicated dye to produce.

There are three types of dye. Those described as 'substantive' or direct dyes produce colour without the use of any additives. They are water soluble and extracted from plants such as turmeric, saffron, onion skins, red cabbage or walnuts. These dyes were often used in the home as they are easy to prepare by simmering the fibre with the plant matter, but some are not fast to washing or light. The majority are defined as 'adjective' or mordant dyes which require a fixative to act as a chemical bond between the dye molecule and the fibre. Mordants are metal salts of iron, aluminium, tin and chromium, alternatively tannins can also act as binders. Alum, potassium aluminium sulphate, is the most widely used mordant that is frequently mentioned in old dye recipe books along with tin which will brighten the colour and iron which will dull or sadden it. Finally, the 'vat dyes', such as woad, indigo and Tyrian purple extracted from shellfish, were developed from a fermentation process which was complex to prepare and required the greatest skill. All these methods are still used today although the vat fermentation process can be simplified with the use of chemicals.

2.3 Faded Jeans

2.4 Botanical Painting
by Lynfa Cameron

In the Middle Ages, fine cloth was exported white to be dyed and finished abroad by skilled Italian and Flemish artisans. The blue indigo dye used in England prior to the 1580s was solely extracted from woad and to date no written English instructions have been found for preparing commercial woad vats. Research in the archives of the Guild of the Arte Della Lana in Florence by Dr. Dominique Cardon uncovered information which describes the setting of a woad vat dating from 1418.[2] John Edmonds has also written on the subject in his book 'The History of Woad and the Medieval Woad Vat'. It was not until 1548 that the first specialist treatise revealing the secrets of dye recipes was compiled by Giovanventura Rosetti entitled *'Plictho de larte de Tentori che insegna tenger pani telle banbasi et sede si per larthe magiore come per la comune'* (Collection of Instructions in the Art of the Dyers which Teaches the Dyeing of Woollen Cloths, Linens, Cottons and Silk by the Great Art as well as by the Common). In his book, Rosetti states himself to have been a *'provisionato'* at the Venice Arsenal, which possibly involved him in the provisioning of raw materials and where he first became sufficiently intrigued with the use of dyestuffs to collect and even pay for information. He declares in his introduction

> *'...I have worked, days and nights, months and years, bearing this studious discipline with risk and discomforts, with my own blood and my poor substance, and God willing, I have brought it to conclusion. As will be seen in certain places, it has taken sixteen years.*[3]*'*

Historically, to dye blue with woad required three stages of controlled bacterial fermentation. The first was done by the growers following the harvesting. The leaves were macerated to a paste and formed into woad balls which were then dried over four weeks. The second fermentation was done either by the grower or the dyer. The woad balls were crushed to a powder and evenly spread about 2 to 3 ft deep on a stone floor. The heap was moistened with water and turned daily to control the heat and ferment in a process called 'couching'. This took up to nine weeks and if done correctly the composted woad turned into a black tar like substance which could then be dried and stored. These two stages concentrated the strength of the indigo precursors of isatin B and indican[4] molecules in the plant matter to about twenty times the dyestuff of the fresh leaves.[5] This dye matter was now ready for the third fermentation in the vat process.

In a commercial medieval dyehouse the setting of a woad vat took about three days. The couched woad was placed in the vat with lime or wood ash, boiling water was poured over and the liquid stirred. Once it cooled to 50^{0}C, bran and madder were added and it was fermented for a day and a half to render the indigo soluble. Any red colourant from the madder was lost in the process as it fermented in the vat. Expertise was essential to adjust and maintain the correct temperature and alkalinity, because woad vats were temperamental and the indigo could be easily destroyed. The readiness of the vat was tested in one of several ways as the right pH was crucial for this final fermentation. If alkaline, the liquid would feel slippery when rubbed between finger and thumb, if not, it felt rough. There were slight changes in the smell or taste if the vat was either too alkaline or acidic in which case small amounts of bran and madder were added. When ready to dye the residual plant sludge settled on the bottom of the vessel and the indigo would be thoroughly dissolved in the liquid. Wetted fibres were introduced to the vat and as they were removed and exposed to the air they would change from yellow/green to blue as the indigo oxidised and reverted back to an insoluble blue pigment on the surface of the fibre. Unlike the later indigo/woad vat, medieval sources suggest that this vat would be exhausted after three days of dyeing and the contents would have been discarded and the whole process started again. It is easy to see why, woad unlike madder, may not have been as widely used in a domestic setting.

2.5 Dried Woad Ball

By the 16th century, it was felt by some that English dyers lacked the knowledge and expertise for commercial indigo vat dyeing. While similar to processes used by the dyers on the continent, they were not identical.

'...No two woad vat dyers use the same recipe in setting a vat, and each considers he has a secret art by means of which he ensures the successful working of this vat, and this he jealously guards. All these differences in the manner of setting the vat are brought about not by any radical differences in the materials used, but by some unnoticed differences in other surroundings; differences in the mean temperature of the water used, in the general conditions of the atmosphere, all of which have a material influence on the development of the vat, but which are, in the majority of cases, overlooked by the indigo dyer, the result being that a method of working which is successful in one place would not be so in another.[6]*'*

In France, the woad growers washed the leaves to remove any contaminating matter before forming the woad balls called *'cocagnes'* which could explain the letter written in 1553 by William Cholmley of London, a *'grosser and one that selleth spyces'*. He suggested that while the best process for dyeing with woad may have been known in the earlier Middle Ages the skill had been lost for at least a hundred years. He asserts that in his view, English dyers did not know how to dye correctly using woad and that their working practices were wasteful, contaminating the rivers and resulting in uneven colouring on the cloth as a ground for black or for other colours which they claimed was due to the poor state of the water rather than their lack of knowledge. He says *'...I am not able, neyther hath it been my bryngyng up to furnishe a dyehouse with all thinges thereto belongyng'*. Instead, he and his partner, engaged from Antwerp, worked together for three years to prove that kerseys, broadcloths and capes could be dyed in England with woad *'...as substantyallye, truly, and perfectly well, as ever it was, is, or can be done in Flanders or in France, or any other parte of the whole worlde'*.

He was also of the opinion that the merchants and drapers had a vested interest to keep the finishing and dyeing of white broadcloth overseas so they could increase their profit by charging considerably more when importing it back to England. He refutes the many arguments put forward to justify the continuation of dyeing in the Low Countries with a generally negative view of his fellow countrymen:

'...We beynge beastly mynded and sekyng to gayne so much by doynge so lyttle, every man sekeyng his owne pryvate commoditie, without regarde of the weale publike, do not diligently applye oure good wyttis to the serchyng

oute of good knowledge, but to the inventing of subtyle dysceyte to our pryvate avancement, but the decaye of the puplicke weale of oure countrey.[7]'

From 1560, the new Indian shipping routes lead to the gradual introduction of indigo extracted from their native plant, *Indigofera Tinctoria* to Europe and England. This plant contains significantly more indigo precursors than woad.

2.6 Indigo Powder

27th April, 1577 '...Whereas one Pero Vas Devora Portoguese is sente from the King of Portogale into this Realme to make shewe and triall of the working of a certain commodity or merchantise named Aneel commonly called in English Blue Ynde which cometh out the the East Yndias and by report is made of the flower and first croppe and cutte of an herb growing there whereof woad is made not before this tyme practised upon wull or clothe in England.[8]'

2.7 Woad Powder

Following this adoption, while woad was still a major ingredient of the vat, indigo was cheaper to use and the woad trade in France started to decline. The popularity of blue remained unabated and a list of blues, published in 1669 included many shades

'...White blue, pearl blue, pale blue, faint blue, delicate blue, sky blue, queen's blue, turkey blue, king's blue, garter blue, Persian blue, aldego blue, and infernal blue.[9]'

The extraction of indigo from *Indigofera Tinctoria* used a different fermentation process. In a tier of three large tanks, bundles of the cut plants were steeped for ten to twelve hours, after which the water was drained to the next lower tank and the plant matter discarded. The water now containing the indican was agitated to introduce oxygen and

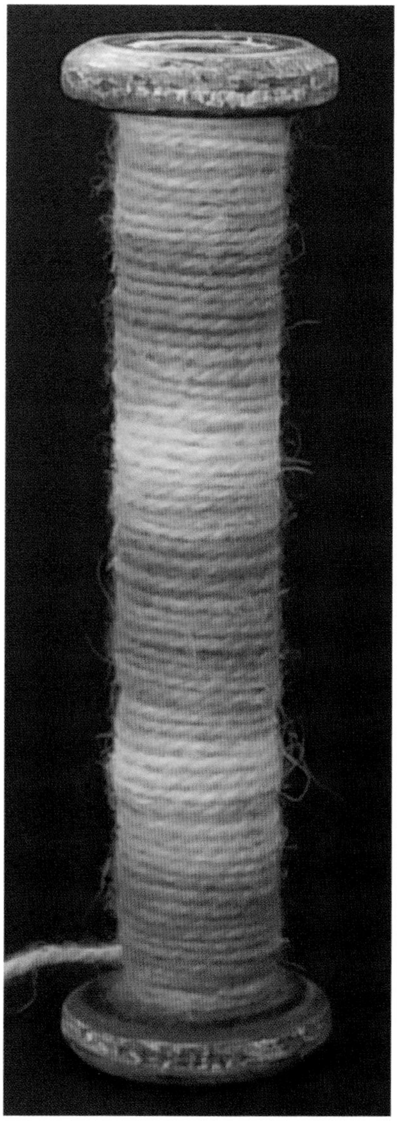

2.8 Shades of Blue

precipitate the indigo pigment. Once it had settled at the bottom of the tank the water was drained from the top into the third tank and the indigo sediment was collected. It was left to dry and solidify before the paste was cut into blocks of a dark bronze blue colour, packed into casks and sold to the dyers. Once purchased by the dyer, lumps of indigo were dry ground for half a day in a mortar with a 12-18 pound cannon ball or with a small millstone inside a stone trough with a spout. Water was then added to make a paste. To obtain the finest colour it was washed well in hot water to remove any residual dirt leaving the clear blue sediment to settle, any remaining lumps were removed and ground again.

> *'...This drug is so dear that these directions aught to be strictly adhered to. If they are well followed, and the indigo carefully and laboriously ground into perfectly fine powder, 6 pounds and a quarter of the best East India indigo may be made to dye 100lbs weight of cloth a full deep blue.*[10]*'*

From this period, the preparation of a combined indigo/woad vat changed as it could be kept active for many months by adding dissolved indigo powder rather than the previous use of composted woad matter.

When the white cloth export trade of West Country was replaced by the manufacture of the lighter medley broadcloths, these were dyed 'in the wool', and the correct setting of the indigo/woad vat was essential.

> *'...All other colours may be done by a receipt, and when once well performed, may be repeated with the utmost certainty, provided the water and dyeing wares are the same; but it is not so with woad dyeing, in this a constant judgement is required. It depends altogether on a given stage of fermentation being equally and constantly preserved, and as this is ever liable to vary from a variety of causes, the operation is thereby rendered very difficult.*[11]*'*

2.9 'Dyed in the Wool' with Woad

In the 18th century the vats were made of wood bound with iron or copper hoops. The bottom half was covered in hard clay and sunk in the earth. The equipment was described as

> *'...The size of the blue vat will be in proportion to the business you expect. The common size should be 5 ft deep, 3 ft in diameter at the top and 20 in at the bottom. For the sake of conveniency, place your vat 2 ft in the earth; observe that its cover fits close. That a hoop is suspended 2 ft from the bottom with a net stretched over it to keep your wool from the grounds which lie at the bottom. A dyer's rake is also necessary. A stick should be put across your vat, about one inch below the surface of the dye in order to draw the cloth over, you will also need two sticks about a foot long with hooks at one end, to haul your cloth for it will be inconvenient to haul it with your hands.[12]'*

Wool continued to be *'woaded'* and the term and the occupation of woadman was retained until the 20th century. The woadman was responsible for taking care of the vats in all blue dyehouses.

> *'...Wanted – experienced wool dyer in the management of blue vats and furnaces. Dependent on capability £40 - £100 per annum. Apply RW Sheppard, Frome.[13]'*

The methods used to set a vat varied by country and dyer; an American, Elijah Bemiss in his book of 1806 'The Dyer's Companion', describes English, French and Dutch methods and mentions that

> *'...Blue made from wood alone, according to the opinion of some persons prejudiced in favour of old customs, is much better than that which the woad gives in addition to indigofera. But then this blue would be much dearer, because woad gives much less dye than indigofera. So the using of the indigofera with the woad is a great saving, as one vat with indigofera shall dye as much as three without it.[14]*
>
> *A vat of the size described, is set with five times one hundred and twelve pounds of the best woad, five pounds of umbro madder, one peck of cornell and bran, half of each, the refuse of wheat, four pounds of copperas, and a quarter of a peck of dry slacked lime. When the materials are in, it should be filled with water at 90°C and the contents stirred for half an hour and then put in 15lbs of well ground indigo and cover down close. The vat should be set about 4 or 5 o'clock in the afternoon and be attended and stirred*

again at 9pm. To prevent it cooling too low throw some mats or wool bags over the cover. The person who manages the vat must attend at 5am and remove the covers and plunge the rake into the vat, so as to bring some of the air that is carried down to the surface. If fermentation has progressed, air bubbles will appear on the surface and the liquor a dark olive green. Add another 15lbs of indigo, and a quarter peck of slaked lime, stir for twenty minutes and cover down. Two hours after this stirring it must be stirred again, the bubbles will be a richer purple and the surface covered with copper coloured scale. Add another quarter peck of lime, cover and close down. The liquor must now be stirred every two hours and lime added. By the time eight quarters have been added, the liquor will look very rich in the bead, the bubbles will rise of all sizes. The indigo now when raked up, will show in the liquor, its appearance will be a rich yellow olive clouded with indigo.[15]'

Another type of vat was made as follows: '*...To 50 gallons of stale urine 4lbs of common salt are added, and the mixture heated from 120°F. to 140°F. Then 1lb madder and 1lb ground indigo are added, and the mass is well stirred. Then the mixture is allowed to stand until the indigo is completely reduced, when the vat is ready for dyeing*[16]*... Commercially this may have been the preferred method of some dyers, as apparently it was cheaper than using potash. The author of this paper includes the preparation of this vat under protest that the use of it as troublesome, filthy and wasteful of indigo but it has the advantage, it does not spoil with age, on the contrary it improves'. For domestic household use small quantities of blue dyeing with indigo from woad or indigofera may have continued to use this method, as stale urine breaks down into ammonia dissolving the indigo. By 1815, the urine-indigo vat was seldom used commercially, being unpleasant to work and with few advantages over other vats.*[17]'

While the indigo/woad vat was being set, the wool was prepared. Many variables affected the even dyeing of wool, and it was important to have a ready supply of clean water, quality dyestuffs and well sorted wool. In Frome, as well as the river, the town has many springs. Wool was identified by the clothier's mark. It was sorted into baskets of choice white locks, English, Spanish, coarse and list wools, then brought from the lofts to the dyehouse. In specialist dye establishments, the dyer would not know if the wool provided by a clothier had been scoured properly beforehand, so to protect his reputation, it was customary to give it another wash.

2.11 Indigo Extraction from Woad

'...Cleanliness is undoubtedly the condition which the wool must possess to enable the dye to hold on and not to come off the fibre, this latter causes a loss of dye-stuff, soils the whites, and gives rise to trouble between the dyer and finisher.[18]*'*

For this preliminary wash, stale urine, called '*sig*', and water was heated in a furnace and batches of wool were immersed and gently agitated. This was followed by rinsing the wool in running water with a final rinse in spring water.

'...Any trace of grease which the fibre contains are the causes of nearly irremediable stains in the dyeing operations. ...After wetting and preparatory treatment such as mordanting, it is best to proceed immediately with dyeing. ...If the fibres be left in a heap for too long a time, the moisture may be irregularly distributed, causing an uneven fixation of the colour in the first stages of dyeing. The dyer, however, must not be less careful to see that the dye-bath is what it ought to be.[19]*'*

When ready to work, a blue vat had a copper film and a '*florry*' of oxidised indigo pigment on the surface. This was removed before dipping the wool in the liquid as it could cling to the surface fibres. It was considered good practice to have two working vats at any one time, the new one for priming the wool and a second one that had been worked for a couple of months for finishing. One man would tip about 60lbs of wool over the top of the liquor while the other put it under with the vat stick, where it would be left for less than ½ an hour. The workman would then haul it out on a net wringing cloth and shake it up so that the air would reach all parts of the wool watching it change in three or four minutes from green/yellow to blue.

'...It is not advisable to attempt to get full or deep shades of indigo at one dip, for such would necessitate the use of strong baths. Dyeings produced in this way are liable to rub badly,

because the indigo lies mostly on the surface, to which it is more or less mechanically attached. Light shades of indigo are fast to rubbing, and by repeated dippings in a light vat or a medium shade vat deep shades of fair fastness to rubbing can be got.[20]'

A vat that was set with five hundred weight of woad and five hundred pounds of indigo would colour for six months. If skilfully managed using prime indigo it would colour 220 lbs of wool each week and for the six weeks of working down after the last addition of indigo it would colour 400 lbs of dark blue, 200 of half blue and 200 lbs of very light. It was usual in all regular dye houses to reheat on Saturdays in the afternoon and again on Tuesdays or Wednesdays according to the vat works.[21]

After dyeing '...The goods were taken out of the dye-bath squeezed or wrung to remove the surplus dye-liquor, which could be used again. The dye-bath was not exhausted of colouring matter, and could be reused for another lot of goods simply by adding fresh material to make up for that absorbed by the first batch.[22]'

The early dye-works were on the banks of the river, where from *'washing boards'* or *'bridges'*, the loose dyed wool was washed in tubs then tipped into wicker baskets which were suspended in the water allowing the current to carry away the waste. It was then placed in a drying stove and once dry, it was sorted to remove any discoloured or poorly dyed locks and returned to the clothier. Dyeing in the wool made economic sense for Frome as the river contains lime which makes it difficult to prevent spotting and even dyeing of a whole piece of cloth. The lime has a tendency to combine with the dye molecules preventing the colour from penetrating the fibre. This can be partly adjusted by adding a weak acid such as vinegar to the dye bath. The reaction still occurs, but it forms much more slowly allowing time for the dye to soak into the fibres. The locks of different breeds of sheep also vary considerably in their absorption of dye. Finer wools take up more colour than coarse and, even in the same bath, some will come out a deeper shade. If a broadcloth was woven from mixed wools, it may not have dyed evenly in the piece.

In Lullington near Frome in the 1670s, Christopher Brewer dyed his cloth in the *'say'*. This was when the cloth was cut from the loom and washed but not fulled. In this state, the loosely woven cloth was dyed, but complaints were raised that the process was fraudulent and that the dye was not as lasting as that dyed in the wool because, unlike traditional broadcloth, not all the excess dye was removed by the long pounding of the hammers in the fulling stocks. However, Christopher's cloth could be sold at a lower price and it was very fashionable.

> '... *What is the custom or usage in trade between dyers and clothiers if the dyers spoyl or damage cloth in the dyeing or colouring are the dyer in such case by the custom or usuage of such trade to make good or allow for the same to the clothier in the accounts between them or out of the money coming for dyeing etc. ...And this debt also saith that ye rates and prices of dyeing do differ according ye nature of ye cloth and ye variety of colours. And for woading a cloth sometimes 5s and sometimes 24s and other intermediate prices according ye goodness of ye woad. If the cloth be spoiled by them in dyeing green or blew which is when it is spotted or ye colour so uneven as that ye cloth is to be made black it is the custom to make allowance for the same by charging the clothier no more for dyeing such colour than if he had only put a woad upon it, but such allowance is not made on account of a cloth's not happening in the colouring to hit the pattern, provided the difference be not very great.*[23]'

2.12 Colours for Blue Grounds

Today there are lots of methods for extracting dye from natural and synthetic indigo and many books describe in detail the safe use for colouring textiles at home. In the 17th century household, small amounts of yarn, cloth, and clothing would have been dyed for personal use as dye stuff could be bought in small quantities at market stalls, grown in the garden or collected in the wild, like weld or lady's bedstraw.

A seven page booklet of practical household tips written in the 17th century is held in the Chafyn Grove family of Zeals collection in the Wiltshire archives. It includes methods for pricking out embroidery designs using *'Charkcoole'*, making an alum solution and coloured waters such as scarlet with red wine and brazilwood. There are also a few instructions for poultices, cough syrup and tantalizing food recipes such as *'Coller of Beefe'* and *'Scottish Collops'!* When dyeing, they knew that water affected the colour they wanted to obtain and instructions specified the use of rain, river or well water.

'How to Staine according to the ancient Customs of England.[24]

To make blew water

Light blew: Take florry and alum water and mingle them together as you think best.

Fine Blew: Take florry and temper it with clean well water and seeth it over the fire till half bee wasted away. ...Take a quantity of florry and a quantity of allum and temper them with strong lye and a little water, and let them seeth over the fire a good space.

Take florry and or else if thou will take clean well water and make it warmed and put florry thereto and it then wilte make linnen cloth blue. Look that your cloth be not allumed and dippe it once or twice or often if you wish'.

The notes to make a blue draperie were sadly torn and incomplete but they did mention taking

'indeco and white and make a light blue and then blacke and indeco together...'

These instructions do not mention where the *'florry'* comes from, but it probably refers to the *'flower'* of an indigo vat which is the concentration of oxidised indigo pigment that forms on the surface of the liquid as it ferments. It does

2.14 Flower or Florry of an Indigo Vat

Instruction about dyeing cloth

How to stame according to the auncient Custom of England.

First see that the place wherein you meane to worke be cleane and lighte then take a bottle of hay or barley strawe 2 bottles and strawe it as farre as youre shall bee and the hay above, and then take a good Canvis and naile it round aboute as streighte as you can, then take the Cloth you meane to stame, and pricke it round aboute your Canvis with prickes of black Thorne, but first make a hole with youre Bodkine then youre Prickes will not breake

Take Thornes and shave them and then pricke your Cloth that you are to stame on as streighte as you can then take a Charkcoale and drawe the draughte thereon.

To allume your Cloth take a panne of cleane Water, & putt allum therein and sett it on ye fire untill the allum bee melten & then putt the Cloth therein, & let it boyle, but first wash your Cloth in cleane Water ere you boyle it that there bee no therein, then take ye Cloth after it hath bine boyled in ye Allum, and wringe out the Allum and dry it, And when it is dry assay it with youre spittle for if youre spittle goe thorrowe ye otherside, it is not dry, then take it and lay it under you in bedde one nighte untill it bee stable.

To drawe your draughte perfecte:

Take Brasill and shave it small, and put it into a cleane earthen dish and put Water thereto that it bee overcovered then take a little unslackte lime and put it thereto, and stirre them with your finger together untill it be redde, and drawe therewith.

mention that it should be mixed with alum which is not the usual vat process when dyeing with woad or indigo but may work well with linen. In Franco Brunelli's book: 'Art of Dyeing in the History of Mankind', he refers to *'floraye'* printed in an anonymous booklet published in 1513, the title translated from Low German as *'The Book of Wonders.*[25]'

A second household method found in the Somerset Archives on an undated scrap of paper, probably from the late 17th century suggested that for dyeing Best Blue.

> *'... for 4 of ware, (slaked lime)) 2 of rock indigo ground fine in gin spirits, and 4 of green copperas in half a hogshead of soft water.*[26]'

I may try it sometime, but I am not convinced that using gin for such a purpose is worthwhile!

---

1 Exhibited in Glastonbury Abbey Museum
2 Cardon, D 1992: 22 - 31
3 Brunello, F 1973: 181-185
4 Edmonds, J 2006: 35
5 Edmonds, J 2006: 13
6 Beech, F 1902: 139
7 Cholmely, W 1553:
8 Peachey, S and Hopkins, D 2003: 18
9 Mairet, E 1916: 63
10 Cooper, T 1815: 22
11 Partridge, W 1823: 9
12 Ellis, A 1798: 10
13 Bath Chronicle - Aug 23 1798
14 Bemiss, E 1806: 143
15 Partridge, W 1823: 156-7
16 Beech, F 1902: 146
17 Cooper, T 1815:
18 Beech, F 1902: 77
19 Beech, F 1902: 78
20 Beech, F 1902: 139-141
21 Partridge, W 1823: 159
22 Beech, F 1902: 197
23 TNA E134/4 and 5 Geol/Trin13
24 WSHC ref 865/558
25 Brunello, F 1973: 178
26 SHC DD\SF/9/4/7

CHAPTER 3

WALLBRIDGE DYEHOUSE

'To 106 Wool
Woad to this then waish well
25 peachwood
13 Logwood
Boyle one our
Shot 21 1/4 Copers 5 Allum
Boyl Well, Lay in
for Mr Cockell'

Wallbridge Mill Dye Workbook, March 8th 1745/6

As I read 'The Cloth Industry in the West of England from 1640 to 1880' by J. de Lacy Mann I came across a footnote on page 92: Bath Cent. Ref. Libr., Dye Book of Wallbridge Mill Frome. When I asked the librarian for access to these documents, she brought three large green boxes to my table and gave me a pair of white gloves. What a discovery! It was such a privilege to open the boxes, unwrap the tissue paper and take out the oldest leather bound hardboard books. Although in poor condition, the contents were vivid *'dyed in the wool'* samples secured with red wax to sheets of paper and next to each one was a receipt (Receipt was the term for recipe in the 18th century and earlier) written in oak gall ink. These were 250 year old commercial workbooks that had belonged to local dyers. The pattern books from a mill, or more specifically a dyehouse in Frome, Somerset dating back to 1743. Carefully turning each page was captivating, as the words *'Woad to This'* were repeated over and over and samples varied in colours from shades of blues, beiges and browns to beautiful clear and exquisite pinks made from one of the most expensive of all natural dyes, referred to as *'grain'* in the 18th century. Initially, grain was thought to be a plant, but it was in fact kermes, a female scale insect that lives on *Quercus Coccifera,* grown in Sicily, Southern France and other hot countries.

The three books are working documents from the 18th and 19th centuries. The dye books list the ingredients, the instructions and the colours they produced. The pattern book was kept as a record of the inventory of cloth manufactured and sold. The first leather bound book has a Bath Victoria Art Gallery paper label stuck on the front, which mentions that the books were from Wallbridge Mill but there is no indication of the provenance on the documents. It was probably a passing comment, written on an index card when they were donated to the Bath Reference Library in 1953 by Captain Arthur Batten-Pooll V.C. M.C. on behalf of Henry Batten-Pooll, a previous owner of Scutts Mill in the nearby village of Rode. The Batten and the Pooll families were cloth manufacturers in the 18th century who may have had business and personal connections with the owners of the Wallbridge dyehouse. Along with these books, there would have been corresponding account ledgers for cloth sales or returns and letter books for correspondence with suppliers, factors and customers. As valuable tools of the trade, dye books were passed from father to son as an inscription in one of them suggests but once the business ceased to operate most were simply thrown away. So, these books may have been given to Mr Batten or Mr Pooll in 1840 when the dyehouse was demolished to build the Wallbridge Mill.

The Wallbridge site has an interesting past which is difficult to unravel. Located on the outskirts of Frome, on what was the turnpike road to Warminster, it covers the area of the confluence of the river Frome and

3.2 A.H. Tucker Ltd - Wallbridge Woollen Mills

the Rodden brook. A mill had possibly existed on the site since Domesday and later there were two mills, a causeway across the marsh, and a bridge was built over the river in 1634. One mill which dates to the late 16th century may have been a fulling mill for a time and later converted to a grist mill which was leased by Thomas Dunning in 1765. The other, a dyehouse at Wallbridge, was a short distance away from the mill and may have been built in the early 1700s by John Harris and his business partner Thomas Bunn,[1] who was the grandfather of the 19th century gentleman of the same name, whose ideas and charitable benevolence influenced the classical buildings of Frome.

Until the 19th century, candles were used for lighting these buildings and fires were always a risk. Wood stoves were used to dry the wool which was then spread on the floor and oiled. *'...fire broke out in the dyehouse of Mssrs Meares in Frome last Wednesday, overheated stove... Bath Chronicle 29th March 1792'.* The provision of insurance had been developed in the 17th century and companies such as the Sun Fire Insurance were founded in the early 1700s. Their policies provided brief descriptions of commercial buildings. In 1727, John Harris insured the dyehouse and its contents for £500; he paid a premium again in 1730 and 1732 when it was described as a stone and tiled dyehouse valued at £800. The policy

3.3 Sun Fire Office House Mark to Show a Building was Insured

included his stock but excluded outhouses and adjoining buildings. There may have been other policies covering his drying stove building, workhouses and storage sheds. It was insured for £800 in 1734 by his partner Thomas Bunn[2], and was also listed in the town tithing rates. The dyehouse was a large single storey building equipped with vats and furnaces. There is no further mention of it after but in 1751 Richard Holmes sold the freehold to the Meares from Corsley[3] whose family held it for three generations. John Meares sold it in 1834 to Samuel Allen Bull, a local Frome dyer. According to the 1813 Cruse land surveys, Robert Meares owned a house and land around Welshmill where there was another mill and dyehouse. The Wallbridge dyehouse was eventually demolished and a new cloth factory was built on the site which was bought by the Tuckers in 1863. The firm prospered with the production of meltons, suitings, flannels and overcoatings. They installed new plant and a boiler in 1875 and hung a large enamelled sign 'Tuckers of Frome – Finest West of England Cloth'.

The oldest workbook in the collection mentions dates between 1743 and 1766 in roughly chronological order. The second book from 1809 to 1814 is also chronological and the third is not dated but some numbers of cloth swatches appear to match a few of the samples of dye receipt numbers in the second book suggesting it is from the same period.

The earliest sample book, 13 ½in by 8 ¾in wide and 3 in thick, was bound in an ordinary trade binding of brown leather with a fine tooled decorative line and corner motifs when it was new but it is well worn, exposing the disintegrating cotton pasteboards and lacing as the end papers are missing. It has been repaired several times over the years and was possibly patched with more brown leather which wraps around the inner facing or this may have just been the original cover of the pasteboards. The spine shows traces of the support cords which had been

3.4 / 3.5 Images of Dye Recipe Book

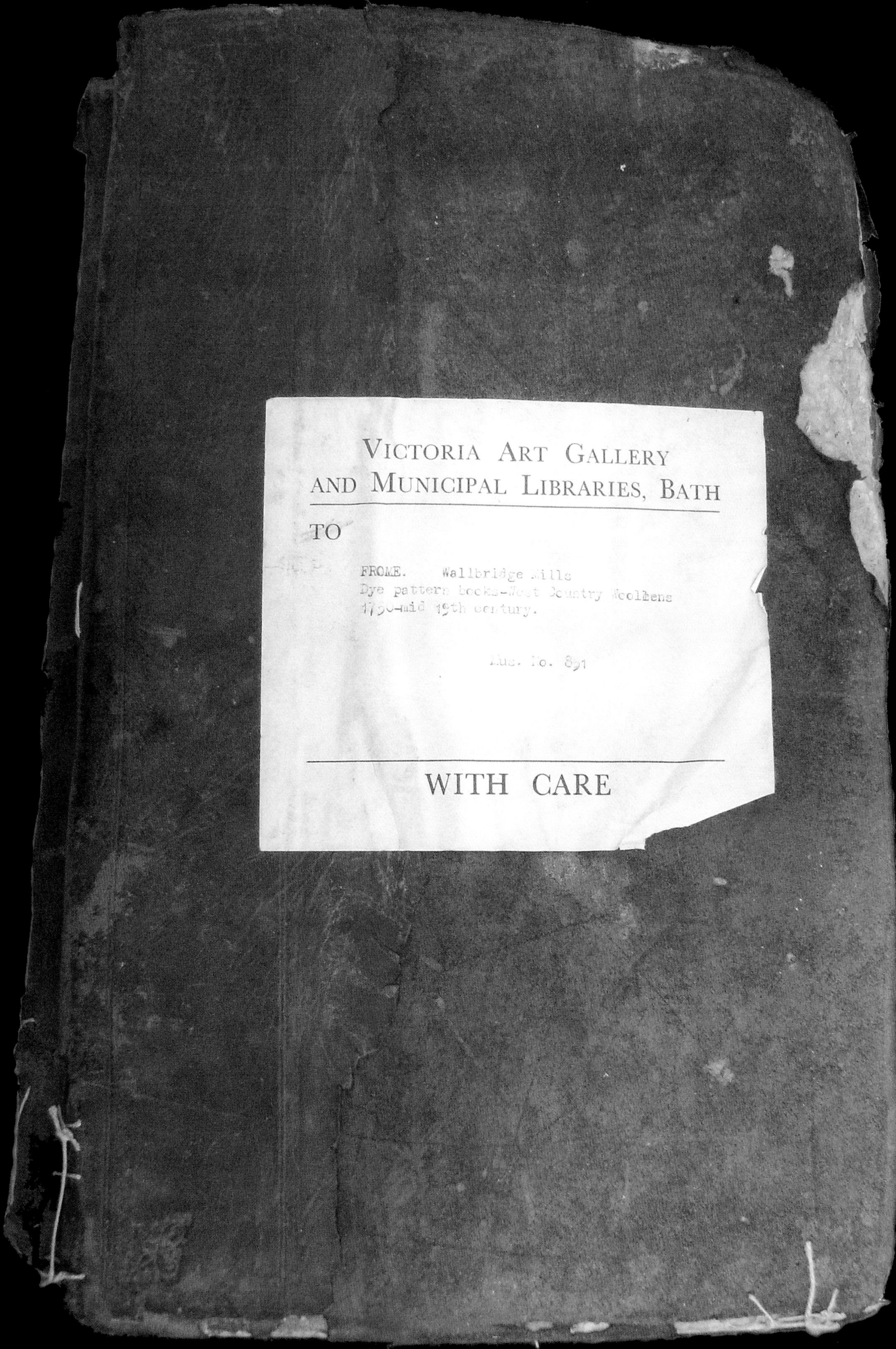
VICTORIA ART GALLERY
AND MUNICIPAL LIBRARIES, BATH
TO
FROME. Wallbridge Mills
Dye pattern books-West Country Woollens
1750-mid 19th century.
Mus. No. 891
WITH CARE

To 44 of Wooll
Boyll 1½ Allum
3 Argll Hon
Well Waich

To 12 of Wooll
¾ Grain ¾ Argll
1½ flover ¼ Brawll
Boyll Well Don

The sam Lickr then to 12 of Wooll
½ Grain ½ Argll
¾ flover ½ Bras
Boyll Well Don

In the sam Licker
to 20 of Wooll
½ Grain ½ Argll
½ flover
Lay In All Night

Go 56 of Wooll
Woad to this
Waith Well
3 pach wood
1½ Brasell
1½ Allom
Boyll & Don

Go 120 Woad to this
1 Gall 1 Argll
4½ Kid
1½ Bras
Boyle ¾ Our
Shot ½ Cop
Boyl 5 Allum
Mr Foard

Go 120 Woad the Sam
1 Gall 1 Argll
5¼ Kid 1 Bras
Shot ½ Copors
Boyll Doon

Go 57 Woad to this
15 fust 3 Log 3 All
¾ Copors All to
gether this Next
Moning Hoord
Mr Gorbury

Go 60 Woad to
this then
3 pound of
Woalls ¼ All
Boyll Well
Don W E

Go 106 Wooll
Woad to this
then Waith Well
2½ pachwood
1½ Logwood
Boyle one Our &
Shot 1¼ Copors
5 Allum Boyl
Well Lay

Mr Hayter Dec 21

Go 57 Woad to this
1½ Log 1 fust
Shot ⅛ Cops Hoord
After to this
Log 7 fust
1⅛ Cop Hoord
and Done Mr G

57 Woad to
Waish Well this
Boyle & Woodwa
then 3
Argll
Boyll Wa
Hoord
Mr Gorbury

sewn in several places. Inside, the folded papers are stitched together in sections. A few sheets appear to have been strengthened with glued strips of old vellum covered in writing, and in the folds, the wool fibres have accumulated into thin black trails of dust. The workbook had been well used, it is stained and the sheets torn out from the middle section allow it to be kept partially closed. The sample batts of dyed wool are attached to each page with red sealing wax causing the spine to splay and distort and some are missing entirely. Perhaps in later years it sat on a shelf, rather than hidden away in a drawer, to be used for the occasional reference by an eager apprentice.

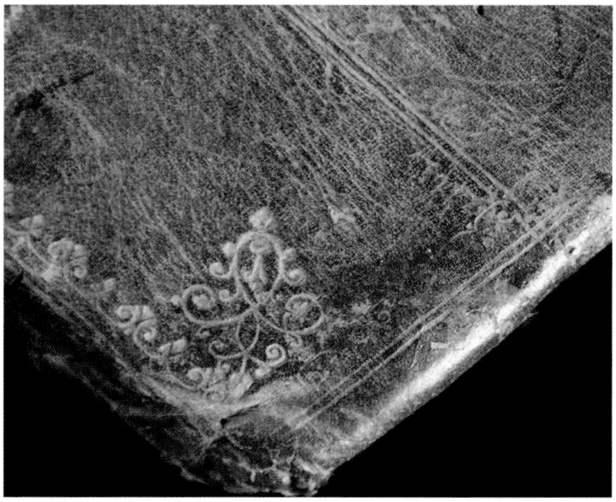

3.6 Tooled Detail in Corner of Leather

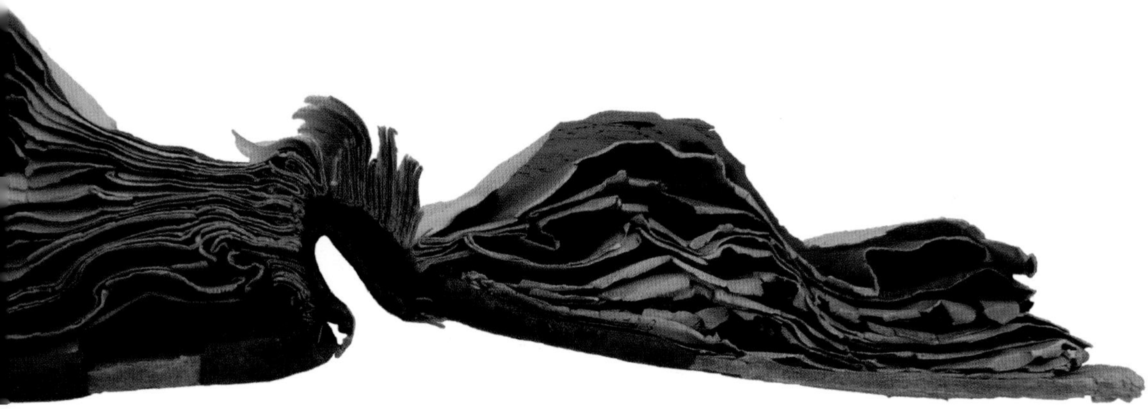

3.7 Torn Pages

Several books describe the best practices of the period and the following is an excerpt from an academic study rather than a practical one:

> *'...Every dyer should keep by him a specimen of every colour he dyes, with ingredients and proportions. These should be pasted or sewed in a book, having a book for each class of colours; he may then know at any distance of time, the ingredients necessary, with their proportions, for any particular shade of colour. In this way, he will never be at a loss to dye a pattern, which otherwise he can never be sure of without previous trials, which always occasion waste of time.*[4]'

The book is in need of conservation but it proudly and honestly reflects the ravages of more than 250 years and remains a fascinating working document of the 18th century dye trade of Frome. The book has remained shut for so many years that when opened at first glance, the samples are strong and vibrant especially those dyed a deep pink verging on scarlet. Venetian scarlet, a type of cloth, coloured with grain, was one of the most important and expensive materials of ancient times, and later gave its name to the colour rather than the material it previously described. The blacks, browns, blues and occasional yellows and greens, while strong in colour, may have been affected over the years by the mordants, by the chemical reactions and the oxidation of the dyes, and wax or just natural degradation of the materials. Some of the blacks have a distinct green or blue hue which may have been the fashionable raven or corbeau colours.

Work books of the period use the word receipt rather than recipe so my descriptions use these words interchangeably. The recipes in the first book are divided into two sections. From the front of the book, the samples are of the distinctive blue grey colour of woad, dating from 1743 onwards. Turning the book upside down and starting from the back they are shades of beiges and browns dating from 1750s onwards. In the middle there is an odd page dated 1805 with no swatches at all. Each sheet of paper in the book only has samples on one side and is divided in half lengthwise with 3 to 5 dye receipts in each column. Where the recipe has required the first step to be a woaded ground for a second colour, two samples of dyed wool are attached and some have fallen off, or have been removed, leaving the tell tale dark red wax mark. The only exceptions are two sheets with samples of pink on the reverse of other pages, one set of samples has been dyed with grain and then woaded and the

3.8 Dye Pattern Book of West Country Woollens

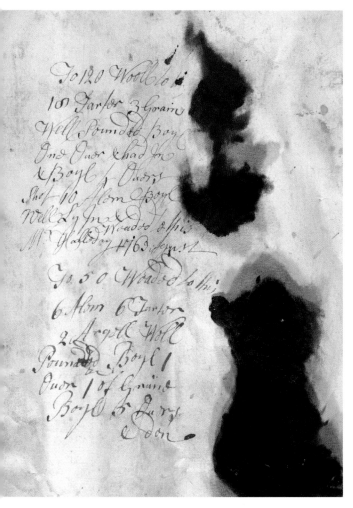

3.9 Grain Overdyed with Woad and a 'Woaded' Ground Overdyed with Grain

other the reverse, dyed with woad and then grain. Others are single samples that have not had a ground of woad, mostly shades of rich browns and beiges where the use of the different dye woods would impart blue and yellow undertones to the colours. The entries, written in oak gall ink, were probably entered by clerks of work or the dyers themselves as they are written in several styles of handwriting and each is separated by a line from the next. They may have been written by candlelight at the end of a day's work after washing the dye from their hands or perhaps first thing in the morning as several recipes mention that the wool should *'lye in all night'* or at least for several hours. It would be very impractical to write during the process and they would have to wait until the sample was dry before attaching it with wax. Spelling was not standard and the recipe books have their own short hand and abbreviations which may be individual to the dyer. It took a while before I understood for example, that *'...shot 4 Copperas'* meant to strew the substance over the liquor in the vessel. These instructions imply that the fundamental processes to prepare dye stuffs and set the vats were already known and taken for granted, and most probably had been learned as applied skills from the long apprenticeship under the guidance of the master dyer.

The format of each receipt is roughly the same; these are possibly the original recipes for standard colours ordered by a clothier. Further batches may have been produced on a regular basis so there are no

3.10 Dye Recipe Book

Bo-131 Woad to this [illegible]
stoord
1½ Galls
2 Madr
½ Brasell Shot
⅜ Cop ⅜ All
Mr Foard Nov-14-17[illegible]

Bo-112 Woad to this
then 1½ flower
½ Bras
1½ Madr
1½ Galls Shot
⅜ Cop Mr Vand
Novr 21-1743

Bo112 Woad to this
¾ Gall ¾ Argl
¾ Kid ¼ Log
¼ Bras Shot
½ Cop
Mr Houghton

Bo112 Woad to this
then 1 Kid ¾ Gall
¾ Argll ¼ Log
¼ Bras Shot
½ Cop Mr Road
Decr 8-1743

Bo120 Woad to this
¾ Gall ¾ Argl
1 Kid Shot ⅜
¼ Log & Don
Wm Moody
Jan-4-1743/4

Bo1[illegible]
to this [illegible]
then 40 Log
Shot 4lb Cop
Mr Langly
Oct-17-1743

Bo-112 Woad to this
¾ Gall ¾ Argl
¾ Kid ¼ Log
Shot ½ Cop
Mr Adry Lon

Bo-112 Woad to this
¾ Gall ¾ Argl
¾ Kid ⅛ Bras
Shot ¼ Cop
¼ Allom Mr
Shreder

Bo112 Woad to this
then ¾ Gall ¾ Argl
¾ Kid ⅛ Log
⅛ Bras Shot
¼ All Mr Bou[illegible]

Bo68 Woad to this
½ Gall ½ Argl
¾ Kid Shot ¼ Cop
Wm Everett
Jan-10-1743/4

Co-116 Mr [illegible]ittmore

3/8 Gall[illegible]

1/4 Log[illegible]

Shol 1/4

Jun Boyl [illegible]

Co-116 Mr [illegible]tman

6 Log[illegible]

3 Fu[illegible]

Boy 1 Our

Shol 2 Cop [illegible] Alm

Lay In this Word

To 60 Mr Hayter

1 Shu 1 1/2 Log

3 fust 3/4 Lix

1/2 Sand 1 1/2 Madr

Shol 1 Cop Lay In Word

Co-145 Mr C Hinton

1 3/4 Galls 3 1/2 Madr

1 3/4 Lid 3/4 fust

Boyl 1/2 Our

Shol 1/4 C 1/4 All

Jute Boyl Dra the

fir Ly In All Night

Jan-10-1754 No-89

Co 116

3/4 Log

1 1/2 Log

3/4 Bra[illegible]

Shol 3/10 C 3/[illegible] All Boyl

Don [illegible]

Co 120 Mr [illegible]rett

1 1/2 [illegible]

1 1/2 Log

3/4 Dach

3/4 Madr 1/4 fust

Shol 1/4 C All Ly In Word

To 118 Mr [illegible]

1 1/4 flour 1/2 Gall

Bras 3/8 Log

[illegible] 10 Cop

3/16 All Boyl

Dra the fir Ly [illegible]

forns With Out [illegible]

Grain Culler

Co-120 Mr Baskerfild

1 1/2 Galls 3 Madr

2 1/4 Lid 3/4 fust

Boyl 3/4 Of Our

Shol 1/4 Cop 1/4 Allam

Jute Boyl Dra the fir

and Ly In Jan-11-1754

reference numbers unlike the later recipe books. There are two types; one where the sample is first dyed with woad in a vat process, along with a few others such as the russets which have a ground of a different colour and are then over dyed. Wool may have been supplied to the dyer already coloured such as the yellow shown in the picture which was then over dyed to produce green. The other, single samples, where the colour is obtained from dyes and mordants which are dyed at the same time.

A dye establishment in the West of England owned by William Partridge in 1799 used about 400 lbs of indigo a

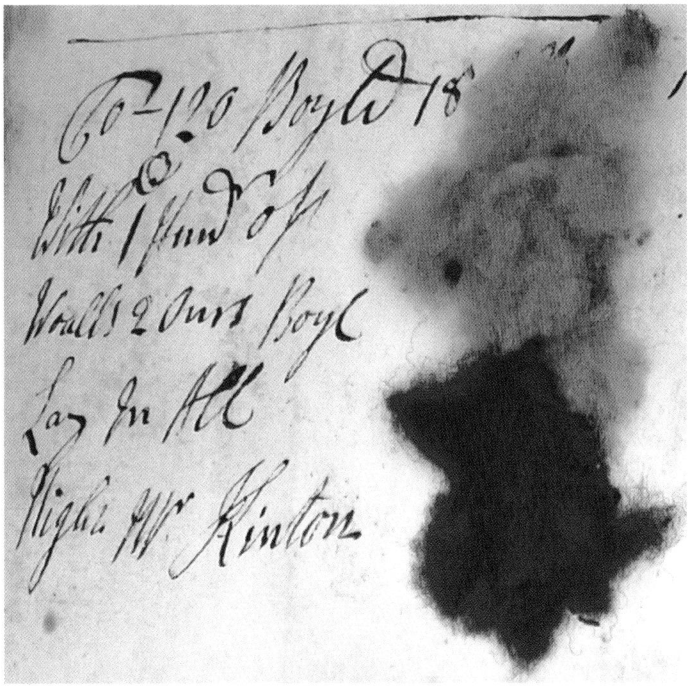
No 120 Boyld 18
With 1 pound of
Woalls 2 Ours Boyl
Lay In All
Night Mr Hinton

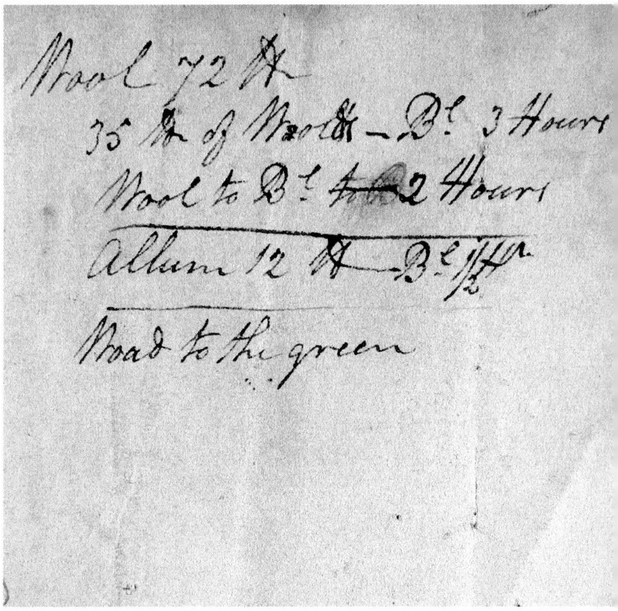
Wool 72 lb
35 lb of Woald – Do 3 Hours
Wool to Do 2 Hours
Allum 12 lb Do 1/2
Woad to the green

3.12 3.13 Examples of Overdying with Woad

week for woading. He emigrated to America and wrote a book in 1823[5] which suggests, that while there are thousands of subtle variations of hue, two thousand recipes would be sufficient for any dye house. In total there are 285 recipes in this book 104 of them have been dyed with woad, in addition, 166 were also dyed with logwood of which 55 had been previously dyed with a ground of woad. Logwood was first imported in Elizabethan times but was quickly banned as it was considered a fugitive blue colour. At the time, the best blacks were woaded and to prevent

3.11 Dye Recipe Book

fraudulent practices, it was enacted that the corner of each piece of cloth should be left undyed so buyers could see a blue rose that showed that it had been dyed first with woad.

The first line of each entry reads: *'to 12, 24, 120, 200 and some to 240 of wool'* this was the weight in pounds of previously scoured wool. Most recipes mention *'to 120 wool'* which may have been the standard dye batch. This would have been easy to scale up for a larger quantity and worked well in the size of vats and furnaces that were available on the premises. It was also a multiple of the weight required to make up the warps and wefts for standard lengths of cloth which required about 60 lbs of wool for each. Lower amounts suggested that the clothier had not provided sufficient wool of a suitable grade. The smaller batches of pinks, may have been experimental colours for a cloth especially commissioned by a clothier for his factor, for a local customer or perhaps a spouse. They seem to have only written down the amounts and methods for the dyes that worked correctly, perhaps having done several tests beforehand, as there are no additional comments about the samples or adjustments to the recipes. The entries don't mention the grade of wool to be coloured either so possibly the dyer did not need to know if it came from his own stock. Wool would have been sorted by the clothier before it was delivered to the dyehouse to match a specific quality of wool for his *'fine'*, *'superfine'* or kersey cloth. In some of the other dye recipe books held by The National Archives the sort of wool is described in more detail, it was also in several inventories of the period.

3.15 'Woad to This'

The second line, and my favourite, *'Woad to This'* with its sample of dyed wool of a particular blue hue attached to the paper with red wax. What does it mean? This term may have originated prior to the mid 1500s when the only English blue was obtained from a woad vat and the phrase remained even though the indigo/woad vat had been in use for more than two hundred years. Woad was sold to the dyer graded by strength and quality of colour depending on the country of origin and whether it was the first, second or a subsequent harvest. The earliest of these books mention woad or 'blew' at 1d and 1 ½d and the later ones at 4d or 5d, these amounts referred to a standard shade of blue that could be ordered by the clothiers.

3.16 Customer Complaint overcharged for a 12d blue instead of a 10d blue

By the 18th century, the woad standard was still in use but the grading related to the

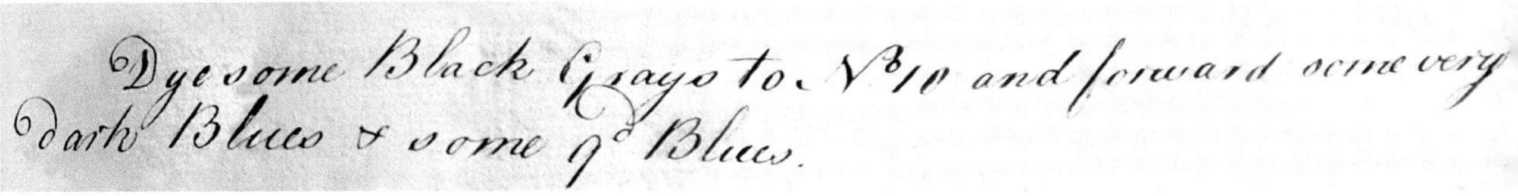

Dye some Black Grays to No 10 and forward some very dark Blues & some 9d Blues.

3.17 Dyeing by Value of the Blue Indigo Standard

quality and value of the indigo. The difference in price may have reflected an increase in the cost of producing the same grade of blue. The recipe does not state how to obtain the particular shade required, but most samples appear to be of a mid tone which would make a good base for other colours. The blacks have a much darker blue ground which would have required repeated dips in the vat. To match the grade of blue, a careful visual check would have been required as the colour of wet wool is not the same as when it is dry. Expertise and years of experience were needed to avoid costly mistakes. Despite our technology, true colour matching today is still very difficult but in the 18th century immersing wool in a natural fermentation vat would be even more variable as it relied on the quality of all the ingredients to produce the best reaction. The recipes suggest that once dyed it was *'Waished Well'* to remove any loose colour and it was not until this was finished and dry that it could be properly colour matched.

3.18 Grades of Blue

To 100 of Mr Pillmans
One Hund.d of furrich
In Boys Boyl 2 Sol
4 5 Sand 6 Brach
Boyl 4 Ours Sho
1 Copp 8 Allom Ly in
Dec 6 1751

To 120 24 fust 3 Bras
56 Mad Boyl
4 Ours Shot
9 All 3 Carbr
Hand this lot Mun
Hon pomp hups had
In with 2 Bras hup
A Bar & Ton
Dec 11 1756 Mr

To 120 : 21 fust
1 Log 9 San
Shol 3 Copp
9 All
Everett Dec 1756

To 120 = 2 Sher 2 Log 2 Fust
1 Rod 1 Sands 1½ Mad. Boyl
1 Quor Shot 1½ Copp Bo
Ly In All Night
Wm Everett 1756

To 120 42 Fust 4½
2 Mad. 3 Log Boyl
Shot 1½ Copp & 2 All Ly
Wm Everett 1756

60
60 Mr 23
Boyl in
1½ 12
Boy 4
Shots
Mr
In Allom Ly
6 lb 3 Log

To 116 Mr Heyto
12 fust 12 Mad
24 Sand Boyl
Sand & Shot 9
6 Carbr Ly
Dec 28 1756

To 70 Wooll to this
Log Boyl 4 Quor
Shot 1 Allom Boyl 4
Sand Mr Sand Licker
Boyl 6 of Woals
Mr Butlor 1756

To 120 36 Fust 12 San
Boyl 2 Quors Shot
3 All Boyl Ly In
Wm Everett 1756

To 120 96 Fust
1 Log Boyl 1 Quo
1 All Ly In Wm Ever

The next few lines include the dyes and mordants to produce the second colour sample of dyed wool, the browns, blacks, violets, and greens. The recipe lists mordants like alum, argol (tartar), sumach, galls and copperas (ferrous sulphate) which fix and brighten or sadden the colours. Some are followed by a little additional instruction such as *'boylle'* for several hours *'till done'* or *'ly in all night'*.

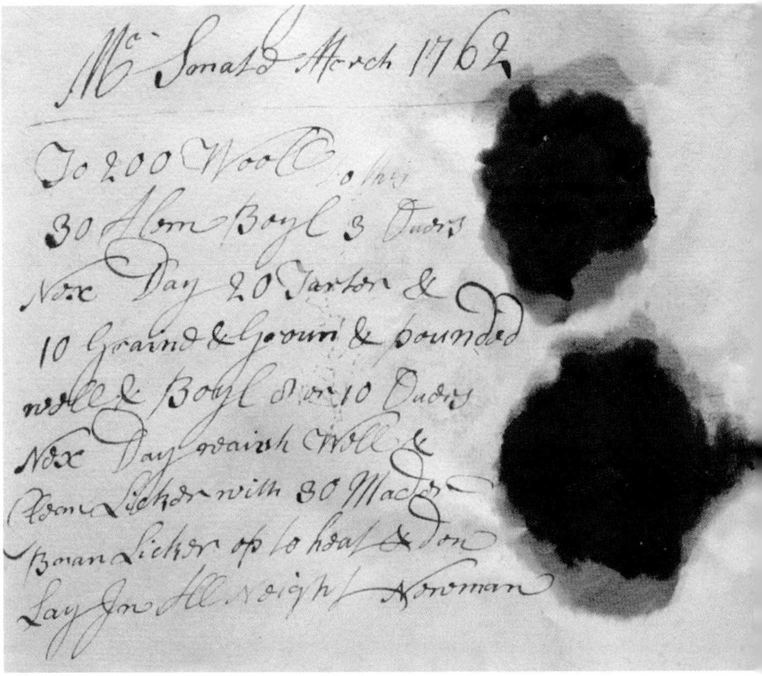

3.20 Dyeing with Madder and Grain

In this book, there are only two samples of bright pink where *'grain'* was added to the dye liquor but without any explanation for preparing the kermes which, like indigo, needed to be finely ground. It is not clear if this scarlet dyeing was done by another Frome specialist or perhaps this batch was coloured on-site. Dyes in this book include madder root and kermes and the tropical heartwoods; logwood, fustick, peachwood, barwood, redwood and camwood, which were *'chipped'* for the dyers in the local mills. Each recipe varies slightly in the different amounts of these substances: some used alum as a mordant and others a combination of several ingredients. Mordanting was not always done in a separate vessel from the colouring except in two instances where it mentions using clean liquor, it was strewn across the liquid in the vessel in small quantities and mixed well. With wool that has been mordanted with alum and copperas, camwood gives a bluer tone to rich claret-brown shades, sanderswood a yellower shade of brown and barwood a mid tone.[6] The measurements for these recipes are very precise, and dyers were aware of wool's sensitivity to alkaline substances which make it feel harsh and if too strong can rot the fibre.

The first or last line of the entry occasionally included a name of a person and a date. This dye recipe book was probably a working record of an independent master dyer, so the names listed were likely to have been

3.19 Dye Recipe Book

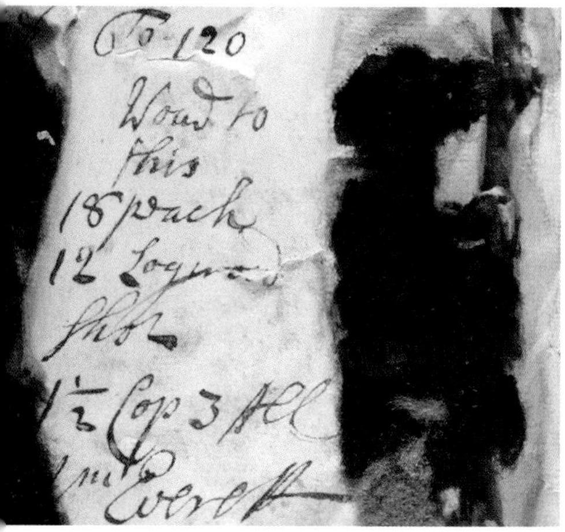

3.21 Mr Everett

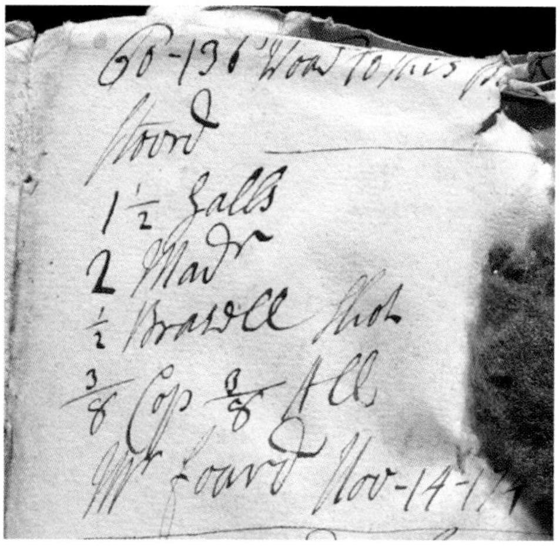

3. 22 Mr Ford

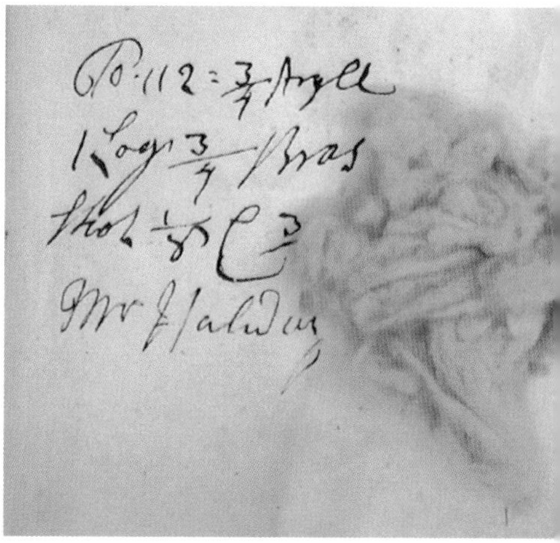

3.23 Mr Halliday

those of the clothier or the factor requesting the work. If the workshop employed several dyers the workman's name may have been noted so he could have dyed additional batches of the same colour. There are however indications that the first suggestion applied as several entries have the name 'Messr's Pittman', one of the many generations of family members working in partnerships. Mr Naish was a clothier from Beckington and Cornelius Batt, a Frome clothier. Robert Hinton married and applied for settlement in Frome parish in 1717. In his application he mentions supervising cloth workers on behalf of Mr Samuel Allen's cloth trade in Frome, as Samuel was a druggist who resided in Bristol. Of the entries with names the majority were for a Mr William Everett who may have been a clothier in Horningsham whose trade supplied livery cloth for the staff of Lord Folkestone amongst others. Wool may have been dyed for Mr Cockell, the owner of a small dye works in Corsley by 1746.

The next two books, one dated 1809 to 1814 and the other undated, seem to record part of the production process of cloth by a manufactory. By this time, Wallbridge dyehouse was owned by Robert Meares, listed as a dyer in Pigot's directory.

The second book of recipes dating almost 60 years later may reflect changes in the dyeing methods. Like the first, it is in need of conservation, however, it is not as badly worn and because the samples are neat little circles of wool and later cloth, the book has retained its shape and can be kept closed. The cover is made from a blue paper covered pasteboard, entitled *'Dye Book 1809 Dark Colours'*, its size is 9 x 13 ½in, and inside there are 32 pages sewn together with a single row of stitching to form the back spine. It contains 377 recipes of which about

120 appear to be wool and the remainder woven cloth, apart from the woad samples which are also wool. The abbreviations of the process are slightly different, '*St*' is used in place of the earlier '*shot*' and '*bl*' rather than '*boylle*'. The colour samples in this book are deep browns, dark blues, blacks and mixed dark greys. Like the other there are two sorts of recipe, some that are woaded and then over dyed with logwood, barwood, fustic etc. and those that are only dyed once with the various chipped dyewoods. There are fewer woaded swatches by the end of the period and those only mention 'blue @ 5d' without a sample. For the cheaper cloths logwood may have been the only dye used as it was less expensive. Five pounds of the best indigo contained nearly as much colouring matter as two hundred pounds of woad[7]. Fifty tons of logwood was claimed to be the equivalent of five hundred tons of woad. Discerning customers were still looking for the distinctive blue rose at the corner of the finished cloth as a sign of a good quality black, but by the 1800s, the method of dyeing black with logwood had improved to such an extent that some dyers just coloured the corner blue to satisfy the perception that it had been dyed properly in the old ways!

The first line of the recipe is '*Wool 254 for 240*' except for one that mentions '*140 of medley locks*' which could be mixed Spanish and English wool or different sorts of wool. It may have been more important for a clothier to annotate the waste in the process of preparing the wool than the dyer who charged for the actual weight he was given to dye. Wool washers handled the batches of 240 lbs at a time. Unlike the previous recipe book, each entry has a unique batch reference number. This could possibly track the inventory back to the specific dye recipe and throughout the process of scribbling, carding, spinning, weaving, finishing; and then, if sold, listed in the accounts

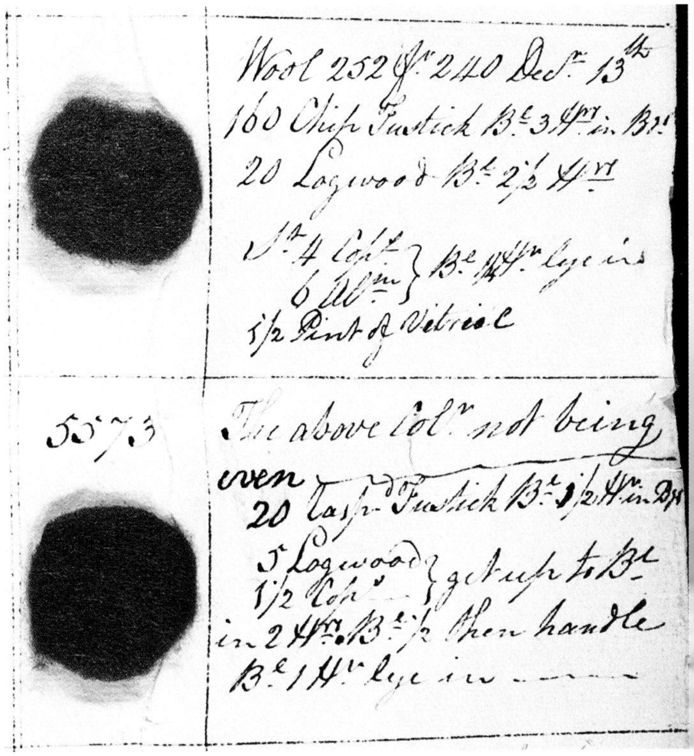

3.24 Uneven Dyeing

receivable ledgers. There is one example in the book which shows uneven dyeing that was redone, which is probably why it does not have a batch number and two that have batch numbers but they are annotated *'bad barwood'* underneath the sample. Presumably the recipes were correct but the ingredients were spoilt or of an inferior quality.

3.25 / 3.26 Wool and Cloth Sample in Different Books with the Same Reference Number

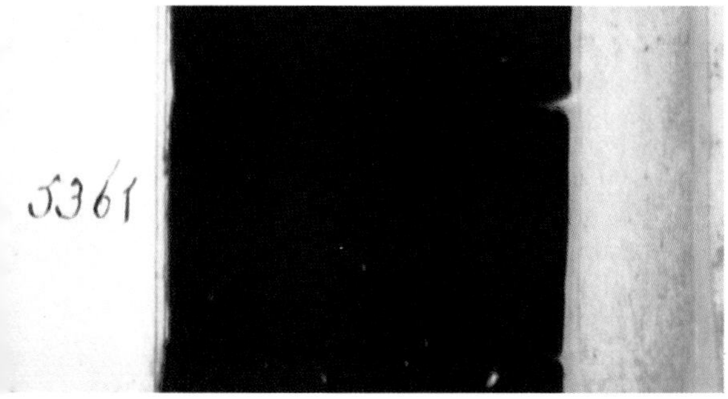

In this book each recipe has a date which may indicate when it was written in the book or the day it was dyed. The entry dates are sequential, but as before, the sample could not be attached until the wool was dry or the cloth was woven and finished. There is an increase in the number of entries year on year, perhaps due to the additional demand for uniform material. To avoid contaminating light colours, it is possible that there were certain days for dyeing dark colours. It may have been more efficient to dye at different times because some of the weaker solutions were used for dipping the lighter colours, once a dark grey brown was obtained other wool could be dyed to obtain a lighter shade of beige, or as a ground on the wool for a different colour.

The process required a great deal of accuracy; because some old dye solutions may have been exhausted and new ones prepared, others like madder contained residual colour which may have been used as a base for the woad/indigo vat or could be modified with mordants. This practice may have reduced the possibility of accidental spillage of darks onto lights. '*... and the light dove stained by an olive cloth when wet put on it.*[8]' Or, it may have just been from an earlier period when dyeing with woad on set days was necessary to allow the time to bring the vat to work while avoiding Sundays and holy days; or even a simple lack of furnace capacity and insufficient equipment. One question this book raises is

3.27 Dye Recipe Book

Dye Book 1809

Dixon [illegible]

whether some of the earlier samples were dyed in the wool and the later cloth swatches dyed in the piece.

The book has entries for part of the year starting in 1809 followed by four complete years. There does not appear to be a regular routine for dyeing dark colours on set days each week but this may have been introduced later. Perhaps, if a new workshop was just being established on the site and was quite small with few furnaces and insufficient work; or it could have been a commercial decision for the dyer to specialise in a restricted palette of colours. The first complete year is in 1810 and assuming these are the dyeing dates, each recipe appears to be for one unique colour on any given day apart from two entries with the same date, one of which seems to correct an uneven dye batch. The workshop may have just specialised in 'Blue and Medley' dyeing as suggested in a local directory which is possibly the case as these swatches are predominantly blue, but at the time there was an increase in demand for uniform material. If the dyers owned or leased the fulling mill they may have undertaken all the finishing processes as well. The first dyeing day was Monday 1st January 1810. In that year, it would seem that dark colours were only dyed once a week but on different days, Saturday 6th, Friday 12th, Wednesday 17th, Thursday 25th. There were only three dark dyeing days in March, August and October, one in September and a final two in December. As there are no records, dyeing lighter colours may have taken place on the same days. In total for the year there were only 42 dyeing days. In 1811, the number of dark dyeing days had doubled to 81, and there were considerably more dyeing days from April onwards with nine in both October and November. In 1812 there were 11 in the month of June and a total of 110 over the year and likewise in 1813 a total of 114, an average of 9 – 10 a month. This surely reflected an increase in the demand. Frome was known to be one of the towns supplying large quantities of cloth for military uniforms during the Napoleonic wars (1799 – 1815), so the increased number of dyeing days may have corresponded to a business expansion in response to the war.

The third book may provide information on the type of cloth produced as well as the range of colours. The title '*Colour Patterns*' is written on the handmade cover of vellum rescued from another document that had

5349

Wool 252 Jr 240 June 13
Blue @ 4d then
30 Chip Fustick Bc 3 Hrs in Bo[illegible]
10 Logwood Bc 2½ Hrs
Sr Alm 20 } Bc 1 Hr
~~Cop~~ } lye in

5335

Wool 252 Jr 240 June 14
120 Chip Fustick Bc 3 Hrs
20 M Madder } Bc 2½ Hr
12 Logwood }
Sr 5 Cop } Bc 1 Hr
2 Alm } lye in

5366

Wool 252 Jr 240 June 25th
Blue @ 4d then
140 Chip Fustick Bc 3 Hrs in Bo
5 Logwood Bc 2 Hrs
Sr 20 Alm } Bc 1 Hr
2 Cop } lye in

5375

Wool 252 Jr 240 June 30th
Blue @ 4d then
130 Chip Fustick Bc 3 Hrs in Bo
6 Logwood Bc 2 Hrs
Sr 26 Alm Bc 1½ Hr
lye in

5382

Wool 252 Jr 240 July 9th
Blue @ 4d then
1[illegible] Chip Fustick Bc 3 Hrs in Bo
1[illegible] Logwood Bc 2 Hrs
Sr 20 Alm Bc 1½ Hr
lye in

5395

Wool 252 Jr 240 July 17
Blue @
12[illegible] Chip Fustick Bc 3 Hrs in Bo
5 Logwood Bc 2 Hrs
Sr 20 Alm } Bc 1 Hr
2 Copr } lye in

5407

Wool 252 Jr 240 July 26
Blue @ then
125 Chip Fustick Bc 3 Hrs
4 Logwood Bc 2 Hrs
Sr 25 Alm Bc 1½ Hr
lye in

54[illegible]

Wool 252 Jr 240 July 31
Blue @ 5d then
120 Chip Fustick Bc 3 Hrs
20 Logwood Bc 2 Hrs
Sr 20 Alm } Bc 1½ Hr
2 Cop } lye in

5433

Wool 252 Jr 240 Augst 10
Blue @ 5d then
130 Chip Fustick Bc 3 Hrs
2 Logwood Bc 2 Hrs
Sr 25 Alm Bc 1½ Hr lye in

5449

Wool 252 Jr 240 Augst 17
Blue @ 5d then
135 Chip Fustick Bc 3 Hrs
5 Logwood Bc 2 Hrs
Sr 25 Alm } Bc 1½ Hr
½ Cop } lye in

54[illegible]3

Wool 252 Jr 240 Augst 30th
Blue @ 5d then
120 Chip Fustick Bc 3 Hrs
15 Logwood Bc 2 Hrs
Sr 18 Alm } Bc 1½ lye in
½ Cop }

5475

Wool 252 Jr 240 Sept 11th
120 Barwood } Bc ½ Hr
30 Redwood } then the Wool 3 Hr
30 Logwood }
Sr 6 Copr Bc 1½ Hr lye in

6695 Wool 254 Qr 240 Janr 13-1812
145 Chip Fustick Bl 3 Hrs in Bags
35 Barwood
15 M Madder } Bl 3 Hrs
11 Logwood
St 4 Alm
4 Copr } Bl 1 Hr lye in

6709 Wool 254 Qr 240 Janr 16-1812
Blue @ 5d then
112 Chip Fustick Bl 3 Hrs
21 Logwood Bl 2 Hrs
St 18 Alm
2 Copr } Bl 1/2 Hr lye in

6721 Wool 254 Qr 240 Janr 21st
140 Chip Fustick Bl 3 Hrs
56 M Madder
20 Barwood } Bl 3 Hrs
10 Logwood
St 5 Copr
3 Alm } Bl 1 Hr lye in

6735 Wool 254 Qr 240 Janr 24th
150 Chip Fustick Bl 3 Hrs
57 Logwood Bl 2 1/2 Hrs
St 4 Copr
4 Alm } Bl 1 Hr lye in

6745 Wool 254 Qr 240 Janr 25
Blue @ 5d then
112 Chip Fustick Bl 3 Hrs
57 Logwood Bl 2 Hrs
St 18 Alm
2 Copr } Bl 1/2 Hr
lye in

6757 Wool 254 Qr 240 Janr 29th
140 Chip Fustick Bl 3 Hrs
18 Barwood
15 M Madder } Bl 2 1/2 Hrs
16 Logwood
St 4 Alm
4 Copr } Bl 1 Hr lye in

6771 Wool 254 Qr 240 Feby 3
150 Chip Fustick Bl 3 Hrs in Bags
57 Logwood Bl 2 1/2 Hrs
St 4 Alm
4 Copr } Bl 1 Hr lye in
[illegible]

6785 Wool 254 Qr 240 Feby 6
Blue @ 5d then
130 Chip Fustick Bl 3 Hrs
5 Logwood Bl 2 Hrs
St 23 Alm Bl 1/2 Hr
lye in

6795 Wool 254 Qr 240 Feby 11
140 Chip Fustick Bl 3 Hrs
30 Madder in Bags
60 Barwood } Bl 3 Hrs
13 Logwood
St 5 Copr Bl 1 Hr
Boil

6807 Wool 254 Qr 240 Feby 13
145 Chip Fustick Bl 3 Hrs
20 1/2 Logwood Bl 2 1/2 Hrs
St 4 Alm
4 Copr } Bl 1 Hr
lye in

6821 Wool 254 Qr 240 Feby 17
Blue @ 5d then
120 Chip Fustick Bl 3 Hrs
13 Logwood Bl 2 1/2 Hrs
St 18 Alm
2 Copr } Bl 1/2 Hr lye in

6835 Wool 254 Qr 240 Feby 2[illegible]
150 Chip Fustick
50 M Madder } Bl 3 Hrs
10 Logwood Bl 2 1/2 [illegible]
St 4 Alm
4 Copr } Bl 1 Hr
see 7005 [illegible] [illegible]

writing in the top right hand corner of the back cover which was then folded over to the inside. The book leaves are made from sheets of approximately A3 folded in half, each side with three straight columns of seventeen very neat rectangular swatches of cloth, cut from a template and glued to the paper next to a reference number.

On one half, the colours show subtle variations of the dark tones of blues, blacks and browns; a few of these appear to match the recipe of a specific colour from the second recipe book. The other half of the book has three columns of light shades of beiges, sands and buffs. There are no dates and the batch numbers next to each cloth sample follow mostly in order but others don't which may suggest the variable time it took to weave and dress each cloth. As the title suggests, a record of the finished woollen material made by the clothier for his customers and factors to place orders. As an experienced clothier he could no doubt distinguish between the finely finished samples of a *'fine'*, *'superfine'*, *'second'* or another grade of cloth but without a close study of the weave structure it is not possible to tell the difference. These cloths were generally plain weave and after fulling, raising the nap and shearing several times, the structure of the weave would be virtually invisible but the finish would be thick, soft and very smooth. Two interesting loose samples in the inside front cover show a buff coloured swatch about a half inch by an inch and less than an eighth thick with a twill weave and a magnifying glass reveals a plain weave on the dark blue cloth. On the last page of the book there are four samples of a corded weave structure and one 2/2 twill which may be a cassimere rather than broadcloth.

3.30 Sample of Wool Cord

3.29 Cloth Samples Cut from a Template in the Same Book

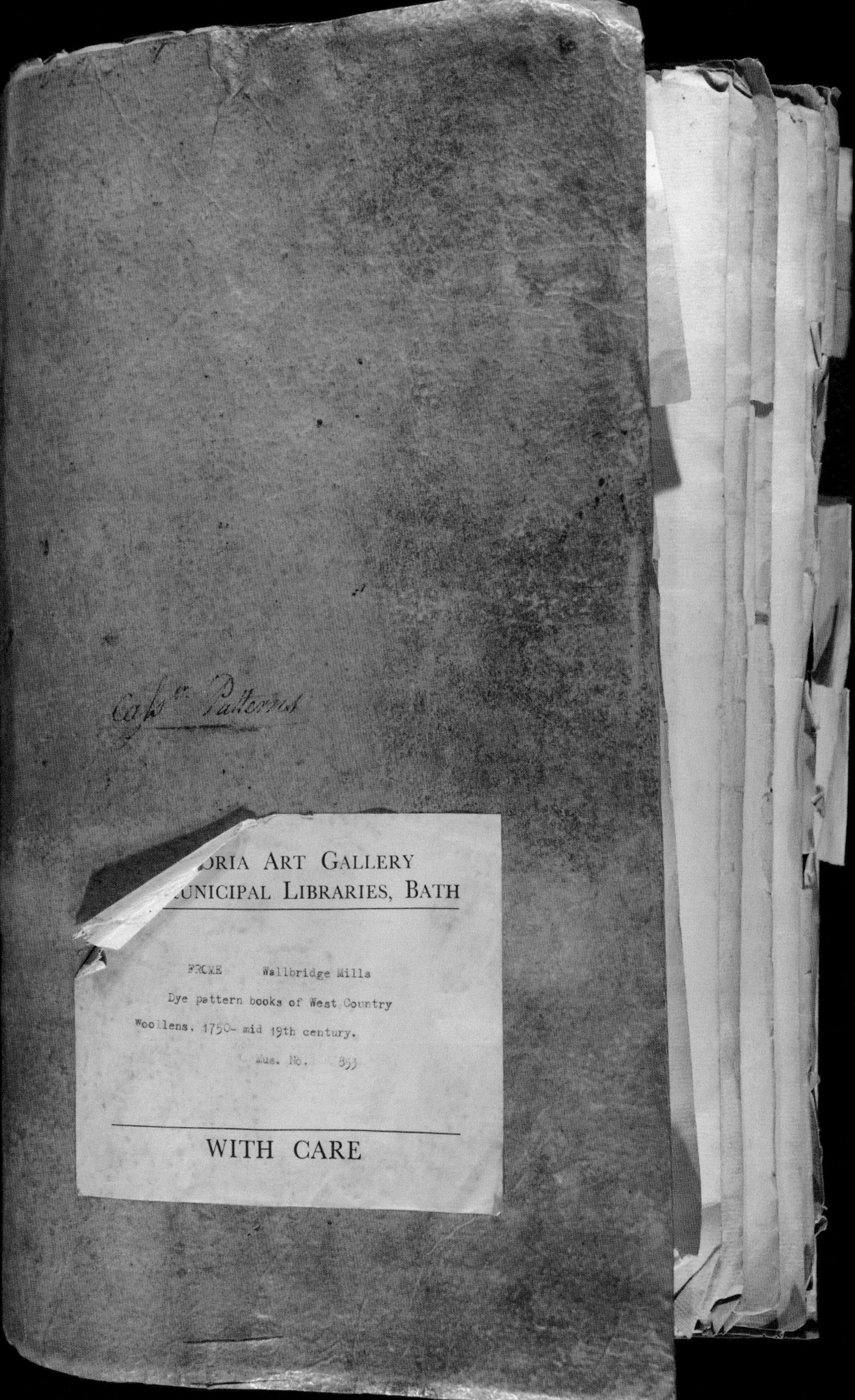
Patterns
ORIA ART GALLERY
UNICIPAL LIBRARIES, BATH
FROME Wallbridge Mills
Dye pattern books of West Country
Woollens, 1750- mid 19th century.
Mus. No. 853
WITH CARE

5750
5707
5752
5706
5733
5775
5797
5765
5785
5748
5551
5774
5801
5766
5783
5777
5719
5839
5768
5842

6082
6109
5968
6122
6130
6121
6129
6107
6132
6120
6147
6133
6123
6131
6146
6088
6148

6159
6100
6160
6158
6171
6173
6172
6169
6124
6149
6174
6170
6216
6224
6137
6202
6213

6197
6217
5540
6575
6304
6250
6190
6231
6257
6240
6195
6234
6271
6209
6232
6233
6247

The two books suggest that the business may have included a dyehouse, but also manufactured and finished cloth. The recipe and production books together indicate that whoever owned them had a thorough working knowledge of every process in the manufacture of cloth and possibly dyed both in the wool and in the piece. Finished cloth was sent to the London factor at Blackwell Hall or alternatively sold wholesale by the piece to a town draper and the seconds were sold directly to customers by the yard at the local market.

These three books were donated to the Bath Reference Library at the same time, but there is no way of knowing if they belonged to the same dyer or clothier or if they were used in the same workshop or how they came to be in the possession of Mr Henry Batten-Pooll.

---

[1] Gill, D 2003: 2
[2] Frome Museum index of fire policies
[3] Gomez Smart - http://www.gomezsmart.myzen.co.uk/
[4] Cooper, T 1815: 186
[5] Partridge, W 1823: 12
[6] Ponting, KG 1980: 30
[7] Cooper, T 1815: 40
[8] Mann, J de Lacy 1964: 2

Small dye workbooks that could fit in the pocket of a leather apron

CHAPTER 4

WELSHMILL DYEHOUSE

'...To this pattern only somewhat grazier and mellow coloured. Save this note, return to me. Deader, snugger and grazier but not too dirty and hevy neither'

Whitchurch wool sample books 1740

A second collection of 18th century wool sample and dye recipe books from Frome are held in The National Archives. These work books pre-date the ones from Wallbridge mill, but some names infer a possible connection with the Wallbridge dyers. They formed part of the evidence for the settlement of a case which was brought to Chancery between 1724 and 1740 and were never reclaimed. The fine cloth trade had started to decline in the South West and Frome was losing its importance in the cloth manufacture, perhaps the family was no longer interested in

4.12 1651 Whitchurch Token Farthing

retaining the business. The Whitchurch family, whose legacies were at the heart of the dispute, were established in Frome by 1573. They may have moved from Shawford where a John Whitchurch had a cloth fulling mill in 1516 that housed two fulling stocks and a grist mill or from Rode where the Whitchurches were numerous as linen drapers.[1] The wills of 1621 and 1635 give the occupation of William as a linen draper and of Robert as a mercer. Over the years, the family had accumulated wealth from extensive property in and around Frome including the manors of Nunney Castle and Maudley Castle. The second son of William Whitchurch, also named William, was bequeathed the estate of Berrow and other lands and had to pay legacies of £500 to each of the eight surviving children; some of these were not paid and as a consequence led to the litigation.

This necessitated a visit to The National Archives at Kew to order one record C104/3. The requested docket brought eleven boxes to the secure room and kept them and us under lock and key. We were only allowed to view one box at a time, with each one secured before the next one was released, which does make it difficult to study the context of an entire collection. These boxes contain another extraordinary source of the day-to-day working documents of Frome's dyeing and clothier trades: six dye recipe books, some scribbled notes, a letter, an indenture and several boxes of loose wool swatches. Some of the dye books are undated but precede the probable closure of the case around 1740. Many more boxes of documents remain to be explored, wills, depositions, bills, answers and pleadings, and other relevant letters and accounts may be untangled to provide a more complete picture.

Working documents like these rarely survive, and like today, when a company goes into administration most are simply thrown away. The records of Bull versus Jesser[2]

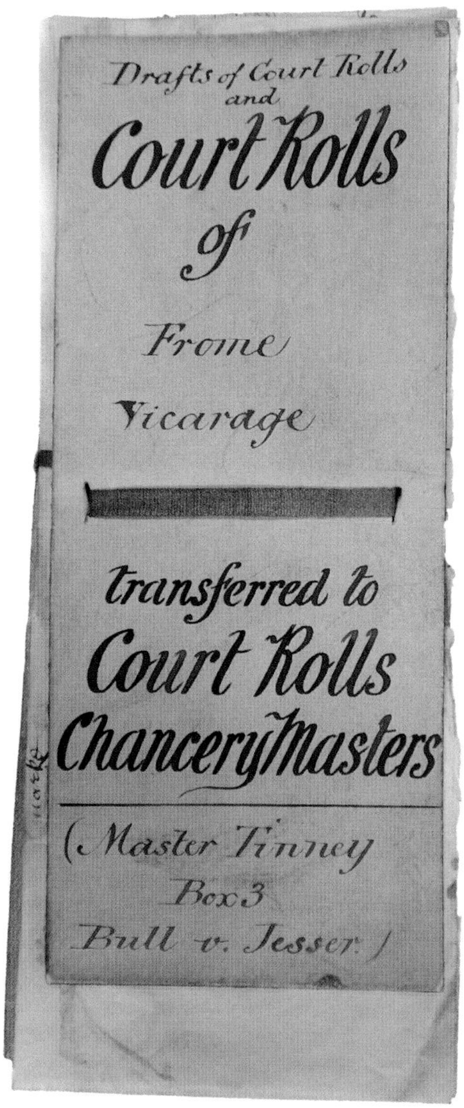

4.3 Chancery Documents

provide a glimpse into the past business history of a wealthy Frome family but the complexity involved in unravelling the details is shown by the number of suits involved. Descendants include members of the Whitchurch, Bull, Jesser, Phelps, Smith and Allen families and many other familiar Frome names. Many members of the families were involved in the dyeing and clothier trades of the 18th century. Two Leversedge daughters married into the Bull family, clothiers of Hall House, one of whom has a handsome monument in St John's church, among the few Frome clothiers to do so.[3] The Jessers were the owners of a fulling mill and dyehouse at Welshmill and may have been responsible for producing the workbooks as evidence.

The will of William Whitchurch, Gentleman, in 1691 bequeaths

> *'...all those my mills called Hapsford Mills to my daughter Sarah.[4]'*

The 1728 will of Thomas Jesser, Clothier, leaves his dyehouse, store, and meadow to his brother Joseph Jesser of Mells. He also leaves £100 for the poor of Frome.

> *'... and to my spinners at Longbridge Deverill £10 in proportion to the quantity of work done for me over the past 12 months before my demise.[5]'*

Separated from the corresponding financial ledgers and accounts of the business, it is impossible to speculate why these dye books, dating from 1724, would prove useful to untangle litigation either for the plaintiffs William and Elizabeth Bull or the defendants Joseph Jesser and others, unless they showed the extent of the inventory. However, in their own right they are fascinating documents of industrial social history possibly associated with a dyehouse at Welshmill. As with the previous collection of dye books, there are no

4.4 The Weir at Welshmill

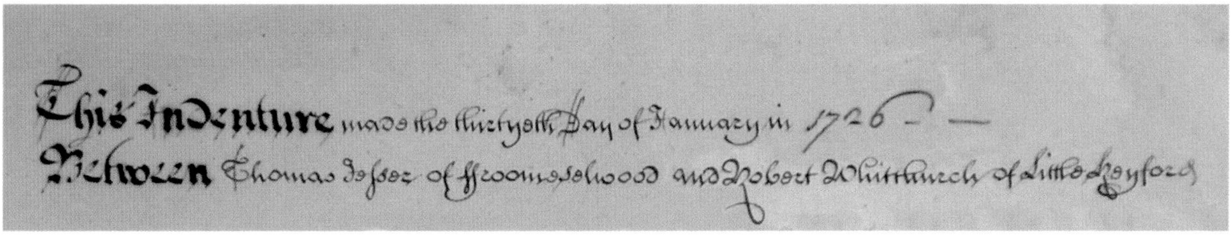
This Indenture made the thirtyeth Day of January in 1726 —
Between Thomas Jesser of Froomeselwood and Robert Whitchurch of Little Keyford

4.5 Indenture for a Lease of a Dyehouse

inscriptions to confirm their true provenance. Edward Whitchurch, a dry salter, was paying a tithing on a part of Welshmill in 1720 and possibly owned more by 1744. In the same years, George Whitchurch was paying a tithing on the Town Mill[6] near the Willow Vale dyehouse which was later sold by the dyer Samuel Allen in 1796.[7] An interesting agreement is mentioned in the indenture of 1726 between Thomas Jesser, clothier of Frome Selwood and Robert Whitchurch, clothier of Little Keyford which grants Thomas the right to rent a dyehouse for £10 a year but if he defaults on payment by more than 20 days, Robert has the right to enter the dyehouse and use the furnaces and utensils to dye four packs of wool in lieu of payment after which Thomas can return to his trade without further interference by either Robert or any of his executors or assignees.[8] I have made an assumption that this document may refer to Welshmill but the specific place name is not mentioned, however, later evidence suggests that a Thomas Jesser occupied Welshmill in 1766.[9]

4.6 Signatures and Seals

These books have hardly been touched for the last 280 years, but heavy usage in the dyehouse and the lack of proper conservation, may have hastened their deterioration. Their condition has been stabilised by textile experts using specialist methods to smooth the pages,

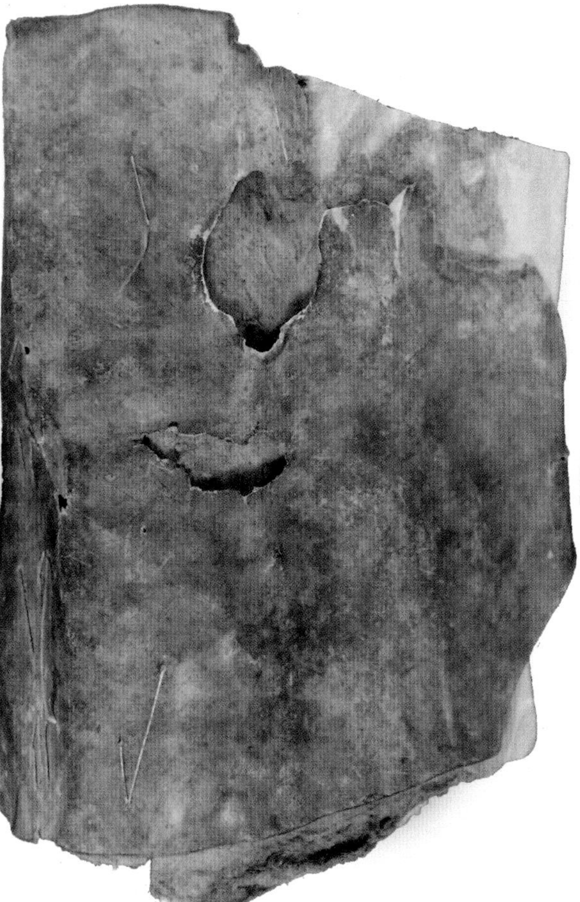

4.7 One of Two Pocket Size Dyer's Workbooks

carefully patch torn sheets and undertake other essential conservation. As they have not been exposed to light for hundreds of years, the true colours of the samples may not have been affected. Each page, as it is turned, reveals the beautiful variety of shades obtained with natural dyes and demonstrates the mastery of the specialist skill of the dyers. These dye books belonged to ordinary working people who may have been dyers, clothiers or business owners experienced in both trades.

Two of the books may have been day-to-day working orders for dyehouse men.[10] They are undated and don't include many samples. Securely cocooned in leather, they are small enough to be kept in the pocket of a leather apron or on a slope desk at the back of the workshop for reference of the day's work. Further detailed study could determine if there are duplicate receipts and if the handwriting might belong to the same person.

The third book is aptly entitled:

> *Dye Book*[11]
> *Commence*
> *August 12, 173(?)*

It is 7 x 8 ¾ in with a heavy paper cover, both the back and front inside face are unmarked. Inside, there are 14 pages, the last few have been left blank. The first page is divided into four columns. I have presumed that

4.8 Dye Book Headers

the headings carry over to the following pages although they are not written down in the same way and some names have been scribbled out.

There are three receipts on the first page but only the middle one still has its small grey wool sample attached. Numbered 739, 741 and 743, the

Copy Book

Commence

Augt 12 [illegible]

wool, described as *'the best throwings'* with the initials *'RH SS @ 18 '*, for a total quantity of 120 lbs of wool; the next entry mentions *'RH SS 60 @ 18 and J. Laws 60 @15 ½ '* a mix of various qualities of fleece from two different suppliers. The third entry mentions more of both *'RH SS 37, and 60 of J. Laws'* and also *'other fine 25'* but does not mention a price. These amounts add up to 120 lbs of wool, which may be the proportional weight for the required dye ingredients in the next column. The quantity of dyestuff column confirms the weight of wool with *'120 wool'* in the top left corner, although some are for less and a few for considerably more. Only one or two entries have a full explanation of how the colour was achieved and others only mention the quantity of dye stuff. Far more than the Wallbridge Mill books suggest, these dyers used a considerable measure of *'sigg'* in their dyeing to obtain different tones of madder red and orange. Perhaps the indigo/woad vat, while very smelly from the fermentation was slightly less offensive.

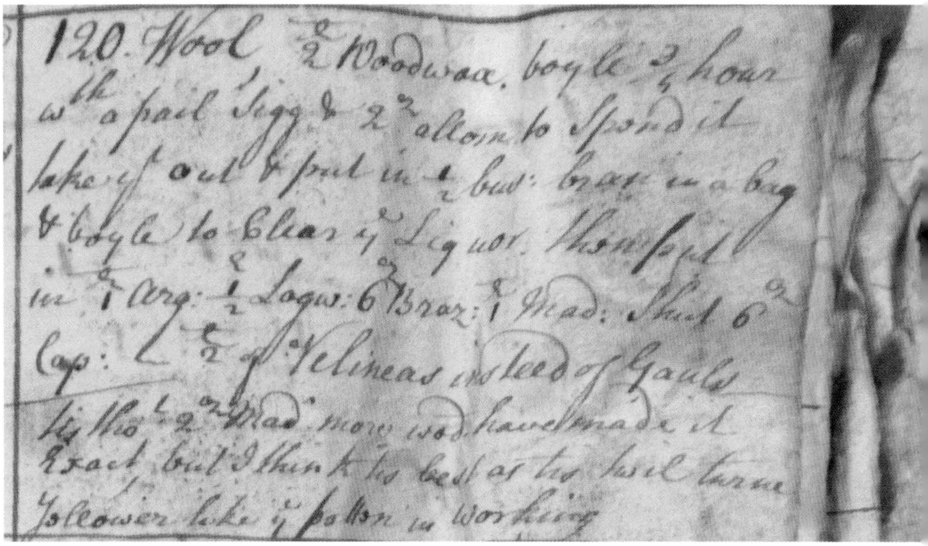

4.10 Detailed Dyeing Instructions

The following five full pages of this notebook have two columns with up to 30 swatches of wool per page of soft greys, fawns, browns and other autumnal colours in neat little rows. The recipes, using the dyers unique abbreviations, denote the quantity of dyestuffs for each shade: All – allum, G – galls, M – madder, written as mather, log – logwood, su – shumac, san - sanderswood, f – fustick, cop – copperas. The next page has beautiful samples of madder reds, one of which mentions *'cropp mather'* which was a better quality than the ordinary, however, the shade does not look too dissimilar from the others. A plentiful supply of *'sigg'* was measured by the pail, tankard or tub full. Sadly there is no mention of the actual process to produce the depth of colour they were able to

250/
36 Allom 30 M 40 pou
15 L 2 pails Sig

120/
18 Allm 15 M: 14 B 4 2 L: a pail Sigg

120/
18 Allm 24 Crop M. 6 d: F

125/
15 Allm 36 d F: 36 M

125/
18 All: 35 M 18 B 3 L

200/
38 All 112 M: 30 d F

250/
36 All 66 M 30 B 1 L

125/
18 All: 42 Mad

125/
18 Allm: 36 M 12 d F

125/
18 Allm 30 d F: put in 1/4 w
4 d allm 15 M:
125/ 18 Ar 36 M 30 B 1 1/2 L
1 pail Sig

120/
18 All 7 M 3 B

125/
18 All 15 M 36 B 2 L a pail Sig

125/
18 All 6 B 36 M
a pail Sig

120/
18 All 15 M 18 B 3 L
a pail Sig

120/
18 All 30 B a pail Sig

120/
18 all: 36 M: 12 B
8 2 L
a Spuggel of Sig

120/
18 All 6 d F: with 2 all
40 M

120/
18 All 36 M 18 B L
a Spugel of Sig

240/
36 All 36 M 36 pou: 3 L
lib of Sigg

120/ 1 G 1 Ar: 2 B 6 F 2 L 7 Sig 16

120/ 1 G 1 Ar: 2 L 2 B 4 F 6 2 L

240/ 2 G 2 Ar: 8 L
4 pou: 5 6

240)

2 G 6 ¼ d ʃ 10 d S 2 [illegible]

250)

4 lb: 14 d S 4 m 2 [illegible]

50) of 1½ blew: Boyled wth
4 ale: grazd wth 1½ [illegible]
a fresh Liquor

120)

1 Vel: 4½ ʃ 3 m: 2 L
1 S 2 C ¼ L

120) Dyed in ¼d Liqr of [illegible]
20 ʃ 2 of [illegible]
is a choice thing in these
Col: 1 m 3 L ½ C
1 ale

120) 1½ Vel: 2½ L 3 B
½ Sau: ½ m ¾ C

120) Dyed after that
next above in a fresh
Liqr 10 ʃ 2 S 3 m
2 L 1 ½ C
Mine Aug: 26: 1734

No 749
120) Mine Aug: 27: 1734
1½ Vel: 2 ʃ: 2½ L 2 m
Shut wth 1½ C 1 ale

No 751
120) Mine Sep: 7
1½ Vel: 1 Arg: 1½ 10 L
1 Sau: 1 Mad: 4 C 12 A
designed to be some of the shine
but browner & Judge the
loss of Sau: & 10 m & the
two Cop: wood make a better
Col. & sorrow the hard [illegible]
Blue [illegible]

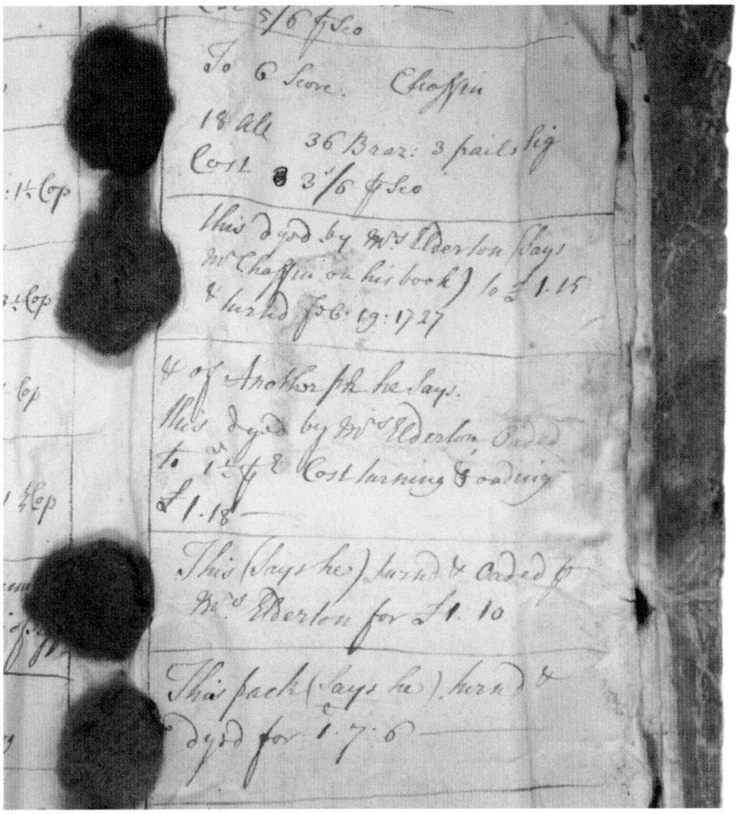

4.13 Entry for Mr Elderton

achieve. Most required simmering for several hours, pre-mordanting and immersing in fresh solutions to modify the colours further.

Some names have been crossed out, these may have been the wool suppliers, the clothiers or the specialist blue dyers. In the second column on page five, a few reds and blues appear to have been *'turned and oaded'* by Messrs Elderton, the cost is also annotated. Page nine reverts back to the format of the first page and some recipes provide a little more explanation to achieve the desired colour, two list batch numbers 749 and 751. These entries raise more questions when compared to the headers on the first page. Was the wool purchased from Mr Ford or is he the recipient of the dyed wool? (While it may not be the same person, the inscription dated 1735/6 on the inside cover of another dye book says that it was lent to a Mr John Ford, whose will of 1754 mentioned that he was a clothier from Nunney.)

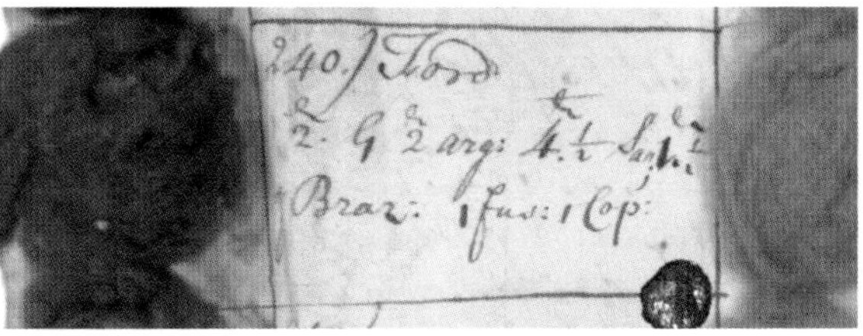

4.14 Entry for Mr Ford

The fourth book,[12] long and narrow, 15 ½ x 5 ½ in, has 46 pages with more than 400 receipts, some sheets are torn and others may be missing. Originally, it may have had more pages as it has no cover and has undergone considerable conservation. Inside, each column lists ingredients and the amount of wool for dyeing. This is mostly for weights of 168 lbs of wool with a few entries weighing up to 240 lbs and several for less than a 100 lbs. This book indicates that it was possibly used in a dyehouse where the furnaces and vats had a greater capacity.

4.16 Dye Recipe Book

168 of wooll
2 Gauls 15 Logwood
1 Fustick ½ Allum
Shadd with 1½ Coprass
4 Logwood ½ Allum

---

168 of wooll
2 Gauls 6 Sanders
5 Mather ½ Logwood
Shadd with ⅔ Coprass

---

168 of wooll
2 Gauls 6 Logwood
5 Brazill 3 Mather
3 Argells Shadd with
¾ Coprass 1 Allum 1 Logwood

---

168 of wooll
Boyled with 21 Allum
A Fresh Liquor with
32 Mather & 2 Brazill
& 6 Payls of Liquor

---

168 of wooll
1½ Gauls 10 Sanders
10 Mather 2 Payls of
Liquor

---

168 of wooll
2 Gauls 16 Sanders
Shadd with 1¼ Coprass

---

168 of wooll
2 Gauls 6 Logwood
2 Brazill 2 Argells Shad
¾ Coprass 1 Allum

---

120 of wooll
1½ Gauls 4 Sanders
4 Mather 1 Fustick
2 Logwood Shadd 1¼ Coprass

---

100 of wooll
Boyled with 16 Allum
A Fresh Liquor with
20 Mather & 2 Brazill
& 6 Payls of Liquor

16℔ of wooll
4 Shumark 60 Fustick
24 Sanders Shott 4 3 Coprass

16℔ of wooll
4 Shumark 6 Sanders
6 Mather Shott 2 Coprass

16℔ of wooll
4 Shumark 8 Sanders
6 Mather Shott 2 Coprass

16℔ of wooll
Boyled with 18 Allum
A Fresh Liquor with
15 Mather & 27 Peachwood

16℔ of wooll
Boyled with 18 Allum
A Fresh Liquor with
40 of Mather

16℔ of wooll
4 Shumark 54 Sanders
Shott with ¾ Coprass

16℔ of wooll
Boyled with 24 Allum
A Fresh Liquor with
56 Mather & 8 Peachwood

16℔ of wooll
Boyled with 24 Allum
7 Logwood A Fresh
Liquor with 48 Mather
& 20 of Peachwood

16℔ of wooll
Boyled with 24 Allum
A Fresh Liquor with
24 Mather & 24 Peachwood

16℔ of wooll
Boyled with 24 Allum
7 Logwood A Fresh Liquor
with 60 Peachwood A
Fresh Liquor with
28 Mather

16℔ of wooll
3 Gauls 60 Fustick
Shott with 3 Coprass

16℔ of wooll
2 Gauls 56 Sanders
Shott with 1½ Coprass

16℔ of wooll
1½ Gauls 40 Fustick
16 Sanders Shott 3 Coprass

16℔ of wooll
wooded two 2 ℔ pound
Boyled with 18 Allum
A Fresh Liquor with
28 Logwood 3 Payls of Sig

16℔ of wooll
4 Shumark 12 Sanders
3½ Logwood 2 Fustick
Shott with 2¼ Coprass

16℔ of wooll
2 Gauls ¾ Sanders
3¼ Fustick 1¼ Logwood
Shott with ½ Coprass

16℔ of wooll
4 Shumark 10 Brazill
14 Sanders 6 Logwood
Shott with 2 Coprass

16℔ of wooll
1½ Gauls 4 Sanders
2 Logwood 4 Mather
Shott with ¾ Coprass

16℔ of wooll
4 Shumark 10 Brazill
14 Sanders 6 Logwood
Shott 3 Argells 1½ Coprass

16℔ of wooll
4 Shumark 12 Sanders
3 Logwood Shott 1¼ Coprass

The quantity of dyestuffs are mostly written out in full in a neat handwriting with few abbreviations. Swatches of wool have remained attached to most of the entries and others that came unstuck may be the ones placed in the remaining boxes of the collection.

Each of these receipts refers to a different colour. There are four hundred beautiful shades of rich medium and dark browns, pink buffs, greyed fawns and deep madder rusts verging on orange. Only two of these swatches required a woad ground and only one has a sample blue black colour still attached. There is very little explanation given with the list of ingredients, but several are two step processes. The wool was first soaked in an alum and dye solution then in fresh liquor strewn with copperas. Interestingly a couple of recipes mention that the wool should be dyed in a liquor containing shumach where it is *'boyled first'* or*'boyled last'*. The two different methods of using the tannin mordant may have affected the final colours. Unlike some of the other workbooks, this one records the ingredients for specific colours but there are no associated reference numbers which tracked the wool batch to the sold cloth.

This book may have been owned by a dyer who manufactured cloth or one who held a stock for sale. Once dyed these wools could be weighed and given a batch number before being carded, spun and woven. A small selection of coloured batts may have been provided on request to the factors or customers to select their preferred shade for cloth or new suitings, but it would make sense if a reference number had been provided. No names are written in this book so the dyer may have financed the purchase of wool and held the dyed stock for sale. If this was a large workshop, he may have spoken daily with the dyers and discussed the samples to be dyed and they wrote the list of ingredients for the dyeing process. Alternatively, this may be the record of the production of the business following the sequence in which the wool was dyed over an indeterminate period of time. The ability to produce a minimum of 400 dark colours could indicate a business of a considerable size, especially if there were additional records for light colours and blues as well. This workbook shows the breadth of experience of the dyers who were able to produce a wide range of colours with subtle variations of shade.

Nº. 7

(F)

Janº 1735/6.
This book was late Broʳ Jnº Collens's
Lent to Mʳ Ford till his Sºⁿ
or the Children shall want it for
their use ———

The next book[13] is the only one that provides any detail of ownership. An inscription dated 1735/6 written on the inside cover showed it belonged to John Collens. He seems to have been of good standing within the community if it is the same John Collins listed as church warden in the town's rate books for the period. This book may have been passed to his children or grandchildren. A Thomas Collins of Marston Bigot is listed as a '*Cloth & Wool Dyer*' in a fire insurance policy of 1808.[14]

This book, bound in off-white leather, has forty pages, each one conserved with tape around the edge. Lists of approximately 250 recipes mostly written in single columns except for the first page which has two columns. The book has wool swatches of mid-tone browns, beiges and rusts with undertones of purples, yellows and greens. There are several sheets of lighter colours with woaded blues over dyed to shades of 'eau de nil', French grey and soft sea greens.

This document also gives a bit more insight to the different wools that were dyed and the type of cloth that could be woven. John Collens may have been a clothier and a specialist dyer for both woad vats and furnace dyes. From page five, some entries mention the use of *'fine wooll'*, or *'75 lbs of Spanish and 47 of English for 3 abbs'*. Abb. is an alternative name for weft, the wool does not need to be as strong as the warp or chain wool

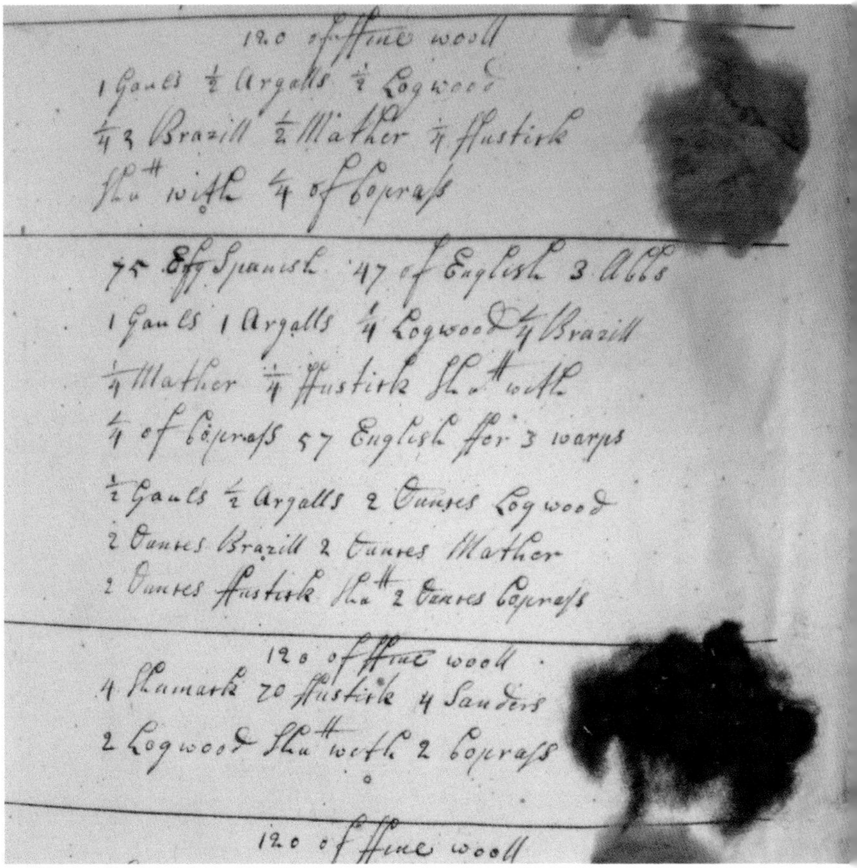
12.0 of ffine wooll
1 Gauls ½ Argalls ½ Logwood
¼ 3 Brazill ½ Mather ¼ ffustick
Sh with ¼ of Coperass
75 lbs Spanish 47 of English 3 Abbs
1 Gauls 1 Argalls ¼ Logwood ¼ Brazill
¼ Mather ¼ ffustick Sh with
¼ of Coperass 57 English ffor 3 warps
½ Gauls ½ Argalls 2 Ounces Logwood
2 Ounces Brazill 2 Ounces Mather
2 Ounces ffustick Sh 2 Ounces Coperass
12.0 of ffine wooll
4 Shumark 20 ffustick 4 Sanders
2 Logwood Sh weft 2 Coperass
12.0 of ffine wooll

4.19 Sorts of Wool

4.18 Dye Recipe Book

which can fray and break with the friction of the reed rubbing the yarn as it is beaten against the fell of the cloth. A mix of Spanish and English chains and others to be spun only of English wool are annotated in a couple of entries, there are also some that mention *'180 of Wooll Super'*, with attached samples dyed a mid brown, woven for the specific type of broadcloth made locally.

Several entries on this page mention the use of coarse wool, but looking at the samples I cannot differentiate between the grades. From page 11 several samples are dyed a strong blue with woad and *'turned'* with logwood and brazilwood to much darker blues. Another example is woaded to a bright blue, almost royal, it was then *'turned'* with logwood, shumach, madder, peachwood, brazilwood and copperas to a much darker greyer blue. The next few pages change to lighter colours, which perhaps reflecting the seasonal demand of fashion, woaded to a much lighter blue, mordanted with alum and over dyed with woadwaxen, fustick and logwood to soft shades of sea greens, light khaki and milk coffee colours. Other pages show varying tones of earthy moss greens and a recipe on page 15 specifically required the use of *'cropp mather'* rather than ordinary madder to produce a soft grey with a pink undertone. Turning a few more pages, the colour samples once again revert to darker browns, blues and greys and some entries start to have batch numbers. This may have been a temporary change in working practice, if the dyehouse had lost their blue vat man as some samples

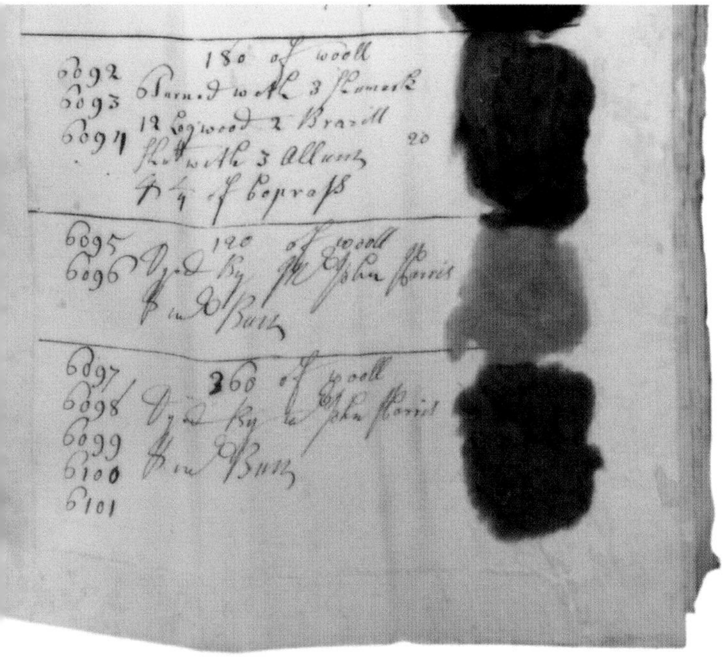

4.20 Entry for John Harris & William Bunn

4.21/ 4.22 / 4.23 Dye Recipe Book Pages

180 wooll
2 Shumack 1 Argells 5 Logwood
3 ffustick 5 woolds ffrottwith
1/4 Cooprass & 1 1/2 Allum

---

120 wooll
7 Allum 1 Argells wash it
Clean 12 woolds 1 1/2 Logwood

---

120 wooll
7 Allum Boyle An Hour
wash it Clean a ffresh
Liquor with 9 woolds 1/2 Allum
& 2 1/2 Logwood

---

130 wooll
2 Shumack 2 1/2 Argells
4 woolds 1 1/2 Allum 1 3/4 ffustick
1 1/2 Logwood 1/4 Coprass 1/2 Mather

---

120 wooll
6 Allum Boyle An Hour
wash it Clean 8 woolds
1 1/2 Logwood 1/2 ffustick

---

130 wooll
8 Allum 1 Argells Boyle
1/2 An Hour 6 woolds 4 Allum
Boyle 1/2 An Hour 2 1/2 Logwood
3/4 ffustick 4 quarts of Segg

---

130 wooll
6 Allum 2 Argells Boyle
An Hour 10 woolds 1/2 Allum
3 Logwood 1/4 ffustick &
qarts of Segg Ly all
Night

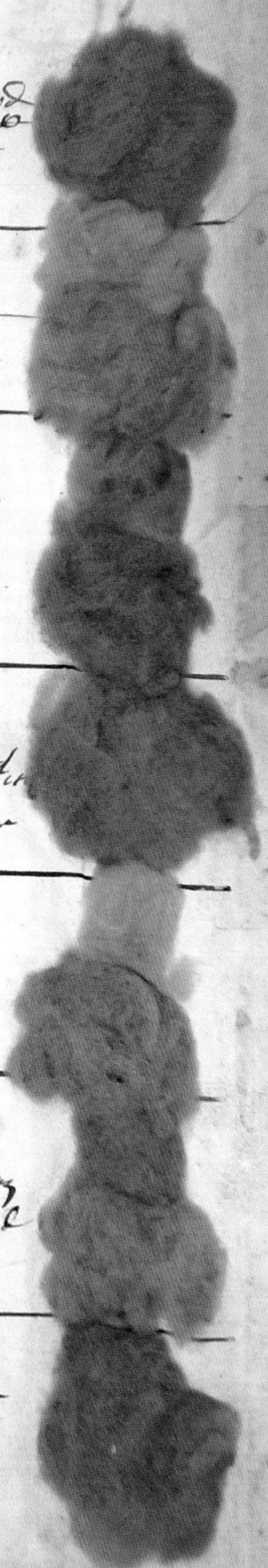

180 of wooll
1/2 Gauls 1 1/2 Argolls 10 of woalds
10 of weeds 1 1/2 ffustick 2 Logwood
Sd with 2 Allum & 1/4 of Coperass

---

120 of wooll
wood^d to 1^d Blew Burned with
2 Shumack 6 Logwood 4 ffustick
Sd with 1 Coperass & 1 Allum

---

120 of wooll
wood^d to 1:1/4^d Blew Burned with
28 ffustick 4 Allum Sd with
1:3/4 Coperass & 1/4 Logwood

---

120 of wooll
wood^d to 1^d Blew Burned with
3 Brazill 2 Allum 1/2 A Bushell
of Bran & 2 Mather Boyle
two Hours x

---

120 of wooll
wood^d to 1 1/4^d Blew Burned with
30 ffustick 4 Allum 6 Logwood
Sd with 1 1/2 Coperass 2 ffustick & 2 Allum

---

120 of wooll
wood^d to 1^d Blew Burned with
5 Allum 1 Logwood 1/2 Brazill 1/2
a peck of Gurgens Boyle one hour
Sd of wash it a ffresh Liquor
1 1/2 Logwood 1/4 Brazill 1 Argall [illegible]

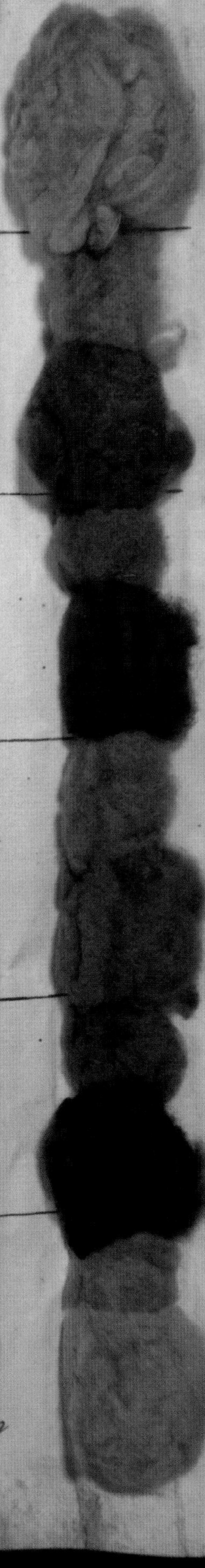

180 of wooll

$1\frac{1}{2}$ Gauls 2 Argalls 2 Logwood
1 Mather shott with $\frac{3}{4}$ of Coprass
and 2 of Allum

---

220 of wooll

$1\frac{1}{2}$ Gauls 12 of weeds 8 Fustick
2 Logwood 1 Allum 2 quarts Sigg
shott with One Ounce & half
of Coprass & 1 Allum

---

120 of wooll

$\frac{3}{4}$ Gauls wooded to $1\frac{1}{4}$ Blew
$\frac{1}{4}$ pott-agsh 4 Logwood 2 Pearkwood
$\frac{1}{2}$ Redwood 1 Fustick shott
with $\frac{1}{2}$ Coprass & $\frac{1}{4}$ Allum

---

120 of wooll wooded 1 Bl

$\frac{3}{4}$ Gauls $1\frac{1}{2}$ Logwood 2 Mather
12 Fustick shott with $\frac{1}{2}$ Coprass
& 1 of Allum

---

120 of wooll

$\frac{3}{4}$ Gauls 1 Argalls $\frac{1}{4}$ whitt
$\frac{1}{2}$ Mather $\frac{3}{4}$ Fustick $\frac{3}{4}$ Logwood
$\frac{1}{4}$ Redwood shot with
$\frac{1}{4}$ Coprass & $\frac{1}{4}$ allum

---

108 of wooll

wooded to 1 Blew 4 Fustick
6 Logwood $1\frac{1}{2}$ Shumark
$\frac{1}{4}$ whitt 1 Coprass

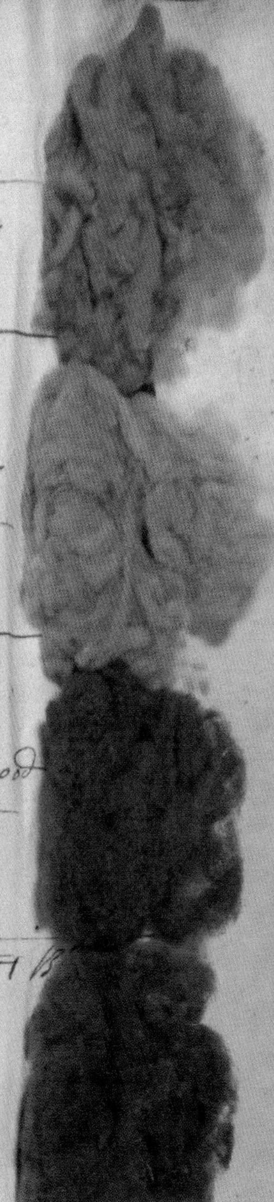

appear to be sent to Mr John Harris to be woaded by him and his partner William Bunn.

Entries in this book are for the most part not dated, the business may have just started and working practices were not fully established. John Collens may have been a blue and coloured dyer, selling the dyed wool by the pound to the clothiers until such time as he had the capital not only to buy better quality raw materials but to oversee production to broadcloth. Looking at the samples with the reference numbers included on these later pages, some entries have no dyestuffs or wool swatches next to them as there are no tell tale wax marks on the paper. A few have been marked with a little x next to them, indicating a bad dye lot or cloth.

One entry has two sequential numbers which would seem to indicate that each batch of 120 lbs of wool could produce two lengths of woven cloth at a standard weight of 60 lbs each. This change of format could suggest that it was at this time that the business was transferred to Mr Ford as shown by the inscription. However, at the top of page thirty four, the first mention of a date ***'September 11, 1732'*** indicates that it was still three years until it was lent to John Ford; and, as this is so close to the end of the book it seems unlikely that there were many entries made by him. Like the others, it may just have passed into the hands of the new owners and left to gather dust on a shelf.

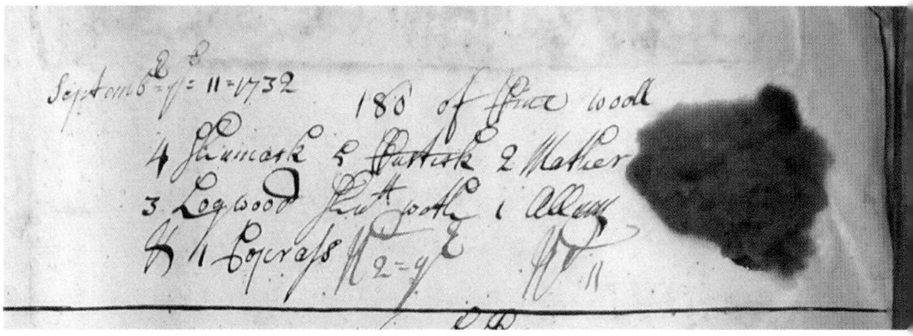

4.24 Dated Entry

The final book[15] in the collection, with a worn brown paper cover just a little larger than A4 size has 24 pages with 8 or 9 entries per page written in single columns with mid tone to dark grey brown swatches of dyed wool. These sheets have been carefully cleaned and flattened, with some stabilised and repaired using a gelatine based solution. With some exceptions, most entries suggested dyeing 180 pounds of wool at a time. The handwriting throughout seems to be by the same person, except for

180 of wooll
40 Shumark 56 Fustick dry 2 allum
5 Mather 1:2 Copprice

---

180 of wooll
Boyled In 18 of allum A fresh Liquor
with 44 Mather & half A Bushell
of Bran

---

180 of wooll
Shumark 55 Sanders 1 Logwood
with 2 Copprice

---

180 of wooll
4 Shumark 16 Logwood 5 Brazill
1½ Copprice 3 Logwood ½ Allum

---

180 of wooll
4 Shumark 40 Sanders 20 Fustick
Lying In all Nightt

---

180 of wooll
4 Shumark 12 Logwood 4 Brazill
2½ Copprice 3 Logwood

---

180 of wooll
4 Shumark 16 Sanders 12 Brazill
8 Logwood 2. Copprice

---

180 of wooll
4 Shumark 5 Redwood 4 Mather
2 Logwood Shott with 1: A Copprice

---

180 of wooll
4 Shumark 30 Fustick 14 Mather
3 Logwood Shott with 4 Copprice

180: of Wooll
4 of Shumak 5 of Redwood 4 of Mather
2 of Logwood: Sh.t w.t 1 of Copprice

180: of Wooll
4 of Shumak 3 of Alloum 70: of Fustick
16 of Sand… Sh.t w.t 1:3 of Copprice

180: of Wooll
4 of Shumak 40: of Fustick 30: of Sanders
Sh.t w.t 4 of Copprice

180: of Wooll
4 of Shumak 56 of Fustick 4 of Sanders
5 of Logwood: Sh.t w.t 4 of Copprice

---

120 of Wooll
3: of Shumake 4½ Fustick 3: of Sanders
3: of Mather Sh.t w.t 1:4 Copprice 60 of Verill

---

180 of Wooll
4: of Shumake 34 of Sanders 16 Fustick
Sh.t w.t ¾ Copprice

180: of Wooll
4. Shumake 60: of Fustick 10: of Sanders
Sh.t w.t 4 Alum 2 oz of Copprice

180: of Wooll
4 Shumake 40: of Sanders 20 of Fustick
Lying In all Night

180: of Wooll
4 Shumak 30 of Sanders 16 of Fustick
Sh.t w.t 1:1 of Copprice

100 of woll

1½ Gauls 4 Argells 4 Mather
4¾ Sanders ¾ Fustick Shott with
2 3 Coprass Mixt with 2 of [illegible]

---

150 of wooll

4 Shumark 5¼ Fustick 3½ Sanders
3½ Mather 1½ Coprass 30 Bearll

---

180 of wooll

4 Shumark 26¼ Sanders
4¼ Fustick 4¾ Mather
1 Logwood 5 of Redwood
Shott with 4 Coprass

---

180 of wooll

4 Shumark 5¾ Fustick 4 Sanders
4 Mather Shott with 2 Coprass

No 4149–4150–4151 180 of wooll

4 Shumark 56 Redwood
16 Fustick Shott with 5 Coprass

4140–4141–4142 180 of wooll

4 Shumark 5 Redwood 4 Mather
2 Logwood 1 Fustick Shott 1½ Coprass

---

180 of wooll

4 Shumark 4 Bra[illegible] 4 ake
4½ Mather Sh[illegible] Cop[illegible]

page five and the first three entries on page six which show an exceptionally neat handwriting with a curly bracket delineating each entry. It then reverts back to the original handwriting for the rest of the workbook. Apart for the occasional *'lying in all night'* on the last line there are only a few recipes with explanations. Two swatches, one of which was perhaps experimental as only 30 lbs of dyed wool was then

> *'Boyled in 4 ½ Allum, change your liquor. Put in 12 of Mather and half a bushel of bran then, change your liquor and finish it with 1 ½ Brazill'. The other for 180 lbs of wool was 'Boyled in 18 of Allum a fresh liquor with 44 Mather and half a bushel of Bran'.*

The resulting samples are deep, rich burnt oranges which must have woven a wonderful cloth possibly referred to as cinnamon in colour.

Turning to page 20, two entries have been given batch numbers, perhaps for work on behalf of another clothier. The numbers are not sequential but may be the order in which the dyer received the wool, so 4149, 50 and 51 are followed by 4140, 41, 42 and on the next page 4143 through 4148.

Athough the general time frame is known, as there are no dates it is impossible to determine the specific days and months during which these books were written which may have provided more information about how the business functioned; for example, if it was seasonal, or if fashion influenced the range of colours that were produced.

Other items in this collection include scraps of paper with instructions. A fashionable mellow colour was described as follows:

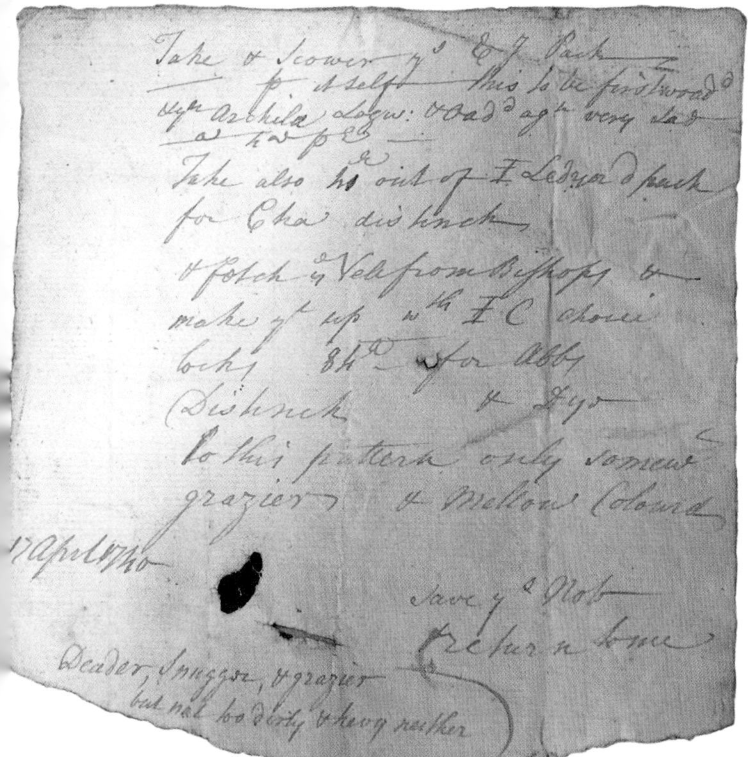
Take & Scower ye [illegible] Pack
[illegible] it self [illegible]
[illegible]
Take also [illegible] out of [illegible] pack
for [illegible]
& fetch ye [illegible] from Bishops &
make yt up [illegible]
[illegible] for [illegible]
[illegible] & Dye
to this pattern only somew[t]
grazier & Mellow Coloured
17 April 1740
Save ye Note
Return [illegible]
Deader, Snuffer, & grazier
but not too dirty & heavy neither

4.27 Loose note

4.28 Coloured Selvedges

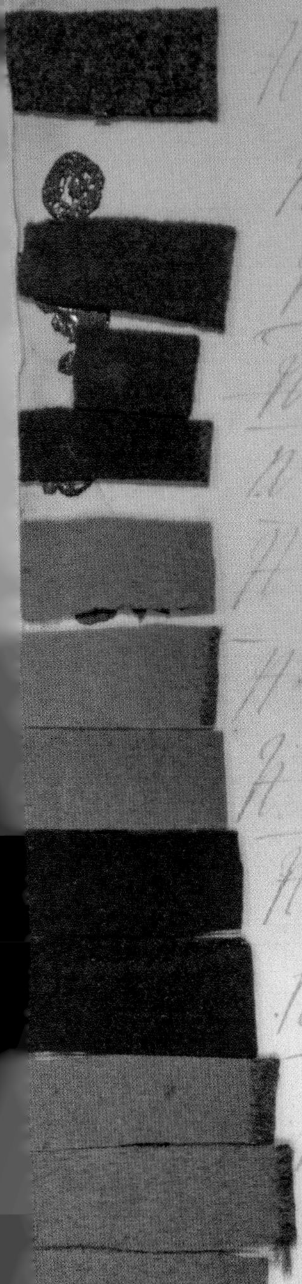

1797

No 178 Supr Yds 24 Janu Yd 30

No 180 Supr Yds 23 } Feby Yd 6th
No 183 Or Yds 28

No 182 Or Yds 25 } Yd 20th

No 181 Supr Yds 20 } March Yd 6th

No 186 Supr Yds 23 } Yd 20th

No 187 Ditto Yds 25 } 27th
No 188 Ditto Yds 21½

No 184 Ditto Yds 24 } Aprill Yd 3d
No 185 Ditto Yds 20½

No 189 Ditto Yds 22½ } Yd 17th
No 192 Or Yds 26

No 193 Ditto Yds 26 24th
No 186 Or ~~pc Yds~~ Yds 24½ a rong numbr

No 198 Green 25 Mayyd 11th

'17th April 1740. Take and scower the E. J. pack to itself – This to be first woaded, dyed Archila, logwood: woaded again very sad ... Take also ...out of ... Ledyard pack for chain distinct. And fetch in ...from Bishops and make it up with IC choice locks. 8 ...for abbs. Distinct & dyed. To this pattern only somewhat grazier and mellow coloured. Save this note, return to me'.

Perhaps on seeing the sample he then wrote the following:

'Deader, snugger and grazier but not too dirty and hevy neither'

I hope the dyer knew what to do!

Other little notes mention an order from J. Ford, to take wool from different sarplers for chains such as *'choice locks white'* and *'short Spanish'* for abbs. and dye them to the attached colour swatches, but the paper has deteriorated leaving the instructions faded and incomplete so only the essence of the note can be understood.

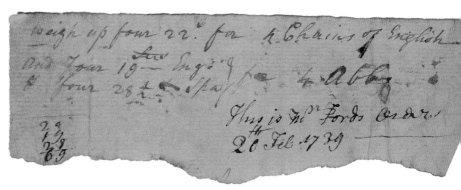
weigh up four 22 for 4 Chains of English
And four 19
for 4 Abbs
& four 28
This is Mr Fords Order
20th Feb 1739

4.29 Order for J Ford

Another sheet of paper, approximately A4, has samples of cloth rather than wool, this woven material may have been the inventory that was collected and sent for sale over a period of 3 months. It is dated Jan 30th 1727, the coloured threads at the edge of each sample show the use of the different colour warp threads for the selvedges as weavers would have used a coarse or waste wool for that purpose. The specific colours may indicate the type of cloth woven although several 'Super' cloths seem to have different colour selvedges so it may have been the weaver's mark by which a faulty cloth could be identified. This record is just a single page, perhaps a loose sheet from another ledger. It lists the amounts of cloth from the end of January to the beginning of May indicating a possible quarterly production of 298 yards. This could suggest that the business was relatively small scale for cloth production but with a much larger dyeing facility to supply other clothiers.

---

[1] McGarvie, M 2013: 70
[2] TNA C 104/3
[3] McGarvie, M 2013: 83
[4] Frome Museum
[5] Frome Museum
[6] Frome Town Tithing Rates
[7] Rogers, K 197: 203
[8] TNA C 104/3
[9] Frome Town Tithing (as transcribed by Stella Young for FSLS)
[10] TNA C 104/3/3/ & C 104/3/5
[11] TNA C 104/3/1
[12] TNA C 104/3/2
[13] TNA C 104/3/6
[14] SHC DD/LW/41
[15] TNA C 104/3/4

Boots
Opticians
Opticians
Repairs
Valuers
Charles Hart
Jewellers & Valuers
Rose & Lyons
Rose & Lyons
RAVES
GRAVE

CHAPTER 5

FROME, A CLOTH TOWN

'...an agreeable appearance of bustle and business everything indicated the presence of manufacturers and trade... with all the labouring men, women and children at Frome as deeply tinged as ancient Britons with dark blue with the manufacture of cloth'.

'Excursions from Bath' Reverend Richard Warner, 1801

Frome owes its heritage to the cloth trade. Like Trowbridge, Bradford on Avon, Westbury and the surrounding villages, the textile industry worked for hundreds of years as if to the rhythm of the looms. There were early Roman settlements in the area, lead and silver were mined from the nearby Mendips, much of which was transported back to Italy until the collapse of the Roman administration. It was not until the occupation by the Saxons, in the second half of the 7th century, that Frome was established in 685. St Aldhelm, the Benedictine Abbot of

5.1 Cheap St Frome

Malmesbury, was said to have founded a small outpost monastery near the site of the present St John the Baptist Church in an attempt to civilise the bands of rogues roaming in nearby Selwood Forest.[1] Frome's cloth trade did not start until the mid 1300s but it is apt that as a poet and scholar Bishop Aldhelm wrote:

> *'...it is not the web of one uniform colour and texture that pleases the eye and appears beautiful but is one that is woven with shuttles filled with threads of purple and various other colours flying from side to side.[2]'*

It was said that during his lifetime, Aldhelm amassed a precious collection of books which ironically was destroyed a thousand years later at the dissolution of the monasteries, to accommodate the looms of William Stumpe of Malmesbury, a successful and wealthy clothier.[3]

In 934, Athelstan, the first King of England, presided over an assembly in Frome of powerful and important ecclesiastical people, earls, barons and thegns[4], which could suggest that the settlement was already important. Its geographical location with access to water and easy river crossings led to tracks converging in the area, which formed a hub for the surrounding rural hamlets. With the arrival of the Saxons, Frome was designated the administrative centre for the largest Hundred in the area, although Selwood Forest and most of the land within Frome itself were held directly by the King.

As towns became secure and trade flourished, they were increasingly regulated. Frome may have been a borough in Saxon times as it had an established market, a mint and paid the third penny taxation.[5] Although not a borough, if a settlement contained a concentration of population which had a wide range of non-industrial occupations especially those derived from participation in trade and industry, it could be defined as a town[6] and Frome may have fit that description. In the larger towns of Winchester, Bristol and Salisbury informal groups of merchants framed regulations, kept the peace, inspected goods and witnessed market sales. These organisations became the recognised authority forming the Anglo Saxon Frith Gilds. Building halls to display their wealth and power, controlling all aspects of commercial trade, they evolved into the municipal authorities.

Frome was small, its market sales were overseen by bailiffs appointed by the Lord of the Manor which may have given the town an early commercial advantage. Moreover, as the restricted guild regulations increasingly strangled the potential for expansion, Frome had the foresight to exploit its geographical location and expand its local trade.

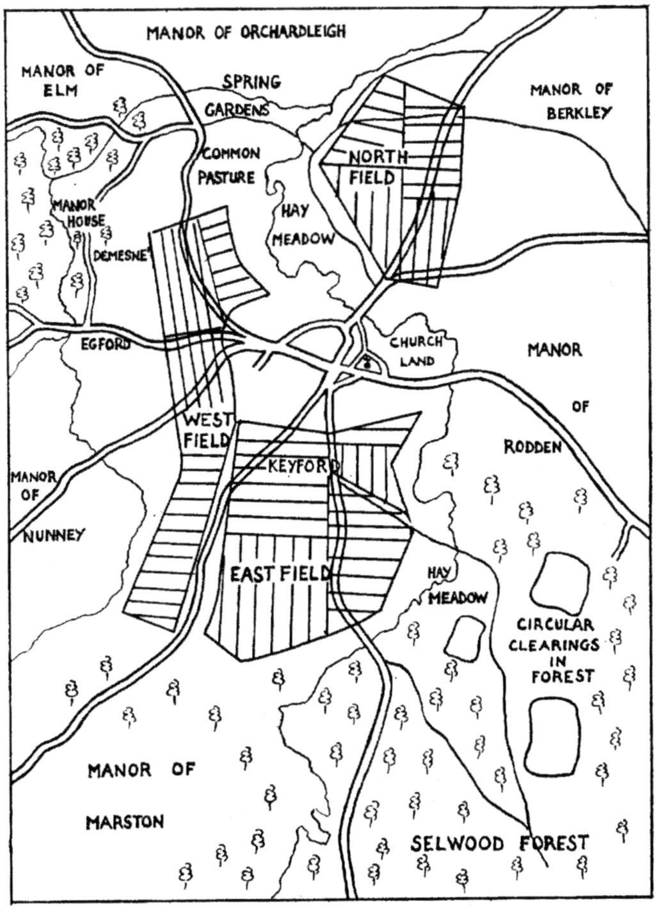

5.2 Frome as a Medieval Manor

William the Conqueror designated sheriffs, who acted as the links between himself and the autonomous shires which were governed by tenants-in-chief or their stewards. By the end of his reign in 1086, a full assessment of the country's land, ecclesiastical and manorial demesnes, landholders, peasants, livestock and mills had been recorded. The Domesday book, while not entirely accurate, recorded the ownership of manors and estates to determine the monies owed to the crown. The Hundreds, encompassed manors which were granted to tenants-in-chief and sublet to under-tenants who managed the woods, arable and pasture land for grazing animals, along with the more valuable meadows and mills by the rivers. These lands had to produce as much income as possible for the lords and a livelihood, although not necessarily a good one, for everyone else. Frome as designated administrative centre for the Hundred had responsibility for law and order, raising taxes and military service.[7] The boundary of Frome included several manors and land owned directly by the King and the church, which later devolved to the merchants and along with the markets, mills and sheep were the foundations of the town.

There are two entries for Frome in the Domesday:[8]

'King William holds Frome. King Edward held it. It never paid geld, nor is it known how many hides are there. There is land for 50 ploughs. In demesne, home farm, there are 3 ploughs and 6 coliberts and there are 31 villeins and 36 bordars with 40 ploughs. There are 3 mills paying 25s and a market paying 46/8d. There are 30 acres of meadow and 50 acres of pasture, 24 swine and 93 sheep. Wood 1 league in length and the same in breadth'.

The second entry:

'Held by Reinbald of Cirencester who was the tenant-in-chief. It was considered very large with a total population of 97 households, 35 acres of meadow, 1 mill worth 2/6d. Other cattle and 228 sheep, with a total value to the lord of £6.00'.

The total population of England at this time would have been less than two million. The views of Historians differ both statistically on the size of regional populations and the influence of government changes on working peoples' lives. Frome had an estimated population of four to five hundred inhabitants and the lands of the manor and church covered an area of approximately five square miles.[9]

By 1189, the town had ceased to be a royal manor, Henry II gave the greater part of it to the family of FitzBernard and the remainder to Wandrill de Courcelles. These families were united by marriage and the manor passed to William Braunche. It remained in that family until his grand-daughter Alianor married Richard Wydslade in the 14th century.[10] Their son Stephen was succeeded by an only daughter, Elizabeth, who married Edmund Leversedge, the founder of an alms house at the beginning of the 15th century, later renamed the Blue House. The ownership of the land subsequently became more widely dispersed and the manorial lands of Caivel, Chaivert (Keyford), Reddene, Berkley, Egford, and Fairoake were drawn in to the expansion of the town.

Fairs were held in late spring and early autumn. A charter granted 28th August 1270, by King Henry III allowed William Braunche to hold an annual one at the manor on 7th, 8th and 9th of September.[11] An earlier charter permitted a Saturday market for the trading of livestock and while Frome's market, like others, was shaped by its surrounding agricultural region, people like Robert the Merchant, mentioned in 1250, would have traded in wool, cloth and other goods. The Glastonbury Abbey records for their Deverill holdings from 1296 to 1345 show that customary tenants regularly carried grain to the weekly market of Frome, Oldford-by-Frome and to the hamlet of Trudoxhill[12] and most likely others living within a ten mile radius did so too.

Markets, fairs and inns were central to the exchange of information. By the 14th century, several abbey wool houses had developed the means to supply hot water systems for their vats and furnaces. The Knights Templar managed landholdings in the region. Their retainers processed some of their wool at Temple Newbury, formerly in the parish of Babington which may have influenced the establishment of the early fulling mills along the river Frome.

An Orchardleigh charter of 1300 refers to John Fullo, who was probably a fuller.[13] The first mention of a fulling mill in Frome was in 1349, an earlier one had been leased in the hamlet of Rodden.[14]

The development of Frome's cloth industry, like elsewhere, resulted from the coincidence of simultaneous events. The restrictive guild practices in towns such as Winchester, Bristol and Devizes to protect their members' interests encouraged journeymen to seek employment

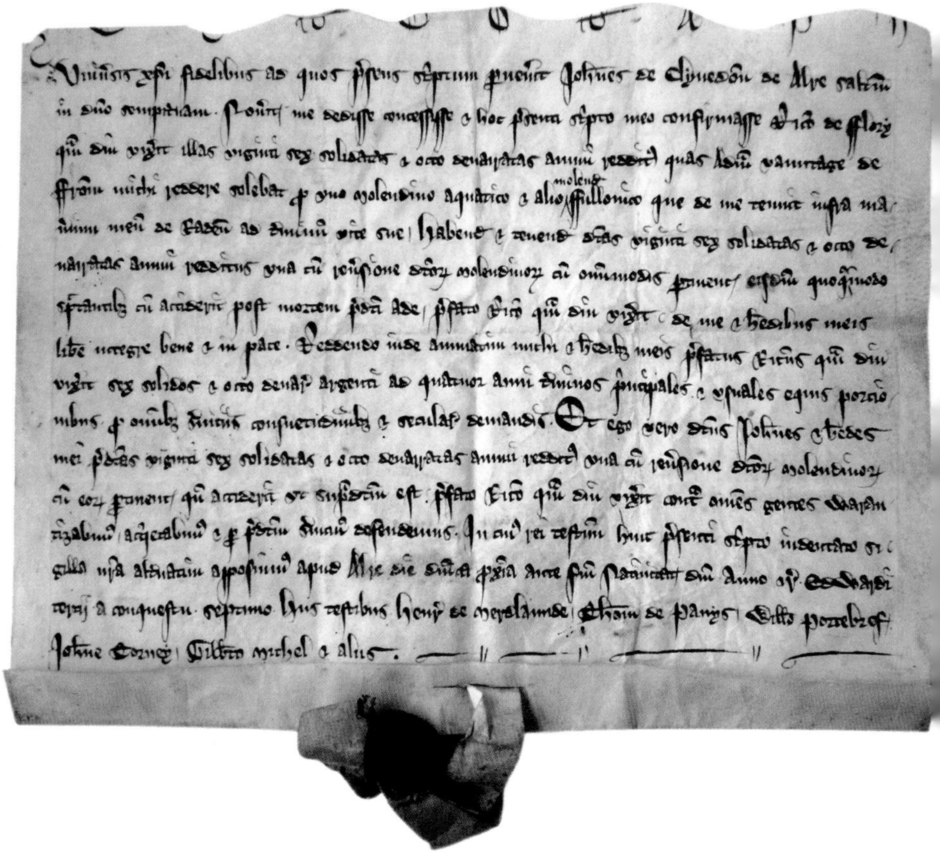

5.3 1333 Lease of Fulling Mill in Rodden to Adam Vauntage

further afield increasing the movement of people and skills to rural areas. The plague was particularly virulent in the 14th century which reduced the population leading to a change in land usage. The high taxation of wool and temporary export bans created a surplus of raw materials. The dissemination of practical knowledge made cloth finishing more efficient and fulling mills built along the river provided financial returns. All these factors led to new opportunities for merchants, the rise of the clothiers and the employment of rural weavers, spinners and dyers.

The people of Frome were engaged in the textile and ancillary trades from the early 1300s, as suggested by occupational names like Poleyn le Webb, a weaver, Walter Le Webbe of Keyver, Walter le Digher and Thomas La Taillour. John Le Pew and his wife Avicia are mentioned in the Feet of Fines of 1307/08 as renting an acre and messuage, comprising a dwelling and outbuildings, from Henry Merlaunde[15] and later records show that John traded in wool. By 1327, the Exchequer's Lay Subsidy[16] list of taxpayers suggests that Frome had around fifteen hundred inhabitants with many new arrivals, some of whom became the successful merchants and clothiers of the town.

Medieval merchants were defined as business people engaged in the retail selling of the more unusual goods such as wine, linen and woad that were sourced from abroad and many would have dealt in wool and cloth. Foreign merchants settled in Frome. The Craas family, possibly of Dutch or French origin, may have been related to John Le Cras an alien merchant of Salisbury who sought letters of protection in 1345.[17] In 1394, John Craas, a merchant of Frome was owed money by a Gloucestershire merchant and in 1397 Richard Crate or Craas, of Frome owed £100 to the Abbess at Lacock.[18] Along with several other entries for the town, Walter Crace or Craas of Frome was mentioned in the 1401 Gascon Rolls.[19] Matthew Craas was described as a Merchant of Frome Braunche whose will of 1408 was proven in Bristol. He may have been one of the Merchant Venturers, willing to underwrite the financial risks for the export of cloth. In 1443 a tax assessment was levied against Patroke and Hugh Graas, immigrants who probably resided in Frome and may also have been kinsmen.[20]

5.4 John, Son of William Twynho

Adam Vauntage, was assessed for tax in 1327 at a comparatively high tax rate of 5s, and six years later he held the lease of the Rodden fulling mill.[21] In 1360, John le March, also from Frome owed a merchant of Bristol £48 16s, for the purchase of wool.[22] Like today, there were speculative investments; in 1365, Stephen Wynslade, then lord of Frome Selwood, was a bankrupt merchant who owed £2,000 for the purchase of wool from Sir John de St Lo, knight and former Sheriff of Somerset.[23] By the close of the century, there were five fulling mills[24] in Frome bolstering the commercial white cloth production; and, no doubt the building of fine merchant houses in Frome.

By the 15th century, Frome's three main strands of commerce, the wool, the cloth and the dye trades were woven into the fabric of the town contributing to its growth and the wealth of its merchants.

A petition in 1402 stated that

> *'...within the parish, there are many merchants, who often, for their business, transfer themselves to other parts, and are thereby hindered from hearing mass according to their wish in the parish church...'*

Six years later Henry IV granted a licence for the founding of the Chapel of St Nicholas in St John's Church by John Cabell, a merchant of Frome and William Twynho of Keyford[25] whose second son John, became a lawyer and a wealthy Gloucestershire wool merchant. Henry Dunkerton, another of the merchants, left considerable endowments to the church when he died in 1419.

Frome was granted a second charter in 1470[26] to hold a Wednesday and Saturday market which could have provided an outlet for Somerset and Wiltshire wool. Merchants and clothiers from the area were supplying the expanding demand for white cloth to the markets of

5.5 Alice, Daughter of John, Founded Fairford Church

the Low Countries. This rising business class came from diverse backgrounds and had working capital to invest. In particular, those who owned or leased a fulling mill could expand their trade by erecting workshops for dyeing and finishing cloth. Most of the region's wholesale production was increasingly controlled by these men as they financed and managed the manufacture, from the selection and purchase of raw materials to the finished cloth for sale.

Over hundreds of years, it is impossible to encapsulate the many events that shaped the growth and trade of small market towns like Frome. In the 16th century, plague and pestilence were rife, poor harvests led to famines, regional land enclosures, taxes and wars all played a part in moulding the social and industrial landscapes. Many worried about the recurrent outbreaks of disease; in his will of May 19th 1538, William Kyppynge of Buckland Dinham, left the residue of his goods to his wife Jone, with the proviso that

> *'...if she departe of this plague now, then his friend Edward Whytt shall have the charge of his children.'*[27]

The town's expansion was limited. While the king and the church owned considerable acreage, it was more valuable retained as agricultural land. Following the dissolution of the monasteries in 1538, this restriction continued as the land was passed to a small number of landowners. To maximise building space, the streets were narrow with a high density of housing.

5.6 Tudor Rose Carved on Ceiling Beam
Cheap Street - Frome

John Leland's observations from his travels around 1540 suggest that the cloth industry was well established.

...There be dyvers fayre stone Howses in the Towne that standye most by Clothinge' later on his return to Bath a possible reference to Spring Gardens *'...I cam to a Botome, where an othar Broke ran into Frome. And in this Botome dwell certayne good clothiars hauynge fayre Howsys and Tukkynge Myles'.*[28]

By the end of the 1500s the town's population was around three thousand. The economic fluctuations brought about by mercantilism were all too common. In 1631 Frome was once again said to be very poor due to the decline in the demand for white cloth. This affected the livelihood of the artisan broad weavers and the spinners living hand to mouth. The clothiers continually reduced wages or paid in kind to compensate for the falling price of their cloth. By the mid 1600s, the possibility of work had attracted many to the area, and

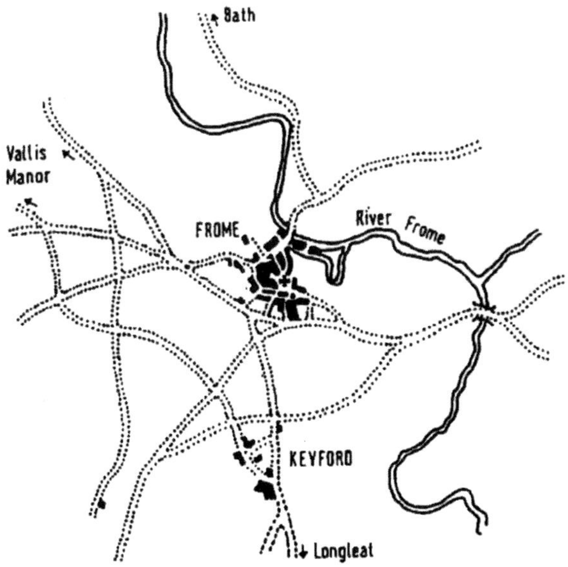

5.7 Circa 1650

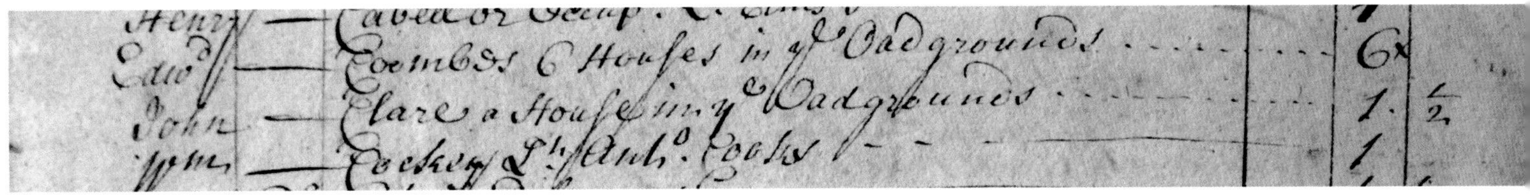

Edw — Coombs 6 Houses in ye Oadgrounds ... 6
John — Clare a House in ye Oadgrounds ... 1. ½

5.8 1727 Town Tithing

the population of the town had more than doubled to around six and half thousand. This influx of workers and their families needed places to live. Landholders financed the development of Newtown, now known as the Trinity area of Frome which has been described as amongst the earliest purpose built industrial housing in the country.[29] The small factories and workshops adjacent to dwellings continued to proliferate as

5.9 Trinity Street - Frome

clothiers were keen to supervise the production of their cloth. A few chose to display their wealth and built grander houses away from the noise, dirt and smell of the manufactory which they left to the management of foremen. However for most of those engaged in the newly introduced medley cloth trades, they only earned a meagre living.

5.10 Weavers Cottages in Trinity Street

Although a large proportion of the town's population was involved in the textile trades from the Middle Ages there is very little written evidence until the 17th century when there are wills, inventories, indentures and other documents. Between 1575 and 1855 there were more than two hundred wills of clothiers and the related trades for Frome and the surrounding area registered in the Prerogative Court of Canterbury (PCC). Before 1858, the PCC had sole jurisdiction in the south of the country to grant probate if the deceased had died in possession of more than £20 of goods, a considerable sum of money. This number of wills suggested a growing class of wealthy clothiers in Frome and the outlying villages which was also indicated by those earning £40 annually and paying towards the poor

5.11 1813 Cruse Map of Trinity Area

rates.[30] By their own hard work, initiative and ambition, many of the families, engaged in the textile trades had risen from artisan workers to landed gentry. Their sons and daughters had married judiciously, encouraged no doubt by parents who were keen to promote business partnerships and financial interests.

The cloth manufacture of the 18th and 19th centuries contributed to an expanding and bustling town but with a growing divide between the capitalist clothiers and the skilled workers. Disputes about conditions and wages may have been discussed at the 'Anker', a building adjoining the Wool Hall[31] backing on to Eagle Lane.

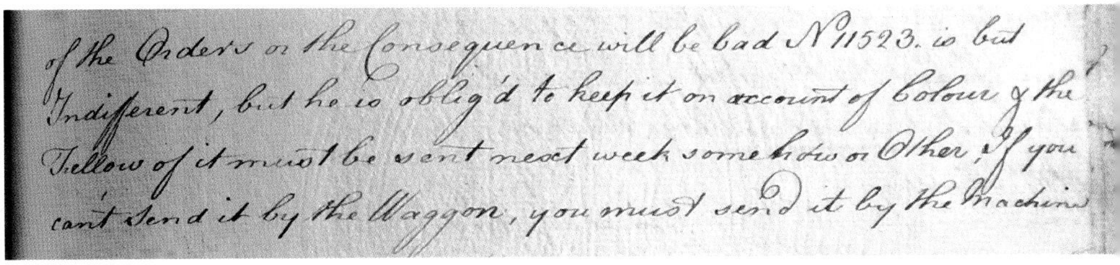
of the Orders or the Consequence will be bad N° 11523. is but Indiferent, but he is oblig'd to keep it on account of Colour & the Fellow of it must be sent next week some how or Other; If you cant Send it by the Waggon, you must send it by the Machine

5.12 The Machine

The hall was once owned by William Whitchurch in 1677 and later by the dyer Henry Allen who left it in his will of 1724 to his wife Mary, his brother Samuel and friends William Hendry and John Harris. The Anchor was a coaching inn and during the 1780s, a post coach to Wood Street in London stopped there every Monday, Wednesday and Friday at 3pm.[32] This may have been '*...the Machine*' referred to in a letter book written by Mr Elderton (See Chapter 14). The inn was partly demolished in 1810 and re-fronted to accommodate Mr Thomas Bunn's vision for the sweeping curve of Bath Street.

'...it was also advantageous in that it resulted in the destruction of Anchor Barton, with 'such an accumulation of dung-hills, slaughter houses and tallow melting houses as to be indescribable.[33]*'*

Although if it was owned by the dyers with the adjacent wool hall they would certainly have

.13 The Waggon & Horses, Gentle Street - Frome

DUNKIRKE
FACTORY

Factory Token

Pack Horse Bridge at Tellisford Mill

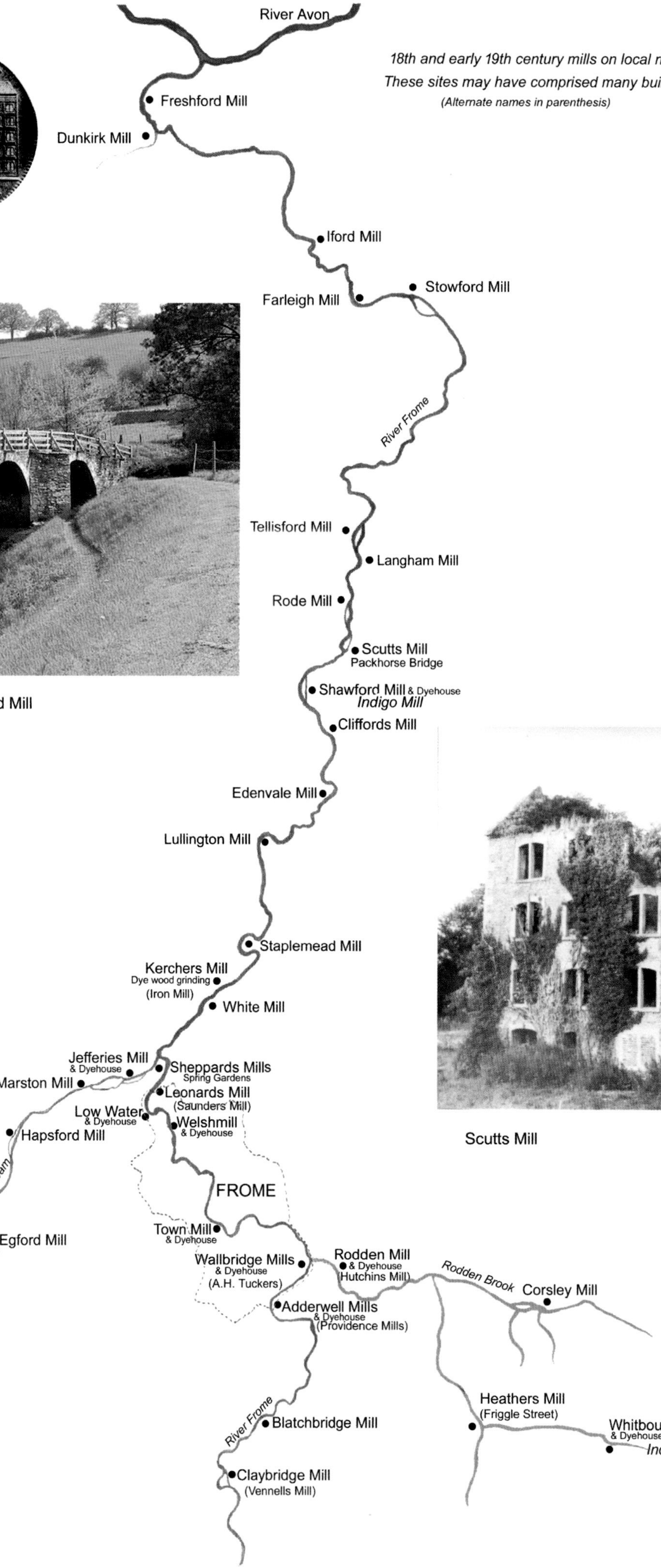
River Avon
18th and early 19th century mills on local rivers
These sites may have comprised many buildings
(Alternate names in parenthesis)
Freshford Mill
Dunkirk Mill
Iford Mill
Farleigh Mill
Stowford Mill
River Frome
Tellisford Mill
Langham Mill
Rode Mill
Scutts Mill
Packhorse Bridge
Shawford Mill & Dyehouse
Indigo Mill
Cliffords Mill
Edenvale Mill
Lullington Mill
Staplemead Mill
Kerchers Mill
Dye wood grinding
(Iron Mill)
White Mill
Jefferies Mill
& Dyehouse
Marston Mill
Sheppards Mills
Spring Gardens
Leonards Mill
(Saunders Mill)
Low Water
& Dyehouse
Welshmill
& Dyehouse
Hapsford Mill
Mells Stream
FROME
Egford Mill
Town Mill
& Dyehouse
Wallbridge Mills
& Dyehouse
(A.H. Tuckers)
Rodden Mill
& Dyehouse
(Hutchins Mill)
Rodden Brook
Corsley Mill
Adderwell Mills
& Dyehouse
(Providence Mills)
Heathers Mill
(Friggle Street)
Whitbourne Moor
& Dyehouse
Indigo Mill
River Frome
Blatchbridge Mill
Claybridge Mill
(Vennells Mill)

Scutts Mill

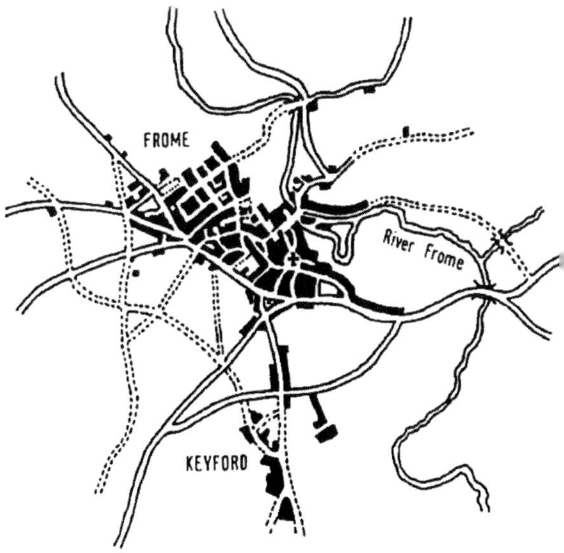

5.15 Circa 1750

contributed to the vile smell by scouring the wool in urine before rinsing it in the nearby spring and dyeing it in the fermenting woad vats.

By the early 1700s, the river was used to its maximum extent as fulling, dyewood grinding and grist mills all had claims on water power. Daniel Defoe suggested that in 1724 Frome was greater than Bath, with more than ten thousand inhabitants. This was probably a slight exaggeration as a more detailed and comprehensive survey was taken by B. & J. Crocker in September 1785. The survey covered East & West Woodlands and the Town Tithings which showed an estimated total of 1,684 families or about 8,125 inhabitants. It lists the occupation by head of household with a distribution for the cloth industry:

> *'47 clothiers, 5 dyers, 12 fellmongers, 3 woolstaplers, 54 spinsters, 6 fullers, 146 shearmen, 141 scribblers, 220 weavers, 5 handle setters, 8 twisters, 4 spinning jenny men for a total 651 and for the ancillary card making industry 5 cardboard makers, 59 card makers and 23 wire drawers.[34]'*

In total seven hundred and thirty eight people, almost half of all heads of household in the town were involved in the cloth trade.

> *'...From an accurate inspection lately made, it appears that one hundred and sixty thousand yards are annually made, of which four fifths are broad-cloths, and the rest narrow cloths and cassimeres. In the above manufacture, 1450 packs of wool of 240lbs each are employed.[35]'*

The town landscape changed in the early part of the 19th century as the mill buildings and chimneys came to dominate the skyline replacing the small shops and workshops adjacent to dwellings. Riots and protests which had started in the previous decades persisted as steam power brought more machinery to larger, purpose built, factories. Frome had a population in excess of twelve thousand people but as new inventions mechanised the production of cloth, weavers, scribblers, spinners, cloth men, card makers and shearers, once paid for their knowledge and skill,

5.14 Mills on River Frome & Tributaries

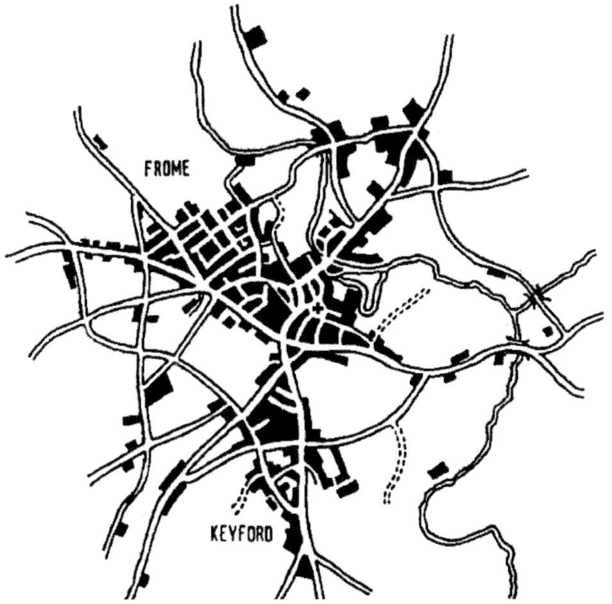

5.16 Circa 1850

became unemployed. The factory jobs were filled by unskilled machine operators, women and children who were paid a pittance for long hours of work in deplorable conditions. It was said that a six mile stretch of the river Frome and its tributaries had more than 200 mills, and while this was an exaggeration there were certainly very many.[36]

The Napoleonic wars brought a temporary reprieve from the inevitable decline of the trade as Frome supplied thousands of yards of blue uniform cloth. Alas, by 1826 the parish had established a blanket factory to provide work for the many poor! Somerset and Wiltshire clothiers were said to have been too complacent and reluctant to invest in upgrading their mills and their machinery. The heavy woollen cloth was no longer fashionable and consumers were happy to buy the cheaper substitutes produced by the Yorkshire factories. The 1841 census showed fewer heads of households engaged in the cloth trades and by the late 1800s many mills had closed leaving the buildings to collapse.

> *'...For sale lot 6: a very spacious cloth factory called Heathers Mill leased by William and John Rossiter formerly owned by Ebenezer Coombs of Corsley; Messrs Harding & Sons, 1840.*[37]*'*

The cloth trade continued to meander into a slow decay which has been written about in detail by many economists, archivists and historians.[38] Tuckers Mill at

5.17 Town View in the 1800s

Wallbridge was the last one to manufacture *'The Finest West of England Cloth'* in Frome and closed its doors in 1965.

---

1 Belham P 1973: 14
2 Aldhelm de Laud 680: 298 305
3 Ponting, K 1957: 46
4 Belham, P 1992: -
5 Darby H 2009: 196
6 Dyer, C 1994: 241
7 Belham, P 1973: 23
8 Belham, P 1973: 50
9 Belham P 1973: 50
10 Belham, P 1973: 52
11 SANHS Vol. 78: 17
12 Farmer, D 1989: 7
13 McGarvie, M 2013: 45
14 SHC DD\SAS\C/795/FR/32
15 SRS Vol. XII
16 McGarvie, M 2013: 47
17 www.englandsimmigrants.com
18 TNA C241/188/115
19 www.gasconrolls.org
20 www.englandsimmigrants.com
21 SHC DD\SAS/C795/FR/32
22 TNA C241/144/134
23 TNA C241/159/65
24 Goodall, R 2009: 8
25 Belham, P 1973: 56
26 SANHS Vol. 78: 17
27 Weaver, H 1905: -
28 Leland, J 1770: 97,98
29 Leech, R 1981: Back Cover
30 Berg, M 2005: 208
31 The Bath Chronicle 21.X.1.1784
32 Davis, M Pitt, V 2015: -
33 McGarvie, M 2013: 114
34 SHC A/AQP/12
35 Rack, E & Collinson, J 1791: Vol2. 186
36 Belham, P 1973: 69
37 WSA 628/16/9
38 For example see Rogers, K in the Bibliography

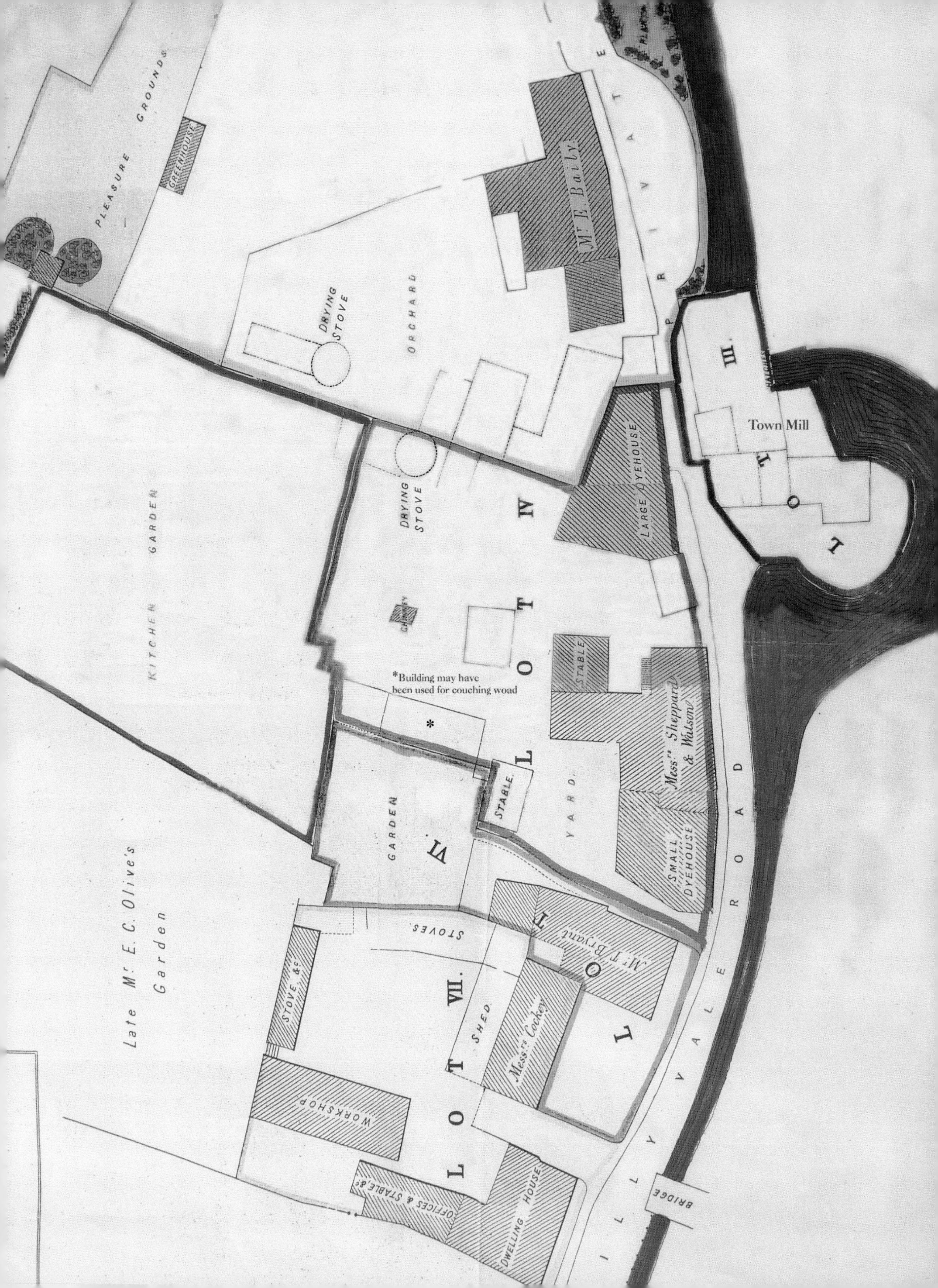

PLEASURE GROUNDS
GREENHOUSE
Mr E. Baily
PRIVATE
DRYING STOVE
ORCHARD
III
HATCHES
Town Mill
LOT
LARGE DYEHOUSE
DRYING STOVE
KITCHEN GARDEN
CHIMNEY
STABLE
Messrs Sheppard & Watson
*Building may have been used for couching woad
STABLE
YARD
GARDEN
VI
SMALL DYEHOUSE
STOVES
Mr T. Bryant
Late Mr E.C. Olive's Garden
LOT VII.
STOVE &c
SHED
Messrs Cockey
WORKSHOP
OFFICES & STABLE &c
DWELLING HOUSE
ILLY VALE ROAD
BRIDGE

CHAPTER 6

18th CENTURY DYE WORKSHOPS

'...Sale: House on the verge of town...Capitol Dyehouse adjoining now in full trade: six blue vats, five furnaces for coloured work, a scouring furnace, washing sheds, dye sheds, stove and drying ground ...two tenements, stable for horses. ...This situation is truly eligible on many accounts, Frome being the largest clothing town in the West of England'.

Somerset and Wiltshire Journal, Jan 1796

In the 18th century, the manufacture of woollen cloth was subdivided into specialist concerns which could either be under the management of individuals, partnerships, or family firms like the Sheppards. There were small independent businesses providing the ancillary services for dyeing, carding and finishing the woollen cloth. In the same way as today's companies, many of these related activities benefited from being close to one another. Sites included fulling mills, dyehouses, scribbling sheds, weaving workshops, drying stoves, pressing and finishing rooms. Business owners bought parcels of land on which they built, sublet premises or operated concessions within larger facilities. Over time, entrepreneurial families expanded and diversified their trades. Arrangements changed as partnerships were formed and dissolved, families were united by marriages and legacies divided land and businesses between spouses, children and relatives.

Buildings for the provisioning of dye workshops comprised a drug house, a scarlet dyehouse, a common dyehouse with furnaces and a separate set of vats supplying the blue trade. (See Figure 6.11) A drying stove house, finishing room, packing room, stores and a 'compting' house were essential for running the business.[1] In 1808 Samuel Allen, dyer of Frome purchased insurance:

> *'...On his dwelling house situate in Long Row, stone and tiled. On household goods, wearing apparel, linen, plate, printed books, furniture therein. On his dyehouse situate at Whatcombe Bottom in Frome aforesaid, stone & tiled. On his stove house detached from the dyehouse about 22 ft, stone &*

6.2 Leonard's Mill with Two Dye Houses with Vented Rooves in the Background

tiled. On his stable and store room about 20 ft from the aforesaid dyehouse, stone & tiled.[2]'

He had a separate insurance policy in partnership with George George and James Clement for the contents of the business.

'...*On their dyeing utensils, dye stuff, wool, broad and narrow cloth, cassimere, coal and stock in trade including goods in trust for other persons in their dyehouse, counting house, store room, tenements adjoining. Stone & tiled. On their stock in trade, utensils, goods in trust in their stove room near the above. All situate at Whatcombe Bottom in Frome.*[3]'

This partnership may have started earlier as a Mr John George of Frome is mentioned in the 1773 correspondence of Mr Hindley, a Mere merchant dealing in linen and ticking which he exported to Hamburg and Lisbon, and, in return, he imported oil.

'...*I expect the arrival of some oil at Bristol in a week's time, which shall order to your house, and sell at same price to you as the last. I hope soon to have two bales of cloth from you.*[4]'

The dyehouse would be located near a strong water supply with plenty of fall to remove the spent dyes but it was more important to have water pressure to turn the mill wheel for thorough cleansing and fulling. A field contiguous to the house provided space for tentering and drying goods in the fresh air or in the shelter of open sided sheds. The buildings were built of brick or stone with thick walls to keep them

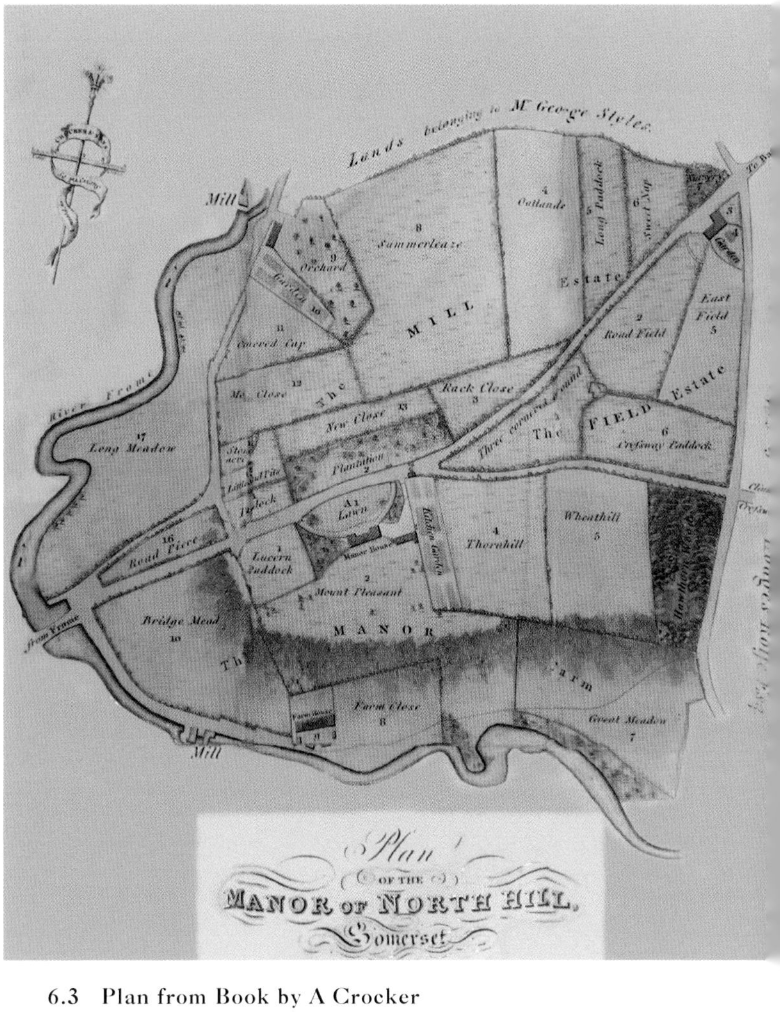

6.3 Plan from Book by A Crocker

cool in summer and warm in winter. The roof was high with air holes over the furnaces to let out the steam. Plenty of light was required but not too much sunshine with the windows about the width of the vat and leaning a little forward towards the top to throw the right amount of light on the surface of the liquor. The bottom of the windows were twelve to eighteen inches above the rim of the vessel so the shade of colour could be clearly discerned. The floor of the dyehouse was hard brick closely set with drains and channels to carry off waste liquor and there should have been enough room in the blue-dyehouse to lay six or eight *'wets'* of wool without interfering with the workmen. Business was so different from today it is hard to imagine a dye man's working day. The weavers generally worked from home, but the dyers would have been in the workshops all day heaving hundreds of pounds of wet wool in and out of vats and furnaces before walking home through town at dusk or later.

In 1808, Edward Olive, dyer of Frome Selwood, insured his stock of wool, indigo, dyewoods, utensils and stock in trade in his mill house.

'...His storeroom, rooms over and counting house all adjoining together and situate near the river Frome. Stone and tiled; for £150 at an annual premium of £1.13s. His stove house situate near the above mentioned store rooms in his now occupation also stone and tiled for £150.[5]*'*

This policy still reflected the group of buildings along Willow Vale formerly Pilly Vale when it was offered for sale by Messrs Harding and Sons Auctioneers in 1886.

'...For sale lot 4: Block of buildings, dyehouses, stables, large yards, drying ground, and well constructed and newly built shaft and also newly built stores and counting house in Pilly Vale.'

An important part of the business involved the purchase, storage and preparation of dyestuffs. It was necessary to hold large inventories and

6.4 Willow Vale Workshop

6.5 Shawford Mill in 2008

once purchased, expensive dyes needed to be stored.

'...The drug house should be fitted up with shelves conveniently, and the floor swept occasionally. It should be well furnished with weights and scales, steelyards, stoneware jugs and pans. All the dyewoods should be kept in tight barrels, well guarded from damp and the steam of the dyehouse.[6] *'*

Dyes and mordants were usually purchased locally from dry salters, an occupation of one of the members of the Whitchurch family. Clothiers also traded directly with merchants, importing consignments of madder, indigo and heartwoods from the early Venturers and the East India Company and indirectly via factors buying on their behalf. This required a long term investment of money and time as shipping commodities was a risky and unreliable

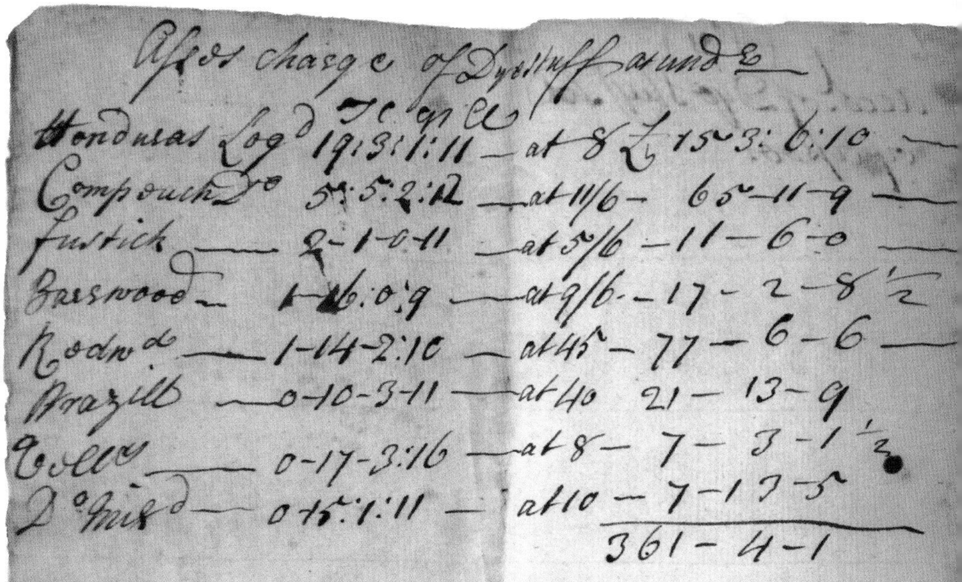

After charge of Dyestuff [illegible]

	Tc qr lb		
Honduras Log^d	19:3:1:11	at 8	£153:6:10
Compouch D^o	57:5:2:12	at 11/6	65–11–9
Fustick	2–1–0–11	at 5/6	11–6–0
Barswood	1–16:0:9	at 9/6	17–2–8½
Rodw^d	1–14–2:10	at 45	77–6–6
Brazill	0–10–3–11	at 40	21–13–9
Voll^o	0–17–3:16	at 8	7–3–1½
D^o Mild	0–15:1:11	at 10	7–17–5
			361–4–1

6.6 1734 Inventory of E Halliday

TO BE SOLD,

At Frome 27th Instant & days following till all is disposed of

By the Assignees of the Estate and Effects of *EDWARD HALLIDAY*, a Bankrupt.

		Yearly Value. l. s. d.
In Fee.	A NEW Built Mansion-House, Orchard, Garden, Stables, Tan-Yard, and other Messuages, and 5 Acres of Meadow or Pasture, in *Froom*, late *Whittock*'s, about - - - -	55 00 00
In Fee.	Two Messuages, 1 Orchard, 2 Gardens, 5 Acres of Pasture, in *Froom*, late *Comber*'s, about - - - -	22 00 00
In Fee.	The Reversion in Fee, after 3 Lives, of 7 Houses in *Vallis-Way* in *Froom*, whereon 1 *l.* 9 *s.* Chief Rent, is reserved, about - -	28 00 00
In Fee.	Ten Acres of Meadow or Pasture, near *Crutchill* in *Froom*, late *Davis*'s, about - - - -	08 00 00
In Fee.	A Messuage, Orchard, Garden, and Lands, call'd *Smith's Barn*, at *Cuckow-Hill*, in *Froom*, about - - -	16 00 00
	A Chief Rent - - -	00 07 06
Three Lives.	Five Messuages against the *Market-Place* in *Froom*, with several Closes belonging to them, late *Bull*'s, about - - -	70 00 00
Three Lives.	Part of an House, and several Lands lying in many Places in *Froom* Parish, late of *John Marchant*, about - - -	46 00 00
Three Lives.	—— Cottages, late *Hunt*'s, in *Froom*, about - -	06 19 00
In Fee.	Lands at *Norton St. Phillip*'s, late *Collier*'s - -	09 00 00
—— Lives.	An Orchard or Close, at *Pelly-Hill* in *Froom* - -	02 00 00
Two Lives.	Twenty-four Acres of Pasture, call'd *Hursover*'s, in *Froom*, late *Edgell*'s, about - - - - -	14 00 00
Three Lives.	Several Parcels of Arable and Pasture, in *Froom*, late *Saunders*'s, about	14 00 00
Three Lives.	Several Plots of Pasture, late *A-Court*'s, in *Froom*, about -	05 00 00
Three Lives.	A Tenement and Lands in *Marston-Bigot*, in Possession of *William Daniel* and *Maurice George*, about - - -	60 00 00
Two Lives.	Several Closes of Pasture in *Froom*, late *Wayland*'s, about -	11 00 00
Three Lives.	Three Houses in *Cheap-street*, in *Froom*, late *Faulkner*'s, about -	
Two Lives.	Two Messuages and Lands in *Froom*, call'd *Luffe*'s *Tenement* -	22 00 00
40 Years after one Life, or one Life and 40 Years.	A Mill, call'd *Kercher*'s *Mill*, in the Parish of *Orchardly*, for dry-grinding Dye-Wood; and Houses adjoining.	
Three Lives.	Some Closes at *Cuckow-Hill* in *Froom*, in Possession of —— *Brit.*	

All the said Hallidays houshold goods & plate &

Many large Quantities and Parcels of the following Goods and Merchandizes.

Madder	Spanish Woool	Purple List Wool	Woool Shears
Shumack	Fine English Wool	Fell Wool	Papers
Allum	Coarse Wool	Blue Wool	Handles
Copperas	List Wool	White List	Teazles
Argalls	Lambs Wool	Lathes	A Press, &c.
Vellony	Spanish Wool Dyed	Bricks	

And other Tools, Implements, and Utensils, belonging to the Cloathing and Cloath-working Trades; and also several large and other Furnaces, Pumps, and other Utensils, fit for Dyers.

Further Particulars relating to the Estates above, and the Names of the Tenants in Possession of them, may be had of the said Assignees, and of *JOHN PHELPS*, Attorney at Law in *Froom*.

Bristol: Printed by *Felix Farley*, in *Castle-Green*.

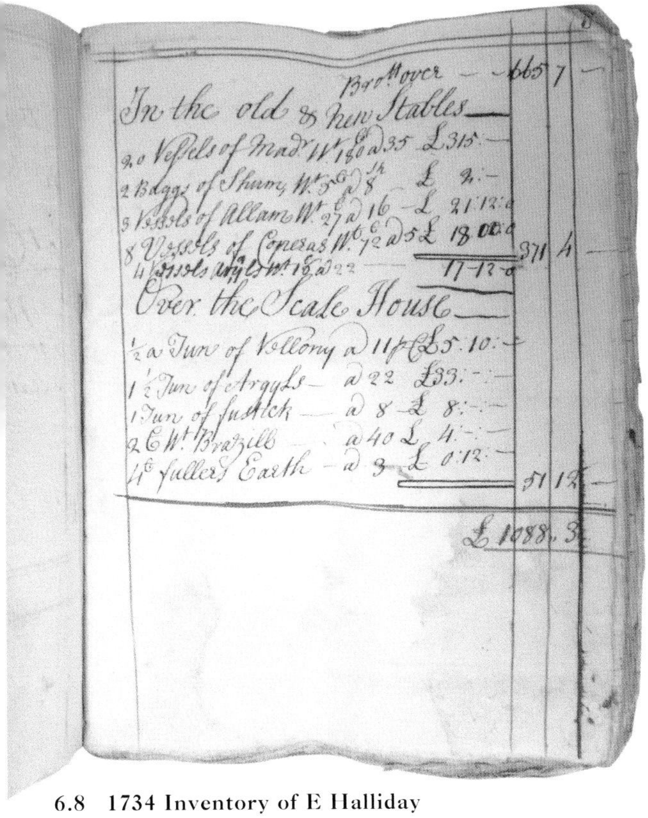
In the old & new Stables

Over the Scale House

6.8 1734 Inventory of E Halliday

undertaking which could take months, if not years, to provide a return of stock and on profit. The dyewoods mentioned in the recipe books included logwood, sanderswood, brazilwood, fustic. Also indigo, although not a wood, was ground in mills to a very fine powder.

Kerchers Mill in Orchardleigh, before it was converted to an edge tool mill, had rack fields in its vicinity attesting to use in the cloth trade. It was mentioned in several inventories for Edward Halliday, dyer of Frome, as a mill for dry grinding logs of dyewoods and the storage of madder, shumach, copperas and alum.[7]

If the the blue dyers undertook the second stage of woad fermentation they required a *'couching house'*. There was not much information to be found on its construction other than a building with an even floor of stone or brick and the walls the same.[8] The buildings would have been similar to floor maltings. Maintaining the correct temperature during the couch was critical so it may have had high vents or opening windows to control the ventilation. Ease of access for unloading heavy cartloads would have necessitated an entryway with wide doors. John Olive processed woad and the vaulted cellar below the counting house in the Willow Vale premises may have been fit for the purpose.

All dyestuffs needed careful preparation:

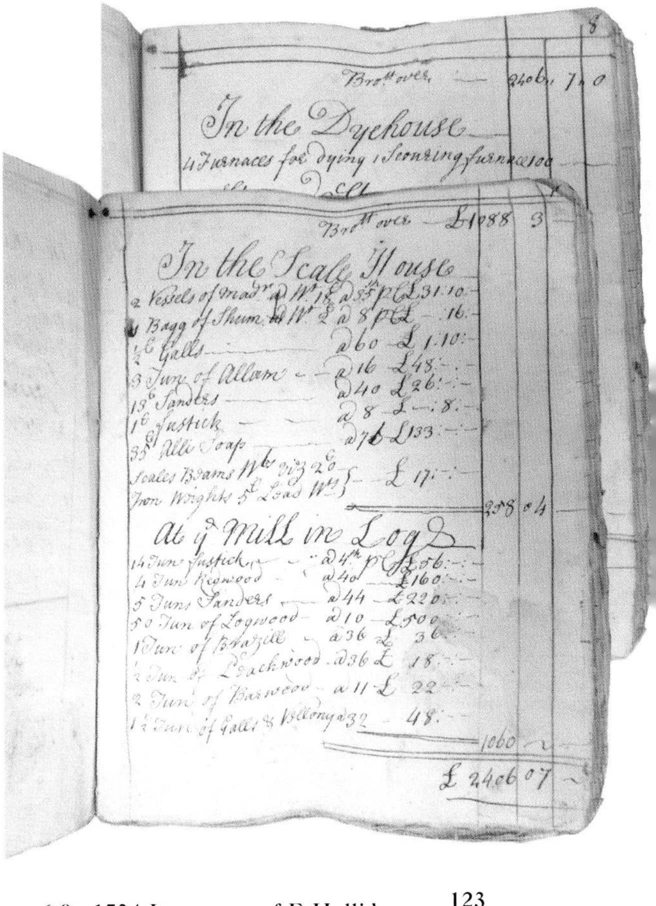
In the Dyehouse

In the Scale House

At ye Mill in Logs

6.7 Auction Particulars

6.9 1734 Inventory of E Halliday

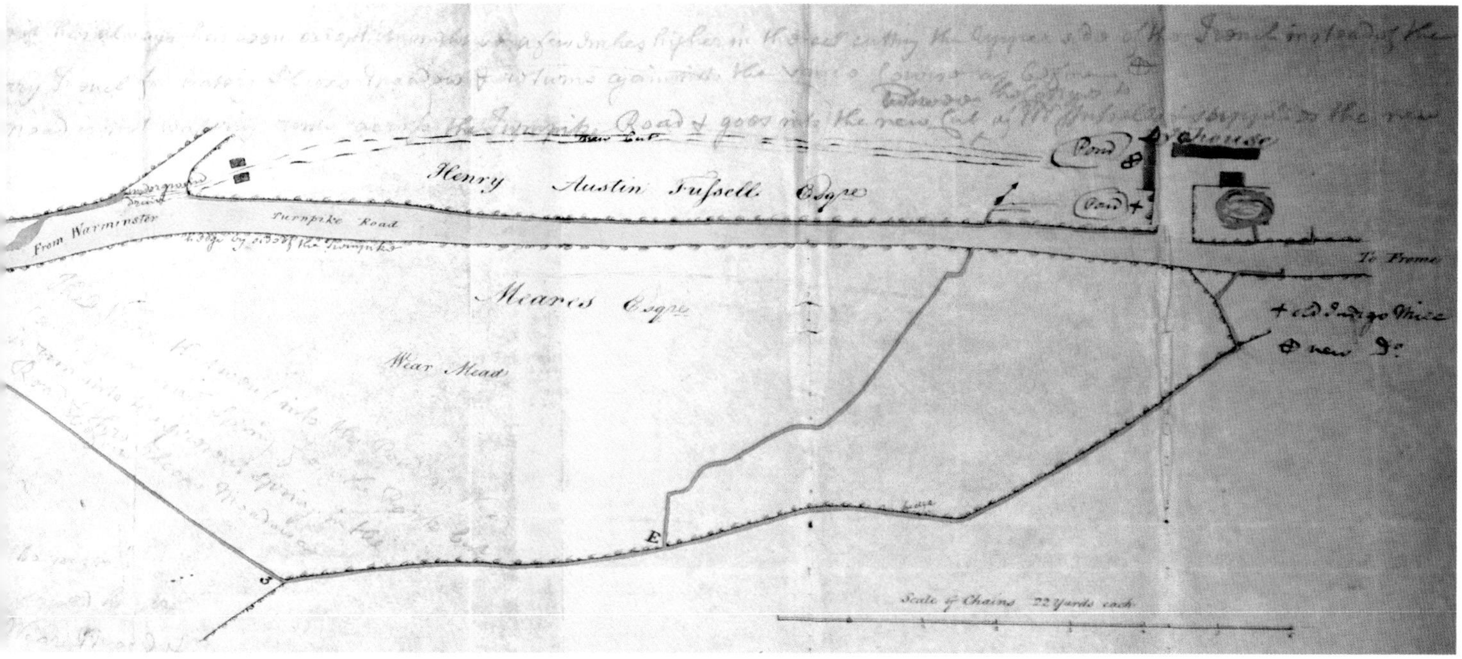

6.10 Sturford Mill, Corsley - Plan for Relocation of the Indigo Mill

> *'In a dyehouse, no step should be taken but by weight or measure as all guesswork surely brings waste.[9]'*

Inventories list brass scales and weights, small vessels and other containers to remove, heat and transfer dye solutions between vats and stoves. There were plans showing a site for an indigo grinding mill along the old Frome to Warminster toll road which may have been powered by a water wheel or a horse. The larger vessels for the furnaces were made of brass or copper with no iron nails, the blue vats were made of wood. They all had close fitting covers to be used as needed.

At Shawford, near Rode, the main mill building which was rebuilt in 1805[10], shows a works plan with an Indigo House, a round fire stove, and an air stove for drying wool. Two buildings house the furnaces; Cæsar and Victoria are in one; and, Toby and Great Furnace in the other.[11] Smaller vats for woad and indigo are in a separate building.

> *'... Over the coppers should be poles fixed in the walls for the skeins and hanks to hang on so that the dye-liquor dripping from them may fall back into the copper. Ladles, wooden shovels, barrels, ladders and barrows, nets and crosses for wool, winces and reels for piece work. The equipment should be kept as much as possible to one kind of colour and scrupulously clean. Where there is room and convenience, all the parts of the establishment should occupy their own quarter; The black dye-house may be contiguous to*

6.11 1844 Plan of Shawford Works

Shawford Mill Race

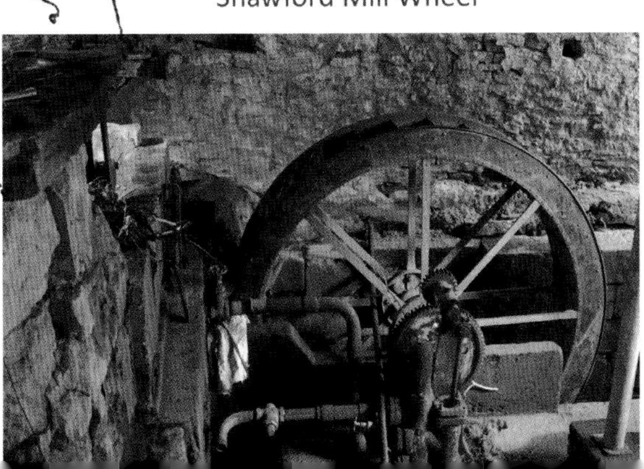

Shawford Mill Wheel

6.12 Early 1900s Low Water Fire Stove Building

the drabs, olives, bottle greens or the chocolates but should not be next to the pinks or yellows.[12]'

Once washed or dyed the goods had to be dried.

'*...It may appear to those who are ignorant of the business, that drying wool is too simple an operation to need any comment, yet this is far from the case. There are points to be observed in many of the most simple operations, which have an essential bearing on the interest of the whole, and one of these must be particularly attended to in the drying of wool, or the staple will be materially injured by being exposed to the sun or the high temperature of the drying stove.*[13]'

This could be done in one of three ways, by open exposure to fresh air, or in fire, or air stove buildings. In Frome there are several listed buildings which were formerly stove drying houses. One was incorporated into a house in Low Water and another in Willow Vale is ruinous. There is one in the town centre on Justice Lane which has been renovated and forms part of the Black Swan Arts complex. These three stand as evidence to the town's industrial past, others were demolished. Typically, the stove houses were circular buildings about 16 ft in diameter built of stone. The upper floors were slatted so the heat could circulate and the steam escaped through vents in a conical roof.

6.13 Ruinous Fire Stove Building in Willow Vale

'...Stove rooms should not be heated by means of a current of hot air as there is a danger of a current of dust![14]'

6.14 2008 Restored Fire Stove Building in Justice Lane

The lower floor was paved with stone or brick; and the stove, with a cast iron flue which terminated several feet above the roof, was placed in the middle of the room. On each floor, situated in a circular arrangement, were upright posts where the wet wool was hung on 20 inch wooden arms projecting at about 20° forming a spiral along the length of the post with just sufficient space between each one to permit a man or boy to collect the dry wool and replace it with wet.

'... It is necessary therefore to take it up in either case as soon as it is dry. In the fire stove, the heat is raised to a very high temperature until the wool is about three fourths dry, then it is permitted to cool gradually until it approaches about 90F degrees at which stage the drying is

6.15 The Wooden Slatted Building was an Air Stove or for Drying Teasels - the Mill at Rode

finished... The stove, if properly attended, could dry 240 pounds of wool every 12 hours with a moderate consumption of fuel.[15]'

Dye materials, yarns and finished cloths were very valuable and if left unattended in sheds and fields were sometimes seen as an ideal opportunity to make a bit of money and theft was not uncommon. In 1795 a court case heard depositions from Thomas Collens, a dyer and George Kingdon a clothier, both from Frome regarding a theft of wool from the dyehouse of John and Robert Meares.

'*...James Butcher, the 'vatsman' had worked there as a day labourer for several years, on leaving work he locked the door and left the key in a place where he and others knew where to find it and let themselves in which they usually did. Around 10 pm on 14th May some person had been just before seen in the dyehouse. James immediately went there to find that 10 or 11 lbs of wool had been taken from several baskets in which it had been placed in order to be carried to the vats to be dyed the next day, wool had also been thrown around the floor and the greater part had been put in a bag to be carried away...*[16]'

6.16 A.J. Tucker's Woollen Mills -Weaving Sheds in the Foreground, Small Dyehouse, Mill building at the Far End

[1] Cooper, T 1815: 25
[2] SHC DD/LW/41
[3] SHC DD/LW/41
[4] Mann, J de Lacy 1964: 116
[5] SHC DD/LW/41
[6] Cooper, T 1815: 5
[7] TNA C 04/221
[8] Partridge,W 1823: 118
[9] Cooper, T 1815: 5
[10] Souvenir Programme 1957 - 1967 Shawford Mill Theatre
[11] Rogers, K 176: 185
[12] Partridge, W 1815: 4
[13] Partridge, W 1815: 36
[14] Partridge, W 1815: 6
[15] Partridge, W 1815:36, 27
[16] SHC Q/SR/363/3/29

The Monthly Rate of Frome Town Tything

To be Collected for the Relief of the Poor according to the Statute in that Case made and Provided 1777.

A

			s.	d.
Richd. Adams		Smiths Mill, and Ground	2	2¾
Do.	2	Tenemts. Late Stars		2
Do.	1	Ditto St. Do.		1
Do.	1	Ditto St. Mundy's		1
Do.	1	Do. St. Norvels		1
Saml. Allen		Wool Hall		6
Benjn. Ayres		Cogshalls Ground	1	6
Do.		Woodards Do.		2
Do.		Late Wises		1½
Do.	1	House and Gro. St. Queels		1
Do.		Part Giffords		2
Do.		Late Smiths		3
Do.	2	Acres Westovers		1
Do.		Pt. Thatchers		4
Henry Allen		Dye House		4
Do.		Dwelling House		4
Do.		Willis's Ground		1

CHAPTER 7

FROME CLOTHIERS & WORKERS

'Frail is the vestment once I made,
death has dissolved this human thread.
My frame I thought so firm so whole,
was but a cloathing for the soul.
The cloth and thread I wove and spun,
by time and weather were undone.
The stronger texture of my frame,
that web of nerves was just the same.
And now the fates which upon the chain,
have cut the thread of life again.'

In memory of John Smith of Fromefield, Clothier,
who departed life November 20th 1745 aged 61

Everyone was expected to contribute to the growth of the family business. Sons and brothers were sent to London, and overseas, to act as agents, while widows and daughters married men in the cloth trade. One example was the 1756 appointment of trustees for Sarah Collens, spinster, on her marriage to Edward Jefferies, factor in Blackwell Hall, both families were from Frome. A record held in the London Livery archives mentioned John Ford of Frome, who apprenticed his son, also John to Edward Jefferies for seven years in 1762. Sarah Collens may

7.1 1777 Frome Town Tithing

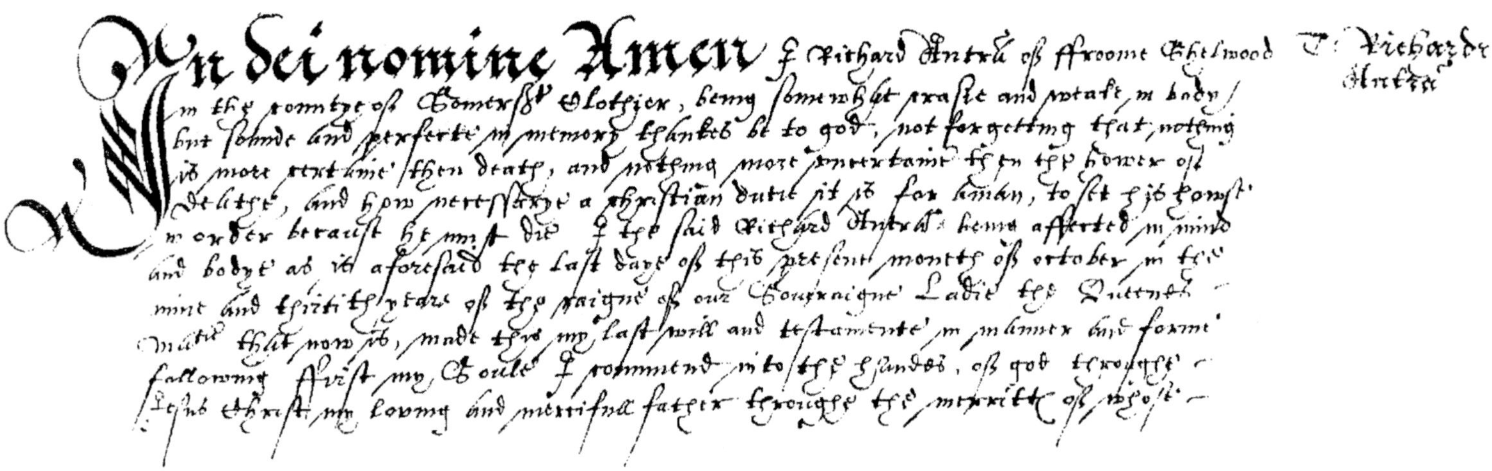

In dei nomine Amen I Richard Antra of ffroome Selwood ... in the countye of Somersett Clothier, being somewhat weake and sicke in body / but sounde and perfecte in memory thankes be to god, not forgetting that nothing is more certaine then death, and nothing more uncertaine then the hower of

7.2 1598 R Antra's Will

have been the daughter of John Collens mentioned in the inscription of the dye recipe book that was lent to his friend John Ford in 1735. As these records raise more questions, I have chosen to introduce only some of the families involved in the 18th century cloth trades of Frome where I have been able to find their wills, inventories, account ledgers and other documents. The Bunns, the Smiths, the Whitchurches, the Jessers, the Hallidays, the Allens, the Sheppards and the Olives, are all familiar local names. I have also touched on a few of the lesser known families, the Antras, the Jenkins and Martha Gibbons who was the freeholder of a dyehouse in Rodden. I have examined some of the records of the parish poor, who contributed their stories to building the layers of ordinary working lives when the dye recipe books were used in the 1700s.

In his will of March 24th 1598, Richard Antra, a Frome clothier bequeathed considerable wealth to his family and:

> *'...I give to each and every one of my spinners six pence a piece. I give 12 pence to everyone of my weavers having a single loomb and to each of my weavers having a duble loomb two shillings a piece...*[1]*'*

7.3 Replica of Cabell Rebus, St John's Parish Church - Frome

The white cloth trade which had provided wealth for a few and work for the many, had ceased by the end of the century. The Craas, the Cables and the Dunkertons had made their money and had left the area but for most of the inhabitants, Frome,'*... for all the treasure of its wool,*' was reported in 1631, to be very poor, its population of around 6,500 being mostly clothiers, weavers and spinners.[2]

Following the disruption of trade during the Civil War, the Restoration temporarily returned commercial stability encouraging a resurgence in the cloth industry. In Frome as elsewhere, there was an on-going separation of religion and politics brought about by reforms from the impassioned arguments of the Non-conformists. For many centuries, they were excluded from universities and holding civic posts, their prospects were limited to those of trade and commerce. These enterprising men and women relied on the fellowship of their church members and their shared views to develop strong networks built on trust and personal reputation to sustain and expand their businesses. This belief in social change, along with the prospect of a livelihood in cloth manufacture attracted many more people to settle in the area. Some of the most resolute clothiers first held meetings in their own houses and later established the chapels that have left an indelible mark on the town. Rook Lane Chapel is a fine example which was built in 1707 on land donated by Robert Smith.

7.4 Rook Lane Chapel - Frome

The people of Frome were resilient, as the manufacture of the fine cloth trades emerged in the 18th century cycles of prosperity resumed and others built on the town's cloth legacy. Demand for cloth grew rapidly with the opening of overseas markets and the import of coffee, tea, and new exotic products shipped by the East India Company were proudly displayed in the best parlours, purchased by the clothiers returning from London with their wool and dyestuffs. In many small towns, those engaged in the cloth trade would travel to London to conduct their business from the inns and the newly established chocolate and coffee houses near Blackwell Hall. Fashion may have dominated some of the conversations, along with the arrivals and departures of the fleets, the quarterly sales and candle auctions, the new business of insurance, the price of wool, indigo and other dyestuffs, or the impending wars and the latest trade embargoes all of which undoubtedly affected their businesses. These topics may have been discussed locally by John Smith, Thomas Bunn, Henry Allen and others at one of the many inns of Frome shown on a map of 1774. The Angel, the George, the Blue Boar, the Three Swans and others that are still trading.[3]

7.5 Door of the Three Swan

The third son of William Bunn, a yeoman and tallow chandler of Frome, Thomas, was born in 1684. He was a dyer, who built on the family's prosperity.[4] He had six children, the portraits of two of his sons hang on a wall in the Frome museum. Both men were probably in their late twenties or early thirties as the portraits date around the 1740s. From an entry in his diary, Thomas's grandson, also Thomas describes his father *'as the neatest of men in the care of his apparel I believe from a principle of duty.*[5]*'* At the time, the common dress suit for men of business such as Thomas, a doctor, and James, a solicitor, were breeches and a waistcoat, over which they wore a coat, all made of the finest cloth perhaps selected by their father and dyed to a fashionable colour of their choice. Coats were of a similar style until the late 18th century when fitted doe skin breeches and swallow tail coats became the height of fashion, only small details changed such as the

7.6 Dr. Thomas Bunn

7.7 James Bunn

neckline, collars and cuffs. Coats and waistcoats were closely fitted at the waistline extending to just above the knee with side pleated vents. Thomas is portrayed wearing a single breasted coat with a round neck, the cloth woaded, then over dyed or saddened to a pale blue grey colour with a matching waistcoat. The large buttons on the coat match the smaller ones of his waistcoat, the close fitting sleeves expose the lace cuffs of a fine shirt. The suit worn by James is a warm mid brown, of a similar cut and he is wearing a white silk or satin waistcoat. Both men wore a stock, the piece of folded linen that formed a high neckband fastened at the back of the neck to display the ruffled shirt front which was fashionable after 1735. The scratch bob or cut wig covered part of their heads, the natural front hair being brushed back over, completed the stylish attire of learned professionals. Like today's younger generation they may have dressed in the latest style while their father, the dyer, perhaps also the neatest of men, retained the old-fashioned dignity of a bygone era wearing a frock coat and a full bottomed wig as he went about his business.

7.8 Mid 18th Century Buff Broadcloth Coat

The Smith family had settled in Frome by the 1500s. Henry Smith was listed as a weaver in the early parish records. Robert Smith, a wealthy clothier who lived in Rook Lane House and who, in 1607, owned all the lands previously endowed to

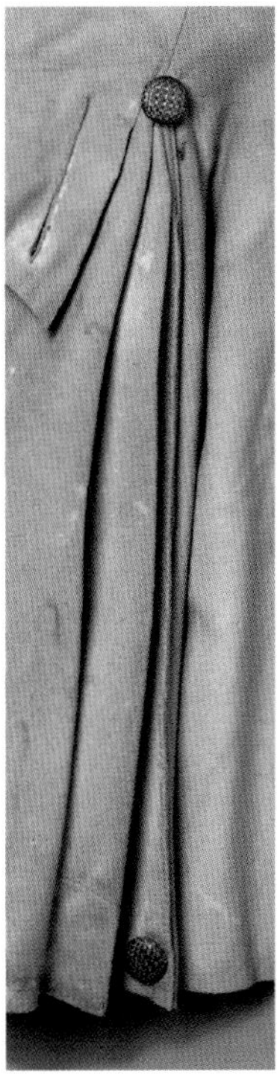

7.9 Pleat Detail

7.10 Stonewall Manor - Keyford, Frome

Frome's Lady Chapel[6] as well as Stonewall Manor in Keyford.[7]

Robert's will, dated 1625, revealed that he had a sufficient estate to leave his wife, three sons and a daughter well provided for

> *'...I give to Robert, my son £200, my greatest silver saulte gilted and my greatest silver bowl. To Henry £200 and my second best silver saucer gilted and one silver spoone, to William £200 and my second best silver bowl, to Edith my daughter £200 and one silver spoone.[8]'*

Like his contemporary Richard Antra, Robert may have been engaged in the export of white undyed and unfinished cloth to the Low Countries. He may also have been instrumental in promoting the coloured medley cloth trade in which John Smith's business excelled. The 1661 inventory of Robert Smith the Younger lists the goods and chattels of an affluent clothier which included wearing apparel and twenty five pounds of ready money. His house had at least four bed chambers with bedsteads, bed curtains, feather bolsters, pillows and blankets some of which were in the little chamber over the parlour, others over the hall and some in the little chamber over the buttery. The dining room and parlour had been furnished with table boards and frames, six *'joyned'* chairs and stools, cushions, rugs and silver plate. In the lofts, there were racks for cheese and the ale that the people of Frome favoured over wine and *'one broadcloth in the yarn loft of mixed make'*. A book of cloths under manufacture and:

> *'one sent this day to London in the hands of Thomas Godman.[9]'*

John Smith of Fromefield, like his fellow Thomas Bunn, was born in 1684. A prosperous clothier, he may have followed in the footsteps of a father also named John, a woollen draper who died in 1685 and whose

7.11 Welshmill House - Frome

will bequeathed all his lands, tenements and hereditaments in Berkley to John, his eldest son. As any caring father today, he was preoccupied for the well-being of his children and he left the remainder of his estate, apart from named legacies, to be managed at the discretion of executors who were to ensure the provision and disbursement of £150 for the *'...maintenance and university education of my sonne Norfolk.*[10]'

The cloth and dye business of the Whitchurch and the Bull families was described in the chapter on the Welshmill dye books. The Jessers, who were involved in the legacy disputes, were first mentioned in Frome in 1602. Many of their wills show them to be engaged in the cloth trade as clothiers, dyers and gentlemen. Joseph Jesser the Elder had a dyehouse at Welshmill and built a grand house nearby, his eldest son became a factor at Blackwell Hall. Amongst their friends they counted Lord Orrery and it was not unusual for Joseph and his kinsman Thomas to meet with his Lordship in the kitchen of the George. In one of his letters Lord Orrery describes a '*merry supper at Bull Hall,*[11]' which formerly stood on Cork St. The family were discerning collectors of pictures, plate and china, and had their portraits painted by the eminent Bath artist, William Hoare. Mary Jesser, another member of the Welshmill branch, had her house built on Gentle Street in 1766 and installed a Chinese Chippendale staircase as she favoured the oriental style furnishings which had become the height of fashion. The Grade II* listed dwelling, now known as 'Argyll House' was named

7.12 Argyll House, Gentle Street - Frome

after the Duchess of Argyll who lived there in 1855. The Royal Society of Arts had promoted the establishment of successful carpet manufacturing on the 'Principle of Turkish Carpets' through subsidies and awards.[12] Carpets made from the weavers thrums was a way to use waste wool from one process and re-use it in another. In 1751, William Jesser received an award for the best Turkish imitation carpet.

Cash flow turned the business mill wheel, which needed a steady supply that was not always available and gave rise to considerable litigation over unpaid debts. Peer to peer lending for a share of the profit was successful as friends, church congregants and others including family members helped to set people up in trade. Higher costs and delays in the provision of raw materials, late deliveries, long term credit notes, shortages of coin and other events held up the receipt of cash in hand by months and sometimes years. Although a form of insurance was available from the late 1600s, the option to be a limited company was not common until the 1850s. Business owners were liable for any debts they incurred and from which they faced potential bankruptcy; this was the case for Edward Halliday, a dyer of Frome. He first came to notice in a marriage settlement agreed between Edward Halliday the Elder, dyer of Warminster and John Hippie, tanner of Frome, for Edward Halliday the Younger and his intended, Mary Hippie,which in 1682 included a farm in Frome and:

> *'...All these his dyeing furnaces and other implements of dyeing belonging to the said trade situate and being at his house at Frome. ...Together also with all such debts of money which are now in owing to the said Edward Halliday the Younger in and about Frome Selwood aforesaid that which together with the said implements of dyeing.[13]'*

in all worth about £200. John Hippie also promised another £100 to the couple. This sum of money worth several hundred thousand pounds today would have provided a good foundation on which to build a business. With an element of luck, and a good head for business, some clothiers became wealthy. The harsh reality of bankruptcy however was also suffered by many including Edward and Mary's son who had followed in the family dyeing trade. Edward's business was once extensive, he owned or leased land and premises from Lord Weymouth at Longleat, from the Earl of Cork and Orrery at Marston Bigot, from the Champneys at Orchardleigh and from the former Leversedge estates. By 1734 the Court of Exchequer at Westminster was seeking to recover a tax payment of £8,000. Two unpaid bonds dated 1727 and 1732, were also mentioned in the names of Henry Bull and John Jesser who had sufficient resources to repay their debts. A letter sent from Chancery to the Bristol bailiffs, requested the valuation and seizure of all his household goods and belongings and demanded his arrest and '*...keep him in prison until we are satisfied he has paid his debt.*[14]'

'January 3rd, 1734 letter to the bailiffs in Bristol on behalf of Mary Halliday of Frome Selwood.

> '*...We are informed that Mr Halliday's mother desires to pay down the full sum for all Mr Halliday's goods. She feels the value put on them is insufficient and desires two sworn appraisers to revalue them. We think the proposal is worth your consideration as the Chancery cannot suffer by such a sale and doubt not your humanity and good nature will influence you to allow so small a request to a gentlewoman unfortunate enough to excite the pity and compassion of not only all her neighbours but all who yet know her story.*[15]'

There are more documents about the case at the National Archives and in the Bristol Records Office which deserve further investigation, but it seems that a lack of cash flow, perhaps from an uninsured loss on exported cloth, contributed to the situation. There are several inventories of his goods which provide insight to the size of the business and a final auction sale describes his stock in trade which included tons of dyestuffs.

By the 9th July, 1735, Mary Halliday had seized and distrained the goods of her son for unpaid rent arrears of two years

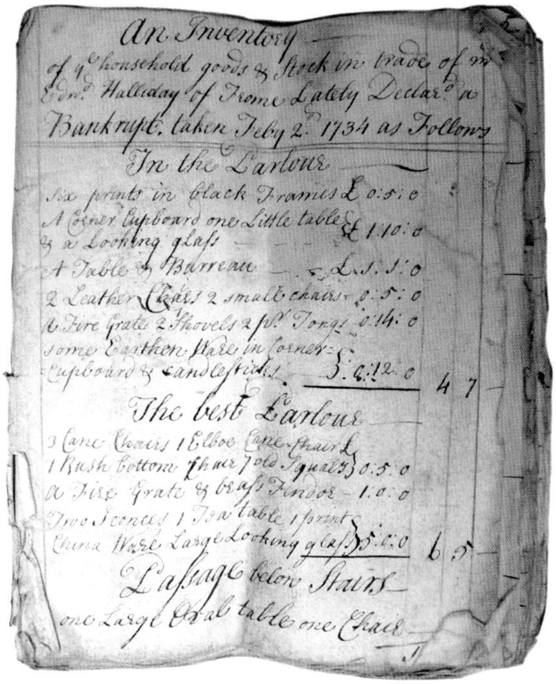

An Inventory
of ye household goods & Stock in trade of Mr
Edwd Halliday of Frome Lately Declard a
Bankrupt taken Feby 2d 1734 as Follows
In the Parlour
Six prints in black Frames £ 0:5:0
A Corner Cupboard one Little table & a Looking glass £ 1:10:0
A Table & Burreau £ 1:1:0
2 Leather Chairs 2 small chairs 0:5:0
A Fire Grate 2 Shovels 2 pr Tongs 0:14:0
some Earthen Ware in Corner Cupboard & candlesticks 0:12:0
4 7
The best Parlour
3 Cane Chairs 1 Elboe Cane Chair 1 Rush bottom Chair 7 old Squabs £ 0:5:0
A Fire Grate & brass Fender 1:0:0
Two Sconces 1 Tea table 1 print China Ware Large Looking glass 5:0:0
6 5
Passage below Stairs
one Large Oval table one Chair

7.13 1734 E Halliday Inventory

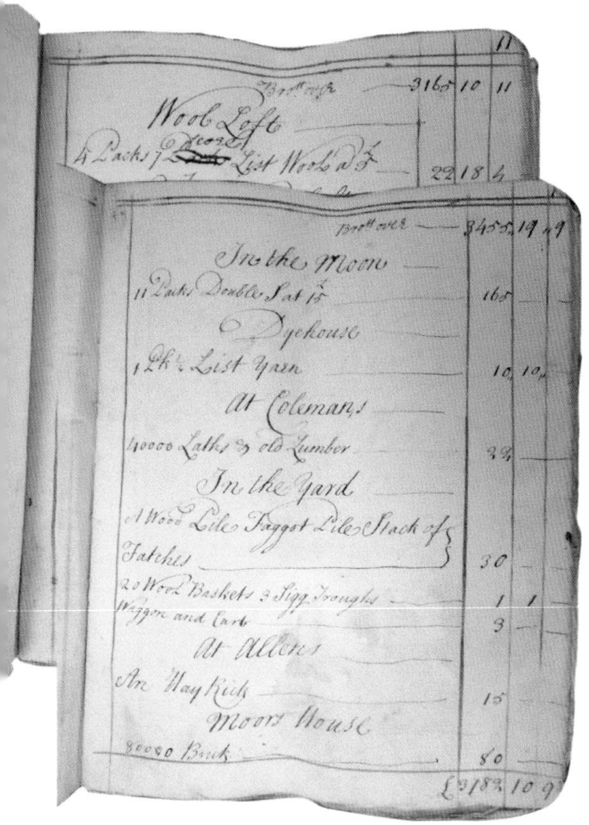
Wool Loft
In the Moon
Dyehouse
At Colemans
In the Yard
At Allens
Moors House

7.14 1734 E Halliday Inventory

amounting to £210. The paperwork lists fashionable household effects in two counting houses adjoining the dwelling house. Furniture, looking glasses, prints, china and one copper *'chocolett pott'* from the parlour. In the passage one storey high, an eight day clock and case. In the best chamber ten prints in gilt frames, bedsteads and bedding, silver spoons, salts and salvers, along with several broadcloths and remnants worth £80 and a few effects from the maid's room. In the passage between the two counting houses, one hundred yards of broadcloth. In the first cellar, four casks with about three hundred gallons of beer, a cask of cyder, many empty vessels and eight tankards.[16]

A separate undated inventory lists items in the new counting house such as a writing desk, a table to till money, a pair of scales and weights, a copper money *'shovell'* and brace of pistols, a tinder box, two fowling pieces (shotguns), three old chairs, a fender and large oval table in the passage. Although a dyer himself, Edward appears to have kept a stock of blue wool bought from a specialist supplier along with a large quantity of English, Spanish and list wools in the yarn and wool lofts, the total weighing more than one hundred and twenty tons. A mix of fines, superfines and coarse blacks of more than six hundred and thirty yards in the perching room, each identified by number and valued at more than £300, an expensive scarlet cloth worth £16 which was unevenly coloured and was to be re-dyed. There was also an inventory of cloths in the mill hands to bray and burl. Eleven cloths worth £60 at Joseph Jeffry's to bray. Twenty six cloths worth £140 with sundry burlers whose names are given along with the number of the cloths in their possession and at least fifty cloths in the loft just cut from the looms. There is no mention of woad but twenty vessels of madder valued at £660 and almost eighty tons of dye woods stored at Kercher's mill . Casks of rape and Gallipoli oil used in the preparation of wool and plenty of *'sigg'* tankards, teasels and handles all necessary equipment for dyeing and cloth finishing. It would seem that he had sufficient goods to settle his debts as his stock in trade was valued at over £6,000 excluding his cloth.[17]

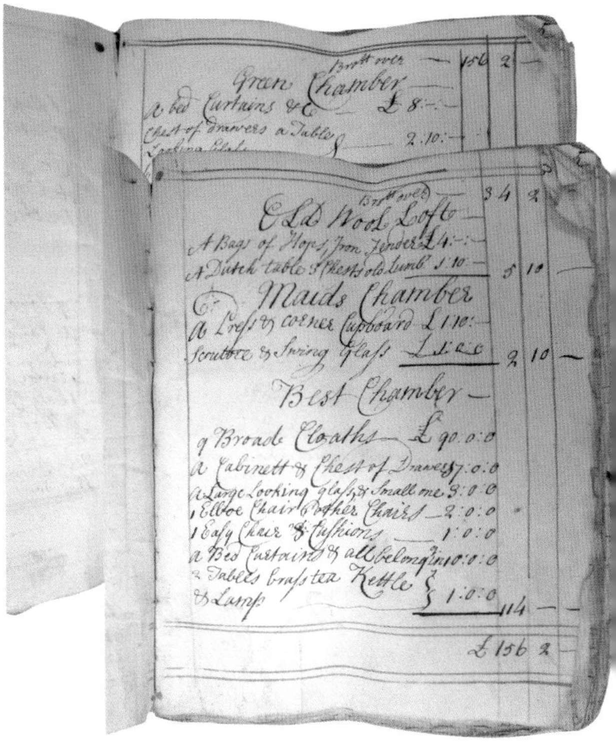

7.15 1734 Inventory of E Halliday

The properties of the Allen families are very difficult to disentangle. The name Dyers Close Lane is all that remains of the large dyeworks that belonged to them at Low Water. The will of Henry Allen, dyer of Frome Selwood, in 1725

> *'...To my wife Mary, my brother Samuel ... and all those wool mills, heretofore fulling mills, and a grist mill called Nettlesham or Nettle Bed Mill or Stapleford or Staple Mead Mill, all of which I lately purchased in fee of Christopher Brewer, Clothier in the parish of Laverton now or late in the occupation of Edward Harris. Edward, only son of my late deceased wife Elizabeth, to have the dyeing equipment to the value of £600 as in a settlement dated 20 Jan 1710.[18]'*

In his will, Henry also bequeathed property for charitable purposes which was to be managed by trustees including James Collens, a church warden, named in the dye recipe book. He also left £10 to his brother Samuel, drug-maker of Bristol, who in 1714, had made an agreement with the son of Robert Hinton a clothier, also named Robert, to serve him as covenant servant, presumably once he had finished his seven year apprenticeship. After three years Robert, who dwelt in Frome, applied for settlement in the parish where he looked after several work people employed in the cloth trade by the absentee Samuel. Recorded in the Frome Town tithing of 1734 until 1742, the widow Allen was paying rates on *'The Wool Hall'* which in 1770 was owned and occupied by Samuel

Allen. Property sales were increasingly common and the Allens' dyehouse in Willow Vale was put up for sale in 1796.

Land at Fromefield was owned by John Smith, and eventually sold to George Sheppard, a clothier who in 1797 built Fromefield House. An imposing Georgian building, in the Robert Adam style, with a symmetrical ashlar front, well proportioned windows, and unusually, it had separate ice and bath houses in the grounds and although at the time it was on the outskirts of Frome, the grade II listed building has now been converted to flats within an easy walk to the town centre.

The Sheppard family[19] had been settled in the town since 1558. The son of an Edward Sheppard, John established the family cloth trade, having started as a wool card maker. From the 1640s, he leased and bought land that had once belonged to St Catherine's chapel, the area known as Sheppards Barton extended to what is now South Parade, where John built workshops and workers houses. He and his wife Elizabeth had seven children, both his eldest son and his nephew were clothiers named John which causes some confusion. There is no will for his son, but his nephew married Philippa who increased the freehold possessions of the family by buying 4 acres in the area of Dyers Close and the dyehouse from John Whittock. Their grandchildren came to dominate Frome's cloth industry whilst some members of the family became factors at Blackwell Hall. There are also connections to the Sheppards of Gloucestershire. In the late 18th century there was a major expansion of their business in Rodden.

> *'...A large body of aggrieved scribblers met on Monday night on report that Mssrs Sheppard of Frome had erected and used scribbling engines at their mill in Rodden. They met the owners and were reassured that they had done nothing to disadvantage the poor and departed peacefully. Bath Chronicle 4th June 1795.'*

By 1814, they had established three mills on four acres of land at Spring Gardens which they enlarged and operated with steam engines by 1824. Like other factories, it was lit by candles and thousands of red stained ones provided light in their premises, *'...if one saw a red candle burning*

The Overseers Paid March 17th 1778 As Under

	£	s	d
No. 1 Column	2	4	0
2 Ditto	2	5	0
3 Ditto	2	16	6
4 Ditto	1	14	6
5 Ditto	4	15	0
6 Ditto	2	15	0
7 Ditto	2	11	6
8 Ditto	1	19	0
9 Ditto	3	1	6
10 Ditto	4	8	0
11 Ditto	2	19	0
12 Ditto	3	13	0
13 Ditto	1	5	6
14 Ditto	3	12	0
15 Ditto	2	17	0
[illegible] Taylor 3/ Betty Ayres 1/6 Thos. Jeffries 2/ Betty Hacket 2/	0	8	6
Jn. Falkner 3/6 Wm. [illegible] 1/6 Benj. Withy 2/ Jos. Rouse 2/	0	9	0
Betty Macey 2/ [illegible] 1/6 half year's Rent of Workhouse	0	3	6
[illegible] Rich. Shepard 5/6 Mary Moor 1/	4	6	6
Nath. [illegible] Jn. [illegible] 6 [illegible] Saml. Williams	0	10	0
[illegible] 1. 14. 8 Jn. Bainton 3/6 Bartholomew 1/6 Mary	1	19	8
[illegible] 2/ Mary Harding 1/ Mary Cross 1/6 Thos.	0	4	6
Turner's fam. 7/6 [illegible] 1/ [illegible] 2/ Simon	0	9	0
Wheeler 6 Thos. West's Bill 3. 1. 10 Bishop's Wife 4/	3	8	10
Mary Porter 1/6 Eliz. French 2/ Wm. [illegible] 1/6 [illegible] 2/	0	6	6
[illegible] 1 Saml. Pope 2/ Betty Parsons 2/6 Chris. Parker 3/	0	8	6
Charlotte Rawlings 2/ Mary Star 1/6 Rich. Gilbert	0	3	6
fam. [illegible] 2/6 Jn. Barter 1/ Ann Grant [illegible] 3 [illegible]	0	6	6
[illegible] 2/ Mary Hacket 1/6 Martha Coles 1/6 Mary	0	5	0
[illegible] delivery 2/6 Coffin for [illegible] Davis 5/ Do. for	0	7	6
Eliz. [illegible] 5/ Do. for Mary [illegible] Child 2/6 Do. for [illegible]	0	14	6
[illegible] 5/ Do. for [illegible] Coomby 5/ Do. for Mary Smith's [illegible]	0	10	0
2/6 Do. for [illegible] 5/ Thos. Cooper 2/ Ann West 1/	0	10	6
Jas. [illegible] 2/ [illegible] for Mary Porter 1/3 Wid. Coombs 1/6	0	4	9
Ann Webb 1/ [illegible] 1/ Jas. Cooper 2/	0	4	0
John Trimby's Disbursments Pr. Book	2	18	6½
Workhouse Bill	8	9	9
[illegible] for the use of the Workhouse 1/6	0	1	6
Mary Porter's Burial Charges 7/6 Betty [illegible] in her	0	7	6
[illegible] 5/ [illegible] Yerbury 1/ [illegible] Yerbury's Child 1/	0	7	11
[illegible] second hand Coat 6 Mary Cooper's Child	0	6	0
Petticoat & Breeches 5/ Jos. Whiting Stockings 1/6	0	6	6
Betty Whittington [illegible] 3/6 Stockings 1/4 Mary Do. Gown 4/	0	8	10
Do. Petticoat 3/9 [illegible] Coat & Breeches 3/6 Do. Shoes	0	7	3
& Stockings 4/6 [illegible] Coat & Breeches 3/ Do. Shoes	0	7	6
Stockings 1/8 Rich. [illegible] making 3 Garments	0	12	2½
[illegible] to [illegible] Rowe's 8 Betty [illegible] 10/2½	0	0	8
[illegible] 1/ Mary Whitington Do. 1/ Jas. Druce 6	0	2	6
[illegible] Presley 1/2	0	1	2
Harvey: Mary Morris 2/ Mary Vigor 1/ Mary Harding 1/ Ann Hawkins 1/	0	5	0
Burlet: Saml. Whiting 2/ [illegible] 2/ Jn. Vigor 2/ Betty Lacy 1/ Grace Carpenter 6 [illegible] 2/ Nath. Vennel 1/ Ann Gifford 1/ Aaron Singer Shoes 6/ Wid. Carpenter 1/ Ann Whitington 1/	0	19	6
Lacey: Ann West 2/ Betty Macey 2/6 Jn. Bainton 3/ Ann Grant 1/ Coffin for Thos. Chapman 5/ [illegible] 3/2 Jos. Yerbury 6 Mary Whitington 2/ Jas. Rowe 1/ John Bishop 1/	0	18	3½
	75	10	10½

The Overseers Paid March 31, 1778 As Under

	£	s	d
No. 1 Column	2	4	0
2 Ditto	2	5	0
3 Ditto	2	13	6
4 Ditto	1	14	6
5 Ditto	2	19	0
6 Ditto	2	19	6
7 Ditto	2	14	6
8 Ditto	2	1	6
9 Ditto	3	5	6
10 Ditto	4	13	0
11 Ditto	2	14	0
12 Ditto	3	13	0
13 Ditto	1	5	6
14 Ditto	3	12	0
15 Ditto	2	12	0
Hanh. Carpenter's Child 1/ Hen. Horease 1/6	0	2	6
Apprenticed 15/ Jos. Taylor 3/ Betty Ayres 1/6	0	19	6
Thos. Jeffries 2/ Betty Hacket 2/ John Falkner 3/6	0	7	6
Mr. Wilkins's Salary	7	10	0
John Trimby's Do.	7	10	0
Wid. Deare 2/ Shepard's Eas Gift 2/ Deacon's	0	4	0
Do. 2/ R. Summers's Do. 2/ Mary Moor 1/ Mary	0	5	0
Cross 1/6 Jos. Tudgey's Salary 10/ Horton's	0	11	6
Do. 10/6 Ann Ames at Trowbridge 9/ Mary	0	19	6
Harding 1/ Rich. Sheppard 4/6 Nath.	0	5	6
Vinel 4/ Betty Macey 2/ Jn. Bainton 3/6	0	9	6
Thos. Turner's fam. 7/ Betty Parsons 2/6	0	8	6
Ann Humphries 1/6 Wm. Daniel's Bill for	0	1	6
Glazing at the Workhouse 11/11½ James	0	11	11½
Brown 6/ Martha Coles 1/6 Wm. Pobjoys	0	7	6
2 Children 2/ Wid. Davis 2/ Wm. Eianor's Bill	0	4	0
13/1 Mat. Bourne 3/ Dina Lane 2/ Jas.	0	18	1
Druce's Wife & fam. 4/6 Grass for Thos. Tagg 1/3	0	5	9
Benj. Withy 2/ Jos. Rouse 2/ Wm. French 1/6	0	5	6
Mary Hacket 1/6 Chris. Parker 3/ Jn. Barter 1/	0	5	6
Deacon 1/ Shepard 2/ Carrying [illegible] Druce to	0	3	0
Shepton for threatening to leave his fam. 11/4	0	11	4
Jos. Rouse Junr. 2/ Wid. Coombs 1/6 Betty Taylor 1/6	0	5	0
Jane Burrel 1/ Eliz. French 2/ Simon Wheeler	0	3	0
& fam. 3/6 Ann Pope's Delivery 2/6 Betty	0	6	0
Dutchers Do. 2/6 Sarh. Tagg's Do. 2/6 Mary Star 1/6	0	6	6
Ann West 1/ Jn. Trimby's Disburs. Pr. Book 4.8.3	4	9	3
Workhouse Bill	8	7	3
Do. ¼ Salary	3	0	0
Mary Hunt's Childrens Clothes redeemed from Pledge 6/2	0	6	2
Making about in Workhouse to keep ye Hall dry 4/8	0	4	8
Pd. for two Bundles of Straw for ye use of ye Poor 4/4	0	4	4
Pd. D. Morgan for Sweeping ye Workhouse Chimneys 1/	0	1	0
Carrying Thos. Tagg to Church 1/ Wid. Deare 6 Sar. Presley 1/2	0	2	8
Jas. Druce 6 Betty Whithead 1/4 Geo. Whitington making a Shift 2/8½	0	4	6½
Aaron Singer Pr. Breeches 3/1	0	3	1
Betty Whitington second hand Apron 1/7 Attending Sessions 1/ Jane Wright's handkerchief out of Pledge 1/	0	3	7
Harvey: Jas. Druce's Wife 3/ Sar. Tagg 3/9 Danl. Pope 1/ Sol. Mead 1/ Wid. Deare 2/ Mat. Bourne 1/6 Jn. Cureznet 1/6 Expences taking Distress 2/	0	15	9
Burles: Mary Moon 2/6 Jos. Whiting's Burial Charges 7/ Sar. Jones 2/ Jn. Vigor 3/ Betty Lacy 1/ Nath. Vinnel 1/6 Grace Carpenter 6 Jas. Isher 2/ Ann Gifford 1/ Ann Whitington 1/ Wid. Carpenter 1/ Ann Harris 1/	1	3	6
Lacey: Ann West 1/ Mary Yerbury 6 Letter 3½ Mary Jenkins 1/ Betty Macey 1/ Hen. Reeves 3/	0	6	9½
	85	6	8½

	£	s	d
March 17th 1778	75	10	10½
Do. 31, 1778	85	6	8½
Thirteenth Month	160	17	7

anywhere in Frome one drew one's own conclusion.[20]' The firm also owned and occupied a dyehouse, a four storey warehouse with a mansard roof, known as the Feather Factory, that has since been converted to housing, and the Town Mill in Willow Vale, which are shown in the plan from a later sale. In full production in 1824, they manufactured 5000 yards of cloth including broadcloths, kerseymeres, doeskins and Venetians each week.

7.17 Fromefield House - Frome

Along with many others, this concentration of mills along the river frequently contributed to a shortage of water power and the factories would lay idle. When work was temporarily stopped at Spring Gardens, the children would play and sing:

'Slade's and Nappers are shut down;
there's no water up to town.[21]'

Workers cottages were built at Innox Hill and as the hours were long and irregular those living nearby could be called to work day or night. In fact sometimes the children went home to sleep during the day and those that lived too far away would curl up under the looms or on the bales of wool in the work rooms. In its heyday, the factory employed more than 1000 people, many were children as young as eight but following an accident in which two boys were killed in the 1830s, the Factory Act legislation of 1833 was enforced making it an offence to hire any child

7.18 2017 Sheppard's Barton - Frome

under the age of nine and reducing the work of those under 13 to nine hours a day. The first two years of employment were considered a probation or apprenticeship and the youngsters were paid a mere two shillings a week. The Sheppards retired from the business in 1878 and the mills were sold for £720 in 1883.

The Smiths also owned land in Pilly Vale where in 1724 a dyehouse and ancillary buildings were built by Henry Allen. The Allens eventually bought the freehold from the Smith estate which they later sold to the Olives; other plots were owned and sublet by the Sheppards. In the mid 15th century John and Thomas Olyffe, alias Olyve were carters for the inland trade from Southampton, they transported goods to Frome and may have been forebears of the Olives who later settled in the town. The first mention of John Olive, clothier of Frome was in 1724 when he was assigned to take an inventory of the goods and chattels of another clothier, John Jelly '*...bedstead blew curtains and vallins.*[22]' In his own will of 1761, John bequeathed all his lands, tenements etc to be equally divided between his daughter Elizabeth Butler who lived in Bath and his grandson John Olive, dyer of Frome Selwood. Thirty years later in 1796 the Allens sold Willow Vale House and the dyehouse to Major John Olive but it is unclear who was leasing or owned which part. The Olives' firm was foremost in the dyeing industry from the late 18th century. They occupied workshops at Willow Vale, Justice Lane and the Town Mill which was purchased by Major Olive from the Earl of Cork. By 1801 the family had bought the Sheppards' former premises at Willow Vale; and, with the workshops they owned in Justice Lane, they had nineteen dye vats and eleven furnaces.[23] In 1808 Edward Olive had insurance

> '*...his wool, indigo, dye woods, utensils and stock in trade only in his mill House; store room, rooms over, counting house all adjoining together and situate near the river Frome aforesaid. Stone & tiled. On his stock in trade only in his stove house situate near the above mentioned store rooms in his now occupation. Stone & tiled. On his household goods, wearing apparel, linen, printed books, plate, liquors in private use in his now dwelling house in River St in the town of Frome. Brick and stone and timber built tiled or slated.*[24]'

By 1813, John Olive was the owner and occupier of a dwelling and dye house on Willow Vale. Holden's Directory in 1814 lists Edward, John and William Olive as dyers in Frome. The Major's nephew, another John, inherited the dyehouse in 1826 and either corresponded with Mr Wheadon in Chard concerning woad and indigo. The business ownership then passed to Edmund Crabb Olive who is said to have used the mahogany from his American dye barrels in the interior of Willow Vale House.[25]

There were many other dyers in Frome, Henry King was a dyer in the late 1600s; John Harris, Thomas Bunn, the Eldertons in the early 1700s. William Rossiter had a dyehouse near Adderwell and his daughter later married John Olive. Mr Button had a dyehouse at Welshmill, and Mr Jeffries owned one at Spring Gardens which had three vats and employed 14 men. Jonathan Noad and John Parrish were dyers at Shawford; later his son William was mentioned in the town rates as a dyer in Willow Vale. Thomas Griffith, dyer, had been a previous lessee of the Willow Vale dyehouse, who employed eight dye men: William Cuzner, James Rogers, Robert and Joseph Francis, John Wise, Robert Carpenter, Stephen Guy and Jas Underhill. John Langford worked for Henry Allen, dyehouse owner. Francis Messiter, Humphries and Major had dye premises. The Meares had their dyeing business at Wallbridge Mill until 1834 which was furnished with twelve vats and six furnaces. The dye trade included a few women who were seldom mentioned as they did not generally run businesses in their own right unless they were widowed. Sam Corp worked for Mrs Beard; and, Martha Gibbons, a widow was listed as a freeholder of a dye-house in Rodden in 1711.

> *'...The said Mrs Gibbons and heirs of her house and dyehouse is to pay an acknowledgement to the Lord of this Manor in the sum of 6d yearly'.*

Two years later

> *'...To this Court came Martha Gibbons, widow and paid 2s 6d for the acknowledgement arrears and for turning the water into her dye-house.[26]'*

And later a complaint was entered at the same hearing

'...We present Martha Gibbon and William Rymell for stopping the ancient way leading to Frome. The same to be laid open before the 10th November next on pain of 20s'.

Most workers undoubtedly coped with a hard life. The few, like the Sheppards, the Bunns and the Jessers described as gentlemen, built the grand houses that still stand today as a testament to their success, but for most, life was a much more precarious existence. As well as paying towards lodgings and monthly expenses, the church warden reports for the relief of the poor of Frome tell the depressing story of injury, sickness, payments for coffins, shrouds and graves for infants and the elderly. The workhouse and relief relied on the benevolence of the parish wardens and overseers of the poor. To reduce their financial burden, they paid for warrants to remove the destitute back to their native parishes. They requested examination papers to approve any settlement. In 1741 for example, the examination

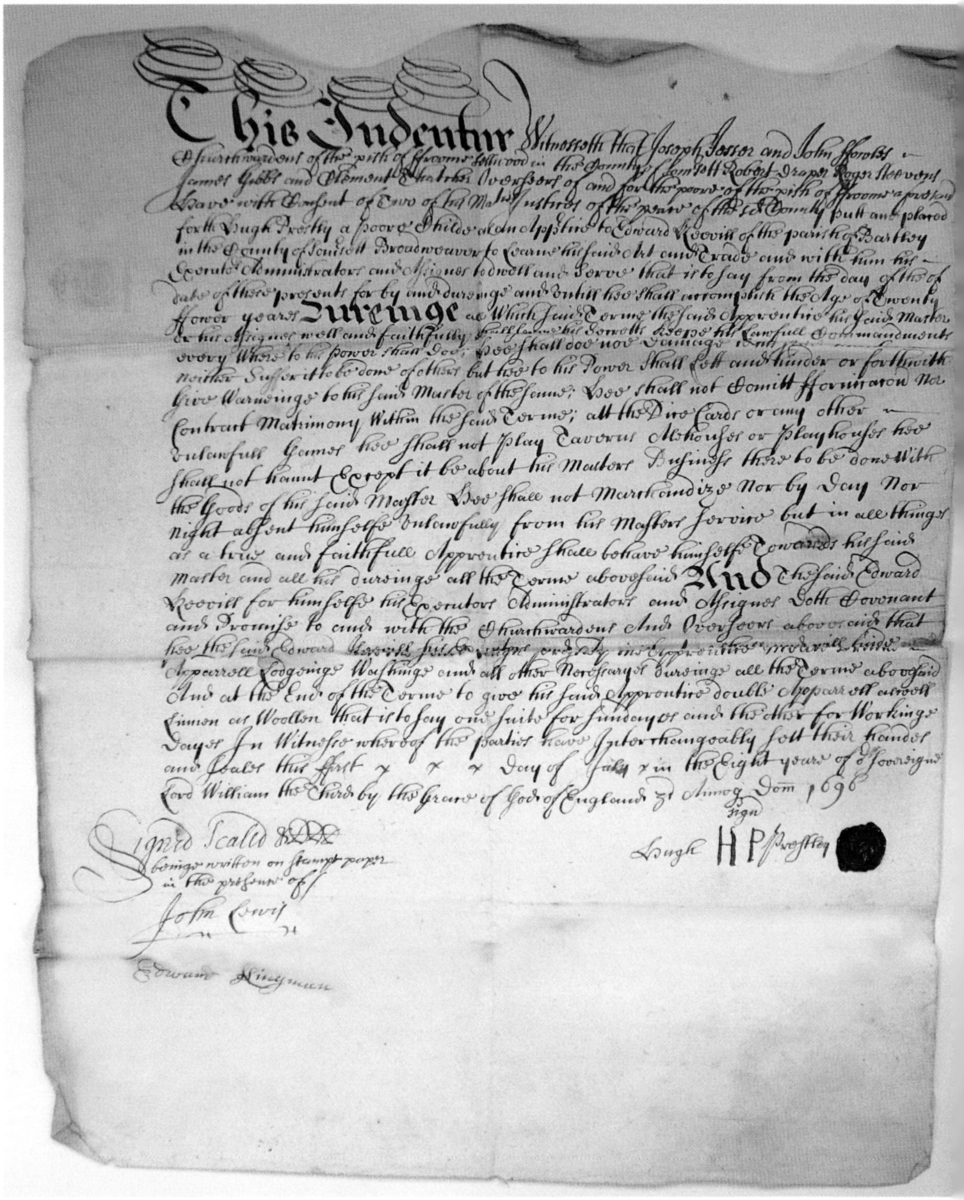

7.19 1696 Apprenticeship Indenture for Hugh Prostley

papers of a French journeyman dyer, *'...John Morel now residing in Frome Selwood, aged 71'* were reviewed by the overseers. John was born in Brittany and sent to Plymouth at the age of 14 *'...to learn the tongue' and live with his tutor'*. He spent some time at sea on the *'Victory'* man of war and after his discharge, he *'...travelled in this kingdom from town to town'*[27] eventually working in Mells as a journeyman dyer of wool. The paper does not provide any information about how he acquired the knowledge and experience of dyeing, only that he worked for Samuel Norman, dyer, as covenant servant in Frome for about two years at a yearly wage of £8 including drink, washing and lodging, after which he returned to Mells to work for Mr Thomas Snook for a year. He was married and said that both his sons, John and Matthew were working in London but that Mary their daughter was living with them in the parish of Frome.

Under the supervision of the church wardens, the overseers bought material for clothing, some perhaps for the elderly ladies and school children of the Blue House. The purchases on one page in October 1727 included thread, 20 ½ ells of canvas at 10d the yard for shrouds, 30 ½ yards of cloth at 6 ½d per yard, 35 yards of striped Barras at 11d per yard. Seven *'ruggs'* at 7s 6d for the workhouse, and three *'coverlids'* at 4s for beds. These were all undoubtedly cheap and coarse materials as they were exempt from any duties. Money was also provided by the overseers for shoes and stockings for Edith Norfolk's child. A small payment of three shillings was made to William Dutch and 1/6d to Kath Frenches for lodgings,[28] perhaps these surnames suggest the earlier foreign influences that improved weaving and card making.

Apprenticeships were another option available to the overseers to gain employment for young children without the need to pay placement fees. In 1696 Joseph Jesser, a familiar Frome name, was churchwarden, and Robert Draper and others Overseers for the Poor, who signed an indenture for Hugh Prostley, a poor child of Frome, to be apprenticed to Edward Koovill of the parish of Berkley, broadweaver.[29] Literacy rates were very low at this time and many broadweavers left their mark rather than signatures on these documents. Hugh was about 11 years old when he was taken on, he was expected to remain to learn his art and serve his

The Overseers paid May 13th 1777 As Under

	£	s.	d.
No. 1 Column	2	9	6
2 Do.	2	4	0
3 Do.	2	10	0
4 Do.	1	13	0
5 Do.	3	0	0
6 Do.	2	6	0
7 Do.	2	13	6
8 Do.	1	16	6
9 Do.	3	4	0
10 Do.	4	0	6
11 Do.	2	10	0
12 Do.	3	16	6
13 Do.	0	7	6
14 Do.	4	2	0
15 Do.	3	1	0
Ann West's Child's funeral at Shepton 5/ Coffin 3/6	0	8	6
James Singer Club Money 3/6 Sheppard 2/ Deacon 1/	0	6	6
Grave 1/3 Mr. Harvey's Expences to Beckington for orders to remove Jas. Crouch & Sarh. Simes 9/1½	0	10	4½
Gave Mr. Cooper with Mary Stevens towards Cloathing	1	1	0
Paid Sto Cradock for his Cart to remove Crouch to Corsley	0	4	0
Ann Carpenter 1/ Dr. Goldwyer's Bill for Curing Wm. Wiltshires Childs Eyes 15.15.0	15	16	0
Ann West Shepton 12/ in full to Jas. Last Jno. Webb 2/	0	14	0
Betty Davis 1/2 one Delivery 2/6 Mary	0	3	8
Cook 6/ Jas. Wright 1/ Jane Burrell 1/	0	8	0
Wm. Harebottle 4/ Mary Whitington 2/	0	6	0
Elizth. Moxham 3/ Mary Wiltshire 3/ Hana Carver 1/6	0	7	6
Thos. Cooper 1/ Widw. Smith 1/ Widw. Wilcox 4/	0	6	0
Sweke's Child 1/ Hann. Carpenter 1/10½ in Cloth	0	2	10½
Josh. Yerbury's two Childrens Clothing	0	10	7½
Robt. Rowles 3/ Josh. Cooks Wife 3/ Jos. West 1/	0	7	0
John Trimby's Disbursmts. pr. Book	4	4	6
Wm. Wilkins 4/ John Wilkins 4/ Thos. Wilkins 1/	0	9	0
Saml. Cook 1/ Thos. Crease 4/ Wm. Brookman 2/	0	7	0
Jane Crouch	0	6	0
Workhouse Bill	6	18	6
Extraordinary to Do.	2	10	1
	76	1	1½

The Overseers paid May 27th 1777 As Under

	£	s.	d.
No. 1 Column	2	4	6
2 Do.	2	2	6
3 Do.	2	7	6
4 Do.	1	13	0
5 Do.	2	16	6
6 Do.	2	6	0
7 Do.	2	11	0
8 Do.	1	15	0
9 Do.	3	1	0
10 Do.	3	18	6
11 Do.	2	17	0
12 Do.	3	13	6
13 Do.	0	7	6
14 Do.	4	0	0
15 Do.	2	14	0
Mary Whitington 4/6 Three Coffins 11/	0	15	6
Six Graves 7/6 Ann Reeves 1/ Jas. Cuff 1/	0	9	6
Susa. Davis 2/ Sheppard 2/ Deacon 1/	0	5	0
Danl. Baily 2/ County Stock £4.18.0	5	0	0
John Trimby's Disbursmts. pr. Book	2	8	7
Putting out 8 Apprentices	6	0	0
Redeeming Hipsibah Taylors Goods	1	5	6
Cloth & making up for old Jas. Brown & Wife 6 Yds. @ 1/6 is 9/ Makg. &c. 7/4	0	16	4
Jas. Wright 1/ Jane Burrel 1/6 Hanah	0	2	6
Carver 1/6 Josh. Bigs's Child 1/ Potter Taylor Do. 2/6	0	5	0
Jn. Wilkins's Do. 2/ Mary Golledge 1/ one	0	3	0
Delivery 2/6 Susa. Wheeler 6 Jane Mount	0	3	0
shire Shoes 3/6 a Crooker for Do. 1/3	0	4	9
Mary George Shoes 3/6 Josh. Cooks Wife 3/	0	6	6
Jas. West 1/ Benony Budget 2/6	0	3	6
Saml. Richards 6 Jno. Bishop 1/ Jno. Webb 1/	0	2	6
Ann Carpenter 1/6 Thos. Crease 4/	0	5	6
Wm. Brookman 2/ James Brown 2/	0	4	0
Workhouse Bill	6	18	0
Extra to Ditto	1	4	0
	65	10	2

	£	s.	d.
May 13th	76	1	1½
27	65	10	2
Second Month	141	11	3½

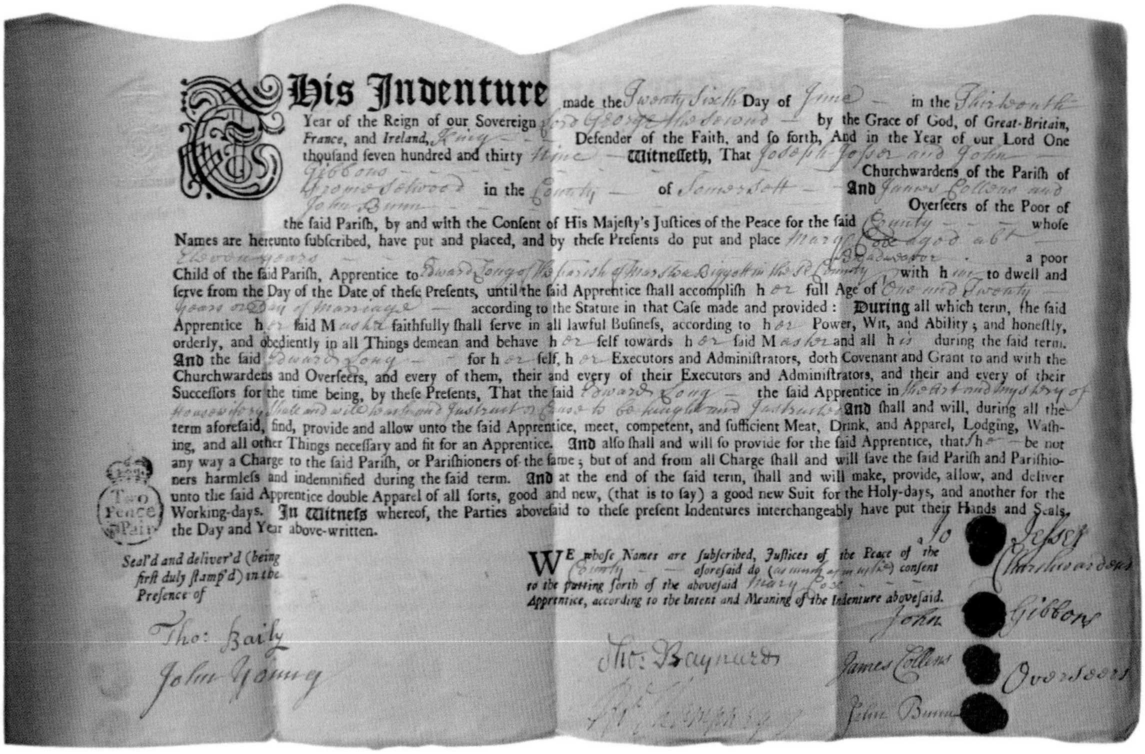
This Indenture made the Twenty Sixth Day of June in the Thirteenth Year of the Reign of our Sovereign Lord George the Second by the Grace of God, of Great-Britain, France, and Ireland, King Defender of the Faith, and so forth, And in the Year of our Lord One thousand seven hundred and thirty nine Witnesseth, That Joseph Jesser and John Gibbons Churchwardens of the Parish of Frome Selwood in the County of Somerset And James Collens and John Bunn Overseers of the Poor of the said Parish, by and with the Consent of His Majesty's Justices of the Peace for the said County whose Names are hereunto subscribed, have put and placed, and by these Presents do put and place Mary Case aged abt Eleven years a poor Child of the said Parish, Apprentice to Edward Long of the parish of Marston Biggott in the sd County with him to dwell and serve from the Day of the Date of these Presents, until the said Apprentice shall accomplish her full Age of One and Twenty years or Day of marriage according to the Statute in that Case made and provided: During all which term, the said Apprentice her said Master faithfully shall serve in all lawful Businefs, according to her Power, Wit, and Ability; and honestly, orderly, and obediently in all Things demean and behave herself towards her said Master and all his during the said term. And the said Edward Long for himself, his Executors and Administrators, doth Covenant and Grant to and with the Churchwardens and Overseers, and every of them, their and every of their Executors and Administrators, and their and every of their Successors for the time being, by these Presents, That the said Edward Long the said Apprentice in the Art and Mystery of Housewifery shall and will teach and instruct or cause to be taught and instructed And shall and will, during all the term aforesaid, find, provide and allow unto the said Apprentice, meet, competent, and sufficient Meat, Drink, and Apparel, Lodging, Washing, and all other Things necessary and fit for an Apprentice. And also shall and will so provide for the said Apprentice, that she be not any way a Charge to the said Parish, or Parishioners of the same; but of and from all Charge shall and will save the said Parish and Parishioners harmless and indemnified during the said term. And at the end of the said term, shall and will make, provide, allow, and deliver unto the said Apprentice double Apparel of all sorts, good and new, (that is to say) a good new Suit for the Holy-days, and another for the Working-days. In Witness whereof, the Parties abovesaid to these present Indentures interchangeably have put their Hands and Seals, the Day and Year above-written.

Seal'd and deliver'd (being first duly stamp'd) in the Presence of

Tho: Baily
John Young

WE whose Names are subscribed, Justices of the Peace of the County aforesaid do consent to the putting forth of the abovesaid Mary Case Apprentice, according to the Intent and Meaning of the Indenture abovesaid.

Jo Jesser
Churchwardens
John Gibbons
James Collens
Overseers
John Bunn

7.21 1739 Apprenticeship Indenture for Mary Case

master until the age of 24. In return, he would be provided with meat, drink, apparel, lodging, washing and instruction in the skill of weaving. There is little information on linen weaving in this area but there was some trade. In 1730, Thomas Moore son of Thomas Moore of Frome, linen weaver, apprenticed himself to John Diss, broadweaver of Shepton Mallet for a term of 10 years. He was possibly one of the Blue School pupils as his father was deceased. An apprenticeship fee of £2 2s was paid by Mr Edward Halliday of the Frome charity school. His indenture states that that as well as receiving apparel, washing, lodging etc '*...He shall not frequent ale houses or gamble, but be honest and faithful.*[30]' Traditionally girls were employed in domestic service and in 1739, Mary Case, age 11, was bound to Edward Long, a clothier of Marston Bigot, as apprentice in housewifery. The document was signed by Joseph Jesser and John Gibbons church wardens and James Collens and John Bunn, Overseers for the Poor.[31] Two unusual indentures for Frome children, one in 1730 for Grace Cass and another in 1809 for Ann Case, both little girls aged 9, were apprenticed as broad weavers; one in Westbury and the other in Trowbridge:

'...with him to dwell and serve to be instructed in the art of weaving until the age of 21 or day of marriage.... Will provide for the said apprentice so that there not be in any way a charge on the parish or parishioners. At the end of their term, the master will agree to provide two suits of good and new clothing, one for holy days and one for work days.[32]*'*

The cloth trade of 18th century Frome was held firmly in the hands of the middling clothiers but it is the hundreds of nameless spinners, weavers, and cloth finishers who deserve our recognition.

---

1 TNA PROB 11/91/271
2 VCH: 412
3 FSLS Map: a Plan of Frome 1774
4 Gill, D 2003: 7
5 Gill, D 2003: 9
6 Belham, P 1973:155
7 Goodall, R 2013: 89
8 TNA PROB 11/146/165
9 SHC DD\SAS\5/2062
10 TNA PROB 11/381/139
11 McGarvie, M 1979: -
12 Rabah, 2004: 14
13 TNA C 104/200
14 BA AC/JS/45/3/A
15 TNA C/104/221
16 BA AS/JC/45
17 TNA C/104/221
18 TNA PROB 11/1268/130 and PROB 11/625/309
19 Gill, D 1982: -
20 SHC DD\LW/134 Somerset Standard Ced 28 1928
21 Belham, P 1973: 113
22 TNA PROB 3/24/42
23 McGarvie, M 2013:
24 SHC DD\LW/41
25 McGarvie, M 2013: 113
26 Frome Museum: Manors of Rodden, Flintford and Grandon Court Book 1659 - 1776
27 SHC DD/LW/7
28 SHC DD/LW/7/4
29 SHC DD/LW/7
30 SHC DD/LW/7
31 SHC DD/LW/7
32 SHC DD/LW/7

Petition of Robert Palace
and others of several
merchants and
Manufacturers praying
leave to import having
manufacturers Cotton Yarn
France

R 16th March 1797
27 do do
2 Indigo

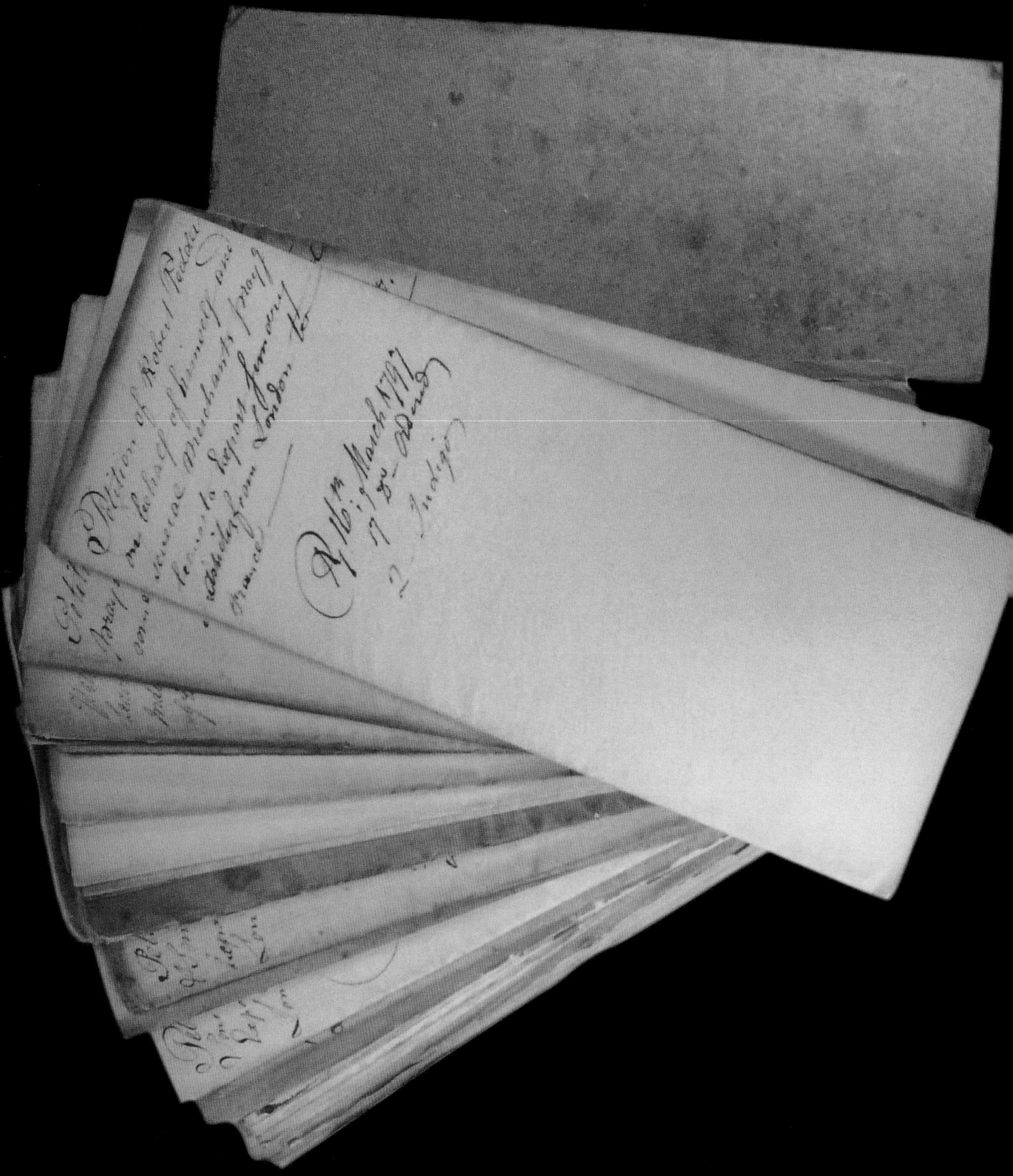

CHAPTER 8

THE WOAD & DYE TRADES

'Thomas Bakere of Frome lately bought three tuns of woad from Ralph Morevyllers of Amyas' of the lordship of France, the king's enemy. Ralph returned to France, Thomas not being able to pay £48 at that time made a bond to William Teynturier the Elder of Salisbury for Ralph's use...'

Calendar of the Fine Rolls Vol 8 Ed III 1369 -1377 October 20th, 1369

Cultures independently derived the means to obtain colour using their native resources. The pigments and dyes embellished objects made of clays, glass, and fibres endowing privilege and status on those who could afford them. The skills, along with the decorated goods and the raw materials, were exchanged and sold as the global trade routes spread across countries and continents.

Textiles were the most important industries of the Middle Ages and the woad trade played its part in the exchange of commodities. Until the 12th century, the English market for blue cloth may have been restricted to areas where woad was cultivated and dyers had acquired the mystery of their guilds. The country may have produced a sufficient quantity for its use as a ground for black cloth. Fine cloths were made from English wool woven and dyed to perfection in Italy and the Low Countries. These and other goods were then sold at the great fairs of St Bartholomew in London and others in continental Europe.

From the 13th century, legislation to increase taxation on wool and the introduction of sumptuary laws encouraged the manufacture of an English cloth. A white woollen broadcloth suitable for export was produced in the border areas of Somerset and Wiltshire in the 14th century and documents attest to the delivery of woad to Frome and other towns in both counties.

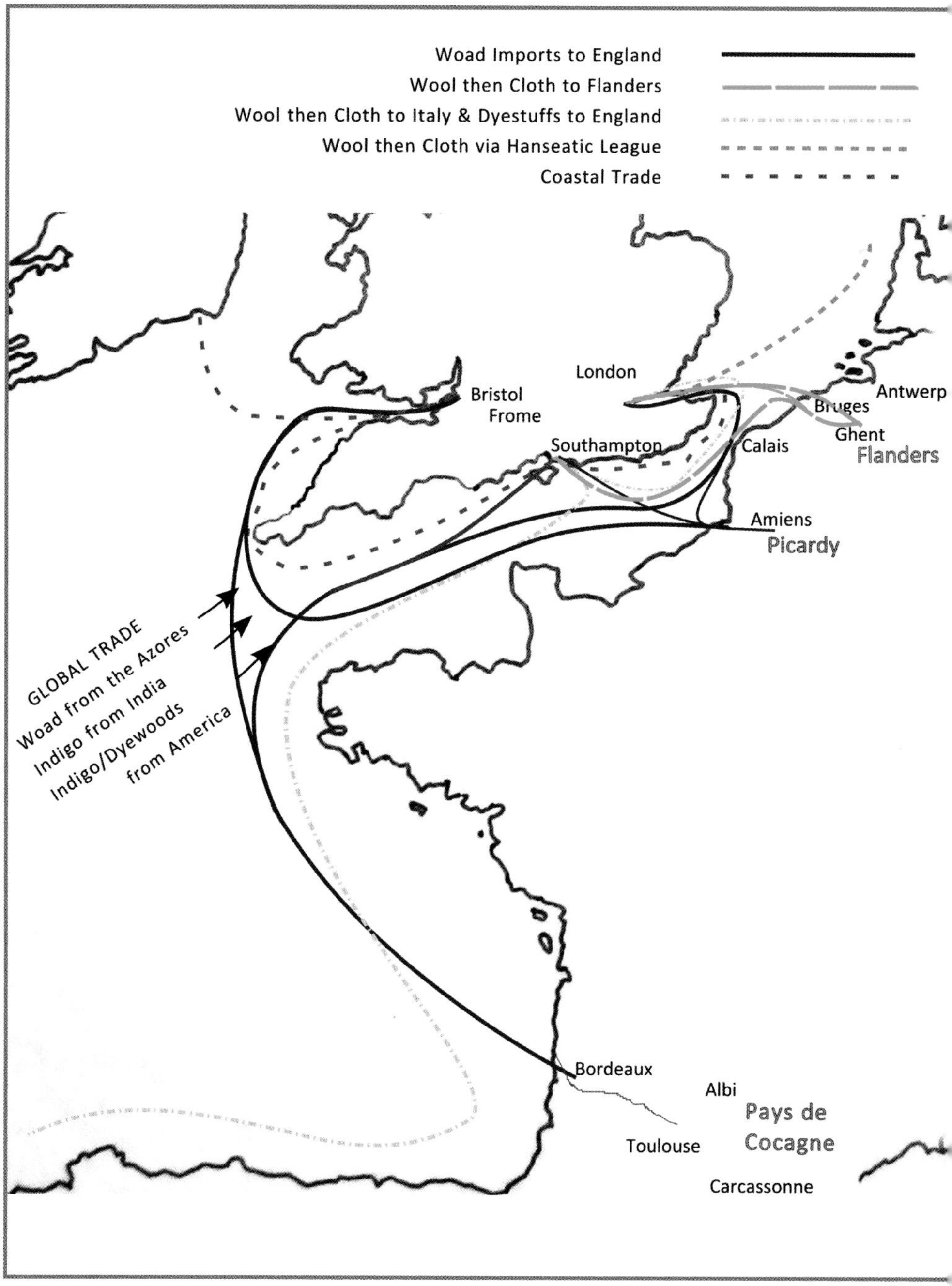

8.2 Wool, Dye & Cloth Trade Map

8.3 Merchant Ship in Chantry Chapel - St Peter's Church Tiverton John Greenway, Merchant 1460 - 1529

The principal coastal trade routes for Europe centred in Venice with spices and goods coming from the Levant and the Far East. Ships sailed to Genoa and Narbonne before loading wine and woad at Bordeaux and continuing to England and the Low Countries. Woad was transported in the cargoes of ships destined for England as early as 1230 and it was imported in significant quantities by the 1350s. English trade until the 15th century was handled by foreign merchants who transported goods via overland trade routes to the staple markets and by sea voyages from the port cities. The merchant galleys were partially unloaded at the ports of Bristol and Southampton in exchange for wool before continuing to London and Flanders. In 1456, as trade disputes in London escalated, the Venetians moved their centre of commerce to Southampton but by 1532 it had declined, and their monopoly was broken by the League of Cambrai. The English merchants increasingly involved themselves in commercial enterprise to finance exploratory voyages and to procure their own goods.

> *'...By 1534 five ships from London, with certain others from Southampton and Bristol had an ordinary and usual trade to Sicily, Candia and Chios.*[1]*'*

In addition to the 14th century wool and cloth trades of Frome and the surrounding areas, merchants dealt in dyestuffs for the domestic market. John Waps,[2] a dyer and merchant owed £17.17s to a Salisbury dyer in 1359. An entry in the Fine Rolls dated October 20th 1369

> *'...Thomas Bakere of Frome lately bought three tuns of woad from Ralph Morevyllers of Amyas' of the lordship of France, the king's enemy. Ralph returned to France, Thomas not being able to pay £48 at that time made a bond to William Teynturier the Elder of Salisbury for Ralph's use.*[3]*'*

To justify the purchase of such a large quantity of woad, local dyers must have known how to extract the colour. The dry salters and merchants of the town would have dealt in the dyes, mordants and wool, purchasing goods at the fairs or indirectly via Bristol, Salisbury and London merchants. The commercial dye workshops would have been established by the dyers with the practical knowledge and financial backing. A bankruptcy case in Chancery in 1372 concerns William Baillif, the younger, merchant of Beckington

> *'...He was not found in his bailiwick, so his goods and chattels which included a kiln worth 46s 8d and a certain vessel called a Wodfate worth 5s, other wooden utensils worth very little were given to his creditors to pay off his debt of £17 7s 8d.*[4]'

The records of debts and litigation state only the facts and not the contributing circumstances of business failures. In 1417, John Martyn[5], a dyer of Frome was unable to pay a debt of £11 11s to a London merchant.

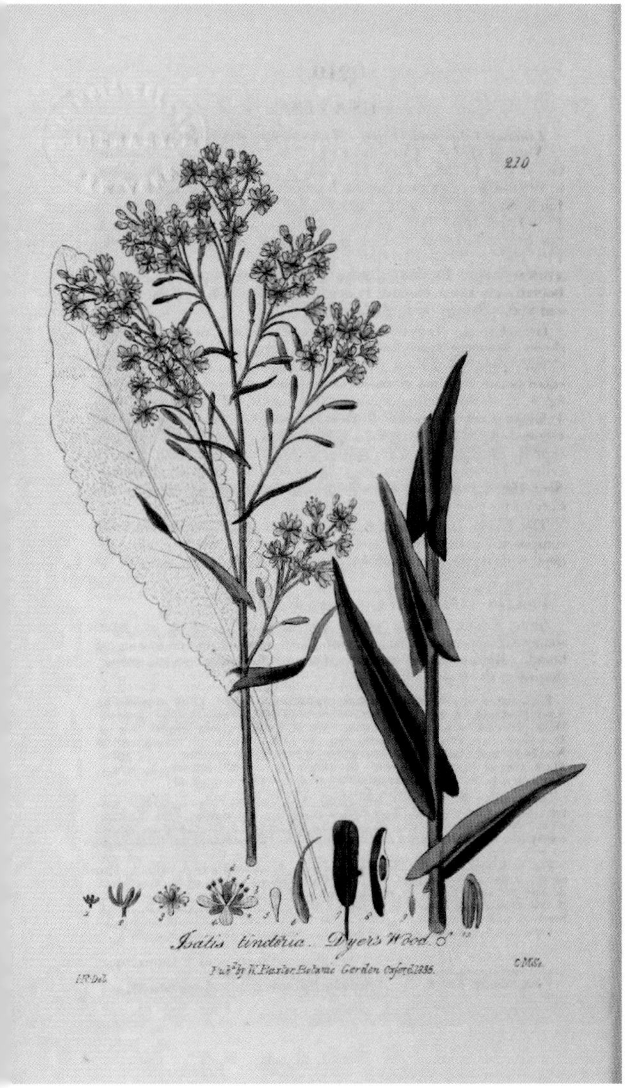

8.4 1836 Herbal - Woad

In the Middle Ages, France was the main woad producing country supplying both England and Flanders with the blue dye. It was not a perishable commodity so it was stored until a fleet of ships was assembled and safe passage was organised for the channel crossing. Once warehoused in Southampton or Bristol it could be distributed to fit the seasonal timetable of the wool and cloth production for the return voyages. Woad was measured in bales of about 4cwt or half bales known as balettes of about 2cwt and pipes[6] which were variable but about equivalent to half a ton. Once consigned to a recipient, dyestuffs were transferred to horse drawn carts of a standard size, carrying 2 pipes of wine (252 gallons) 6 balettes of woad, 5 bales of alum etc. Journeys from Southampton to Salisbury took two days and 4 days to or from London. Wains were larger and pulled by oxen which were slower but could carry up to 20 balettes of woad over longer distances.[7] Some 15th century road traffic recorded in the Southampton Brokage Books has been transcribed from surviving ledgers[8] which indicated that woad was carted to Frome.

> *'...On Saturday 3rd October 1439, according to port records, Henry and John Chawyn carted 4 sarplers consigned by Walter Fetplace from Southampton towards Frome, and paid custom of 2s, brokage and pontage of 16d'.*[9]

The books reveal the contents, destinations and the names of people consigning and carting goods. In 1439 four carts of woad were conveyed to Frome.[10] In the 1440s, the town was one of the most important destinations for woad, although this may have been as a distribution centre for other places.[11]

Thomas Morteyn may have dealt with the woad growers of Picardy or Albi. He was a French immigrant living in Frome, who was paying *'alien'* tax in 1443. In 1461 six carts of woad were transported to Frome and three in 1462.[12] Robert and John Smyth transported oil, wool, cloth, woad and mordants, while John and Thomas Osteler were recipients of woad, madder and alum.[13] In 1460, the Court of Pleas mentions John Osteler, executor for Thomas Osteler, dyer of Frome Selwood as the defendant for a debt owed to Thomas White of Southampton from where he and his brother had received consignments of woad.[14] As a successful clothier, John Compton of Beckington bequeathed two bales of woad to his son in his will of 1484.

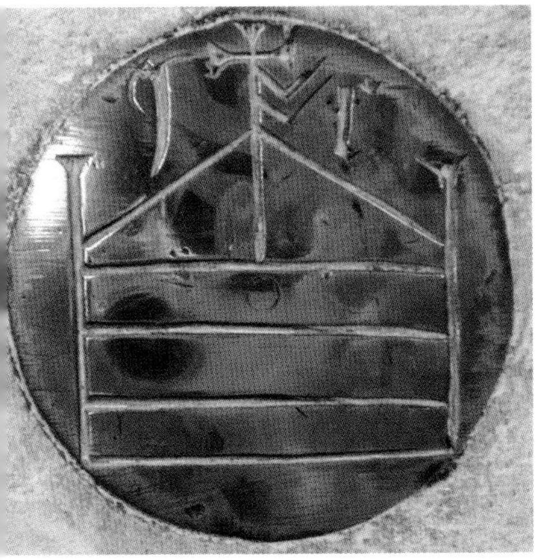

8.5 Merchant Mark of John Compton

Woad, known as *'la guede'* in Picardy or *'le pastel'* in Languedoc, was cultivated in France on an industrial scale between the 13th and 17th centuries. Foreign merchants were granted special privileges and charters by the king, in return for annual payments to supplement the royal coffers. The woad trade, which at first, was dominated by the Picardy merchants of Northern France was mentioned in a Bristol inquest of 1236[15] and an early London charter of 1237 granted the citizens of Amiens, Corbie and Nesle permission to unload, store and freely sell their woad and other

8.6 Statue of Woad Merchants Amiens Cathedral

merchandise, in any part of the country, on payment of 50 marks annually to the sheriffs.[16]

While a major industry centred around Amiens in the 13th century, it was not well managed. The trade of about seven hundred exporters, belonging to some forty families, was supported by a merchants organisation. They each formed small businesses which only lasted for one or two expeditions.[17] Hugh Lenglache and Fermin Auerdras of Amiens in Picardy came to England in 1327 following a proclamation that alien merchants could come to England without impediment and in safety to sell their wares. Despite this surety, their goods were seized by the sheriff at Southampton. Fermin Auerdras later petitioned for the return of his goods and payment from a Walter of Frome.[18] As political upheaval, the ravages of the plague and the Hundred Years War interrupted the supply to England, the competition from new woad production areas had devastating consequences for the region's trade.

By the mid 14th century, the production of woad had shifted to the South West of France and was exported via the English possession of Gascony along with wine from the regional vineyards. Although shipments were affected by war, unarmed galleys were allowed access to the ports to load cargo in return for ready money which was in short supply. Albi was the centre of the pastel trade as it was far more profitable to export the dye than to keep it for domestic use; the growing demand by English and Flemish cloth manufacturers led to export on a much larger scale. A fleet of thirteen ships from Bayonne and four from Bordeaux made their way to England and landed 156 tons of pastel at Bristol in November 1404.[19]

In 1450, production and distribution was taken over by the city of Toulouse from where it could be easily transported on the rivers to the ports of Bayonne and Bordeaux which remained relatively secure under English rule until 1453. The arrival of the Flanders Fleet at Southampton was the social event of the year, in 1470 woad was the second largest import and wine the biggest.[20] The industry was highly organised, underpinned by capital from Spanish and French merchants. Farmers cultivated the plants, *'collecteurs'* bought the leaves and manufactured the dye and merchants organised marketing and export. This collaborative affiliation reduced some of the risk but the whole process could take up to three years before financial investment was recovered.

8.7 Medieval House with Open Loft - Albi

The triangular area of Toulouse, Albi and Carcassonne produced the best grade of woad, sometimes referred to as *'Tullus Wood'* and later as blue gold. By the 16th century, the Languedoc region was known as the 'Pays de Cocagne', translated as the country of woad balls but interpreted as the land of milk and honey. So successful was the crop that commercially astute merchants provided money lending and banking services from the profits as well as building opulent mansions for themselves. There are few statistics but around the 1520s

> *'...At its peak, the annual product of Upper Languedoc alone was 40,000,000 lbs half of which was exported from the port of Bordeaux.[21]'*

To protect their investments against loss, the merchandise was marked with the owner's seal and distributed across the cargoes of several ships in the convoy. On arrival in port, once the paperwork was approved, it was unloaded taxed and inspected for quality at the assay office by the guild's specialist brokers and porters.[22] It was assessed in marks sterling per quarteron, about 26lbs, and from the 1520s on a basis of florins;[23] In 1560, it was sold for 40 florins.[24] Like any crop, the quality of woad was variable as it depended on the weather and the condition of the soil.

Woad could be harvested from the same plants up to five times in the growing season. The lesser value leaves of later batches were mixed together and the second fermentation of *'agranat'* could be adulterated. These fraudulent practices by unscrupulous merchants and three continuous years of bad harvest precipitated the decline of the trade. Tropical indigo was making inroads into the market. *'The dyers estimate that 6 pounds of indigo are equivalent to 300 pounds of pastel.*[25]*'* Despite its use being forbidden, by the early 18th century the pastel mills had all but disappeared.

Before 1500, Italian woad, *'guado'* was also imported to England. The Genoese traders carried large quantities into Southampton, so it is reasonable to assume that some, which came from Tuscany or Piedmont[26], was carted to Frome in that period. Madder and woad were grown in the Low Countries and shipped to England for a short period by the Louvain merchants before the area was besieged by the Duke of Brabant in 1380 leading to a wave of refugee cloth workers settling in England. From the 13th century, woad, *'waid',* was cultivated extensively in many parts of Germany and used for its home industries. Some was exported to England by the Hanseatic merchants via the markets of Frankfurt and Antwerp. Between 1597 and 1603 more than 130 barrels were shipped to England.[27] A considerable amount was transported overland and sold from the staple towns of Nuremberg to Flanders and Görlitz to Silesia, Poland and Hungary. Thuringia was the principal region for the crop. Erfurt, its capital, was one of the five *'waidstädte'* to prosper from its production founding the university from the proceeds in 1379. It was a highly regulated industry from 1351, divided into two branches; the couched and unfermented woad balls. Both products were processed by specialists and it was forbidden to sell either except through a broker in the public market in the staple towns. As elsewhere, the introduction of tropical indigo led to its eventual decline.

By 1527 the west country cloth industry received its imported materials via London and exported cloth the same way.[28] Thomas Kytson's working accounts[29] remain one of the few records to provide details of the period. He was a London merchant in the early 1500s who exported white cloth and imported woad and other commodities for cloth making. His *'Boke of Remembraunce'* [30] furnishes a list of his suppliers and his business transactions. John Clevelod of Beckington was one of his preferred suppliers, who provided him with white cloths and bought woad in return. He also sold considerable amounts of woad to James Bysse and John Horner for dyeing their kerseys and in 1530 John Thycke of Frome took delivery of 26 balettes of woad equivalent to about 2½ tons.[31]

In English wills of the period, besides other goods, cloth and woad were bequeathed to the church for their upkeep and for the endowment of chapels. It was also left for the services of priests to pray for the souls of the dead and their families. Woad, measured in pipes, was left to creditors to settle outstanding debts and given to relatives and servants with the occasional mention that it should be *'of a good and merchantable value'*. One will mentions that each child was to have two pipes of woad unless it was lost at sea, in which case whatever was landed to be equally distributed amongst them.

8.8 Madder Root

As well as woad, imported dyestuffs from Europe had included madder, *Rubia Tinctoria,* a natural source of alizarin that is extracted from the root of the plant which dyes many shades of red when combined with alum, tin, or iron. It was cultivated extensively in Italy, France and the Low Countries. The more expensive deep rich colour of scarlet, obtained from kermes, was adopted as the colour for robes of the high ranking political and religious elite.

Mordants, to fix the dyes,were imported in large quantities; alum was the most commonly used. It was procured from Catholic Italy and the Papal territories and smuggled during the reign of Henry VIII when it was not available by the usual channels. It was not available in crystalline form until it was extracted from alum shale in the mid 1600s in England; it then became available commercially in the latter part of the century. Copperas and ferrous sulphate, used as dye fixatives like alum, were first imported from Sicily and were similarly affected by the religious conflict when English sources had to be found. Extracted from iron pyrites, copperas stones washed up along the Essex, Kent and Dorset shores were collected by pickers. Its manufacture required enormous capital investment as it took four years to refine. The end product of green crystallised copperas, sometimes called green vitriol, was packed into barrels before being shipped for sale. The copperas industry prospered in the south of England until the end of the 19th century, much to the detriment of the workers health. Argol, imported from Spain, Italy, France and Greece, is a bitartrate of potash obtained as a by-product from the fermentation of wine. It was used as a mordant for protein fibres, softening the wool and brightening the colour. When purified, it was sold as cream of tartar which is still used today.

Peace with France had bolstered the woad trade until the last decades of the 16th century when the introduction of tropical indigo created a major competitive threat. Woad attracted strong protectionist resistance and vigorous opposition in most countries where it was extensively cultivated. The merchants were naturally concerned about their loss of trade and governments were keen to retain the money generated from its taxation. Indigo use was forbidden in central Europe and French dyers had to swear an oath that they would not use indigo. In England, despite statutes banning the use of indigo and logwood, by the

8.9 Indian Indigo from Indigofera Tinctoria

1640s, indigo imported from India had superseded woad and by the end of the century it held pride of place among the exports of the Orient. England continued to import small quantities from France as woad was considered essential for fermenting the vats.

However, as war and taxes increased the price to such an extent that Bristol merchants, in partnership with the Portuguese increasingly turned to the Azores for their supplies, saying that woad bought for £12 would sell in Bristol for £20 making it a far more attractive proposition.[32] Despite government intervention the production of indigo from woad in the rest of Europe eventually declined by 1635 as the indigo trade shifted to the Indies and the new world.

Before the 16th century, the voyages of English ships were limited, but commerce proved a powerful motive for exploration. New sea routes to the East Indies had been established by the Spanish and the Portuguese which broke the trade monopolies held by a number of Italian cities. The great Elizabethan age of exploration was underpinned by the inventions of navigational aids, improved shipping and coastal transport and the financial investments of merchants, all of which opened new markets.

According to Hakluyt's Promise

> *'....English dyers would be thrilled to purchase woad and madder which could be grown in Virginia because it shared a climate similar to the Portuguese owned Azores where their colonists sow madder and woad dyestuffs needed for clothing and where these crops flourished.*[33]*'*

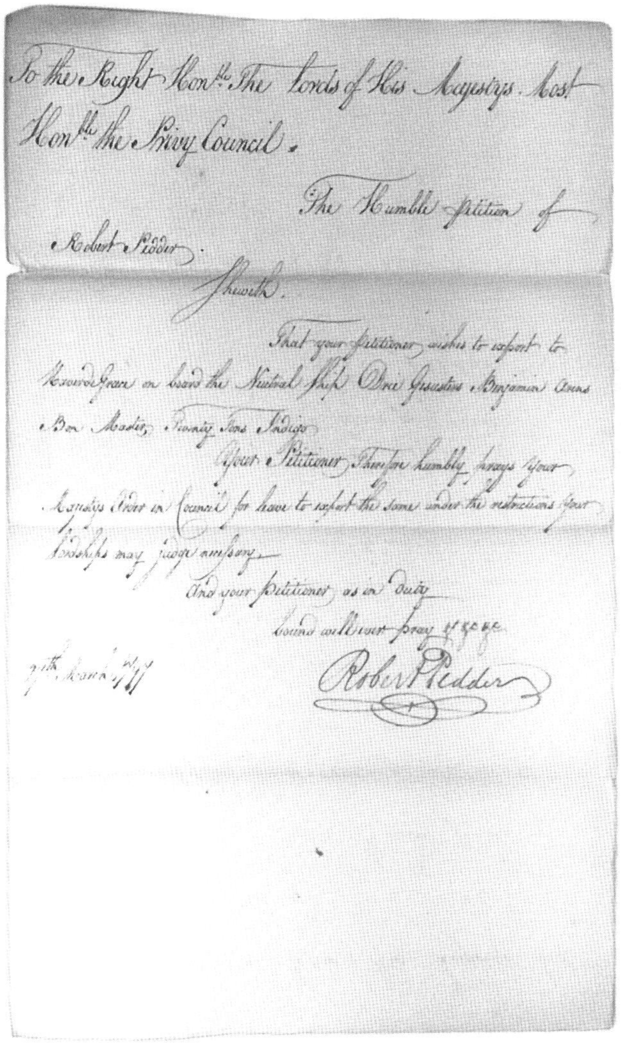

To the Right Honble The Lords of His Majestys Most Honble the Privy Council.

The Humble Petition of Robert Pedder.

Sheweth.

That your Petitioner wishes to export to [illegible] France on board the Neutral Ship [illegible] Benjamin [illegible] Master, Twenty Tons Indigo

Your Petitioner Therefore humbly prays Your Majestys Order in Council for leave to export the same under the restrictions Your Lordships may judge necessary.

And your Petitioner as in duty bound will ever pray &c &c

7th March 1797

Robert Pedder

8.10 1797 Indigo Export Petition

English merchant adventurers were granted charters to form the Muscovy Company in 1555 to trade with Russia, the Levant Company in 1581, and the East India Trading Company in 1600 and the new transatlantic trade opportunities in the new world. Bristol ships traded directly with Spain but as the Anglo-Spanish alliance broke down in the late 1500s new markets to replace the Seville oil for the fine cloth trade needed to be found. As gentlemen, merchants, drapers and dry salters, the Smiths, Whitchurches, Hallidays and other Frome families were probably involved in these new business ventures both at home and overseas. In 1604, Benedict Webb of Kingswood conducted experiments with an oil mill to produce both oil and soap for the cloth industry and by 1618 he had persuaded clothiers to use rapeseed oil in its manufacture.

By the 17th century, English emphasis was firmly on trade and the development of a mercantile economy was dominated by the London merchants. Trade with the Americas was opened up by the Portuguese, Spanish and Dutch and the tropical heartwood dyes mentioned in the dye recipe books were shipped to the European markets as part of the triangular slave trade. These were later grown on plantations in Jamaica, Virginia and the Carolinas and imported directly by English merchants.

Logwood, *Haematoxylum campechianum*, also known as campeachy wood from where it was found, imparts a blue violet colour; it was imported to Europe in 1556 by the Spaniards. Introduced to England soon after the accession of Elizabeth I, its use was not understood, and resulted in the passing of a law

'An Act for abolishing of certeine deceitful stuffe used in dyeing of clothes; whereas there hath been brought from beyond the seas a certeine kind of stuffe called logwood, alias blockwood, wherewith divers dyers, &c, and whereas the clothes therewith dyed, are not only solde and uttered to the great deceyte of the Queene's loving subjects, but beyond the seas, to the great discredit and slaunder of the dyers of this realme. For reformation whereof, be it enacted by the Queene, our Soveraygne Ladie, that all such logwood, in whoes hands soever founde, shall be openly burned by authority of the maior.[34]'

8.11 Logwood

More than eighty years elapsed before the correct mordants to fix the new dye were discovered and it was not until 1661 that the use of logwood was approved as *'The ingenious industry of these times has taught the dyers of England the art of fixing colours made of Logwood.*[35]'

Captain William Dampier from East Coker in Somerset describes the trade in his diaries from the late 1600s. It was planted in Jamaica in the early 1700s and continued to be imported until the 19th century.

8.12 Fustic

Brazilwood, *Caesalpinia Echinata*, traded by the Portuguese, so called from the location of its discovery or possibly from its replacement of the East Indian breselwood. It was also known as sappanwood which had been brought to Europe along the silk road as a red dye in the Middle Ages. Another plant introduced by the Spaniards, Old Fustic, *Maclura Tinctoria*, gives a strong yellow dye. Found in Cuba, Jamaica and some regions of Brazil it was used in Europe from the 16th century. Its European counterpart Young Fustic, *Cotinus coggygria*, is a sumac. The stems and wood produces a fugitive yellow which may have imparted warm undertones to buff colours. Old Fustic may have been so called because the colour was similar but more durable. Barwood, *Pterocarpus soyauxii*, and Camwood, *Baphia nitida*, were imported from several West African countries and are also mentioned in the recipe books. They produce shades of reds to dark browns and in small concentrations enhance cinnamon and tan colours. Sanderswood, *Pterocarpus santalinus,* from India produces a blood red dye which is also for the rich deep browns. Shumack more commonly known as sumac, *Rhus Typhina*, imported from North America dyes a pale yellow but contains tannins well suited to dyeing blacks, greys and browns. It was also employed extensively in the tanning industry. Dyes, such as quercitron from the

8.13 Sanderswood

bark of black oak, *Quercus velatina*, from North America produces a bright yellow dye;

> *'...Quercitron bark, dyeing agent patented by Dr Bancroft, manufactured and sold by Mr Thomas Napper, drysalter, Frome. Bath Chronicle, 26th Jan 1786'.*

The scale insect cochineal was imported by the Spanish following its discovery in Mexico, it soon replaced kermes to produce the coveted scarlet reds.

Pearlash, potassium carbonate, an alkaline substance made from wood ash, was imported from America as a mordant. Trees were burnt solely for the purpose of its manufacture. Water was then poured on the ashes until the soluble parts were dissolved and the clear liquid was decanted and evaporated. The remaining sediment paste was packed in casks of five hundred weight and shipped to England.

8.14 Cochineal

Indigo was one of the main articles traded by both the Dutch and British East India Companies in the 17th century. It was possible that indigo cultivation was taken up in the New World because the supply from India was insufficient. As early as the 1560s an indigenous variety of indigo began to be cultivated by Spanish overseers on the plantations in the Honduras and the Pacific slopes of Central America. The best quality indigo was Guatemalan, and that produced in the French colony of Saint Domingo in the Caribbean.

The English gained their first indigo-producing colony in the area in 1655 when they captured Jamaica. The crop was replaced by sugar within a hundred years and the trade shifted to the Carolinas.[36] The rise of the South Carolinas indigo trade from mid 1740s arose from the depression in growing rice leading to trials of alternative crops. While it proved to be a cheaper product, its reputation was not particularly good as it failed to produce consistent results.[37] While the New World trade provided the British textile industry with virtually its entire supply of dyestuffs and hence its strategic importance, the supply of indigo returned to India.[38]

Frome dyers imported and purchased mordants and dyestuffs until the mid 19th century. During the period in which the existing dye recipe books were used, trade expeditions took many years and privateers were all too common. Most nations took part, which seems to have ensured a good supply of dye woods and indigo for the English. From the early 1700s, records from captured Dutch, French and Spanish ships mention cargoes of indigo and other dyestuff and in retaliation, English ships were pillaged. Such an incident may have contributed to the bankruptcy of Edward Halliday, as the documents from the Bristol excise officials seeking his arrest in 1729, mention his name in connection with a ship called the *'Boston Merchant';*[39] possibly as part of the Triangular trade.

> *The factor, James Elderton dealt with several trading companies.*
>
> May 1763 *'...Please to acquaint Mr Whitaker that some of the ships from the Carolina's have arrived, more expected daily. Indigo mostly sold by private contract, if I can be of service in buying I beg command me'.*
>
> And by June 9th *'...This day sale of indigo 5/- to 5/6d, French from 5/6d to 6/- and Spanish from 10/- to 10/6d, a great favour if Mr and Mrs Whitaker would make our house their home'.*

In 1805, John Olive in Frome corresponded again with John Wheadon concerning the high price of indigo.

> *'..Sir, In answer to yours of the 26th am sorry to say nothing has yett been done to cover the high prices of Indigo, the trade have it in contemplation ... The Wiltshire Dyers are for having a general meeting in London at the home of the Sale as meetings in the country is always known to the manufacturers and considered a combination ... The price we charge for deep Blues is as follows lb English genuine if color'd 14d per lb; 21 to 24d and 26d Spanish genuine Blue.*[40]*'*

These files have undated papers and bills concerning chests of indigo in 1803/4 and madder which give an indication of prices at the time. Dyes and mordants were costly ingredients which were substituted whenever it was possible to use cheaper alternatives, but the new imported dyestuffs must have provided such an array of different shades to satisfy the most discerning customers.

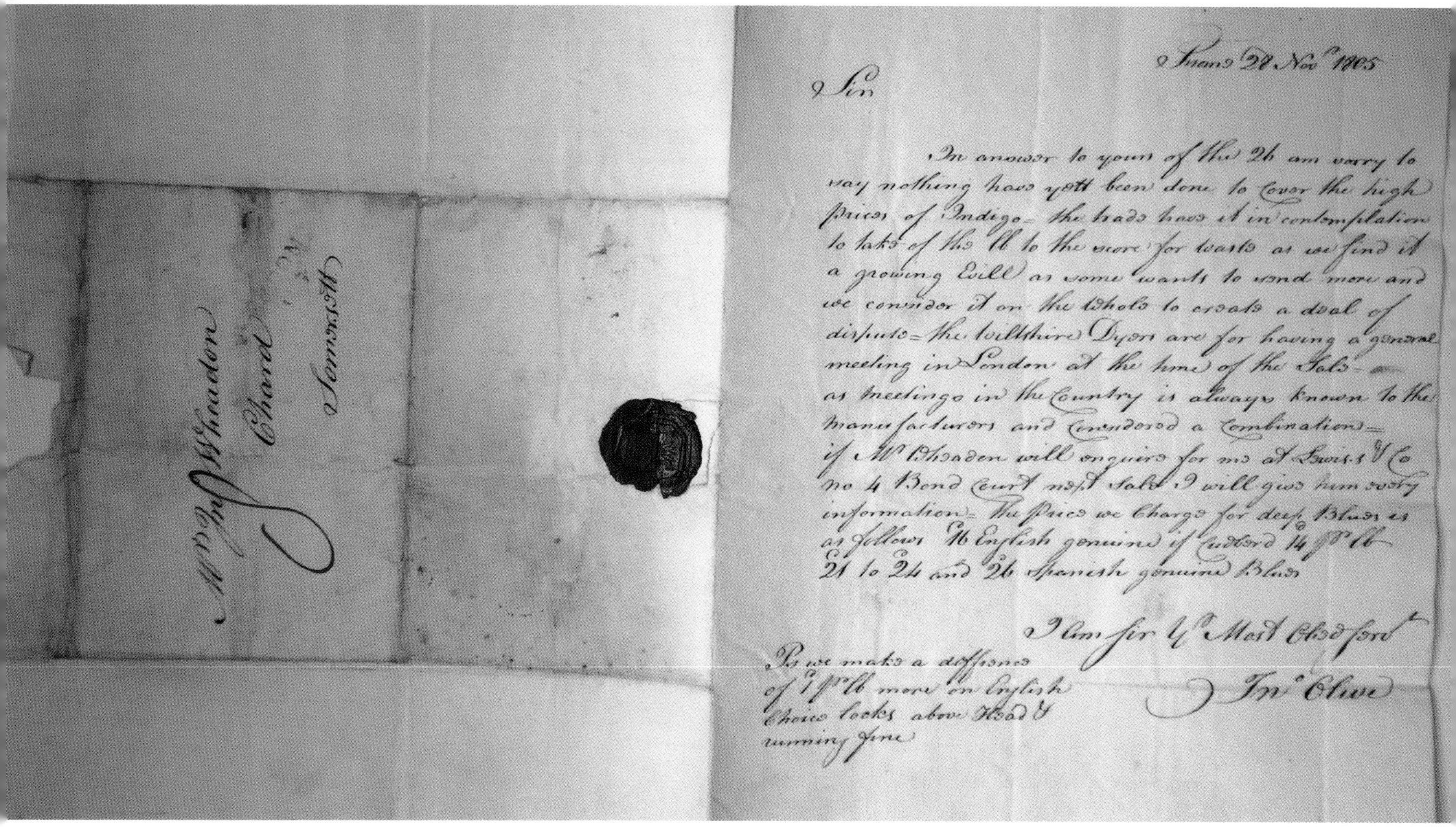

Frome 28 Nov 1805

Sir

In answer to yours of the 26 am sorry to say nothing have yett been done to cover the high prices of Indigo – the trade have it in contemplation to take of the lb to the score for waste as we find it a growing Evill as some wants to send more and we consider it on the whole to create a deal of dispute – the Wiltshire Dyers are for having a general meeting in London at the time of the Sale – as meetings in the Country is always known to the manufacturers and considered a Combination – if Mr Bhoaden will enquire for me at Lewis & Co no 4 Bond Court next Sale I will give him every information – the Price we Charge for deep Blues is as follows 16 English genuine if Cudbord 14/ p lb 21 to 24 and 26 Spanish genuine Blues

I am Sir Yr Most Obed serv

Jno Olive

Ps we make a difference of 1/ p lb more on English Choice locks above Head & running fine

Mr Wm Whaaden
Chard
Somerset

8.15 1805 Letter from John Olive

By the mid 19th century there are few references to Frome's dye trade

> *'...Cuzner's Handbook to Froome Selwood circa 1868, Chemical Works. James Holroyd & Sons has a large premise near the railway station where they prepare ground & chipped woods and spirits of different kinds used in the dyeing and manufacturing of woollen and other goods. They are also dry salters, indigo, cochineal and lac dye merchants. They employ about a dozen hands at Providence Mills, Adderwell.'*

With the closing down of the cloth industry dyeing was now provided by laundry services offering 'blueing' and dyeing of single items of clothing using the new aniline dyes.

8.16 Sign in Milk Street for Blue Product for Whitening Laundry

1 Hakluyt 1522: Vol II 96
2 TNA C241/139/56
3 Calendar of the Fine Rolls Vol 8 Ed III 1369 - 1377 British Library
4 TNA C131/23/1 and C241/157/177
5 TNA C241/210/13
6 SHC DD/LW/109 almanac
7 Hicks, M 2015: 35-42
8 www.overlandtrade.org
9 Douglas, D & Myers, A 1965: 1108
10 Winchester University Overland Trade Project
11 SANHS 2003: 177
12 Winchester University Overland Trade Project
13 Winchester University Overland Trade Project
14 Henry VI Common Pleas 796 transcribed by University Houston Rosemary Simons
15 Sherborne, J 1965:-
16 Calendar of Letter-Books of the City of London: C, 1291-1309. Folio xlv b.
17 Edmonds, J 2006:21
18 TNA SC 8/159/7901 & SC 8/295/14709
19 www.futura-sciences.com
20 Edmonds, J 2006:24
21 Ure, A 1840: 1306
22 Sherborne, J 1965: 3
23 Vanes, J 1979: 19
24 The Ledger of John Smythe 1538-1550 from transcript by John Angus
25 Ure, A 1840:1306
26 Thirsk, J 1997: 80
27 Hurry, J 1939:131
28 Hicks, M 2015: 35-42
29 SANHS Thomas Kytson and Somerset Clothmen – Colin Brett vol 143
30 The Boke of Rembraunce - Cambridge University Library - Hengrave Hall MS.78/2
31 SANHS Thomas Kytson and Somerset Clothmen – Colin Brett vol 143
32 Vanes, J 1979: 24
33 Mancell, P 2010: 198
34 Napier, J 1853: 269
35 Peachey, S 2013: 78
36 Mattson, A 2008 www.lib.umn.edu/bell/tradeproducts/indigo
37 EHR, 63, 2 (2010): 362 R. C. Nash SC indigo, European Textiles and the British Atlantic Economy in 18th Century
38 Balfour-Paul, J 2011: 70
39 BA AC/JS/53/4/a-k
40 SHC DD\SAS/C909

CHAPTER 9

THE WOOL TRADE

Stephen Wydslade, lord of Frome Selwood, Fromebraunche, Merchant of Somerset, owed £2000 for wool bought from Sir John de Sancto Laudo, Knight, Merchant.

Brought before Walter Derby, Mayor of the Staple of Bristol; April 4th, 1365

Wool was a complex story in the economic development of modern Europe and the development of the English cloth trade. Domesticated sheep had been introduced to England since neolithic times, but their wool had only played a small role. The animals were reared primarily for milk and cheese, the meat, manure and hides were the bi-products which assumed more importance as commerce became established. The hairy wool moulted by the sheep, or plucked by the shepherd, was plaited or spun and woven into coarse cloth for settlement dwellers. In North

9.1 Tithe Barn - Bradford-on-Avon

Western Europe, as the flocks were grazed in enclosed areas the sheep grew shorter crimped locks more suited to felting and weaving. The monks, founding the monasteries from the 7th century onwards, introduced improved methods of sheep farming and weaving skills to this country. They adhered to the strict rules of St Benedict who advocated self sufficiency, and as they were endowed with lands each religious community managed its flocks and made its own cloth. The surplus was stored and then transported by customary tenants to be sold at the weekly markets and annual fairs.

There were two forms of agrarian economy based on a cash crop principle in the Middle Ages. The sheep were produced for their wool, cheese and meat and cereals were grown along with small scale agricultural crops such as woad and saffron. Little is known of the medieval flocks, so the type of sheep is a matter of conjecture, but English ones were generally small and had relatively short fleeces. There were two main breeds, a small mountain sheep with a short staple wool that was hand carded and spun into a yarn more suited for a heavy woollen. The other, grazed on rich grassland, produced a longer staple and smoother wool that was combed and spun for a lighter weight cloth. The Exeter Domesday survey which recorded the livestock of the Somerset manors suggested that sheep could be grazed year round on the vast pasture land of the South West. The grazing patterns and stock management of these sheep led to the production of wool that was suitable for export. For three hundred years, there was a flourishing commerce with Europe for 'Lemster ore' from Herefordshire, Lindsey in Suffolk and the Cotswolds.

In the 13th century the English economy was dominated by the market for wool which was considered *'the jewel of the realm'* until its decline in the late 15th and early 16th century. English sheep provided a wide range of fine quality wool suitable for export, medium grades for domestic and foreign markets, and the inferior locks and refuse were used for coarse cloth, sacks and stuffing. The wool producers fell into two categories, the monasteries and landholders whose large scale production was prepared and sold wholesale under contract for cash advances. In many of the contracts, the merchants specified thorough washing, drying, sorting, weighing and specialist packing for the wool they purchased. The owners of small holdings and peasant farmers had recourse to the '*collecta*'. Their wool was gathered and sold collectively as part of the larger wholesale contract or was purchased by woolmongers and broggers, the middlemen dealers for the export merchants and later, the clothiers.

9.2 Tithe Barn - Bradford-on-Avon

Sheep were an efficient method of converting rough pasture into manure, improving the soil for the cultivation of cereals and it was common practice to maintain flocks in permanent sheep folds, erected on the estates. The ewes, wethers and hogasters were each kept on different pastures managed by shepherds and overseen by stock keepers, skilled in animal husbandry. In this area, the manorial records of Farleigh Hungerford[1] show that flocks were run on an inter and extra-manorial basis and that the Manor of Frome took part in these interchanges from the mid 1400s. The grazing patterns meant that in any one year flocks could travel between several manors separated by 30 miles or more. To improve the yield, the flocks were replenished from local markets and further afield, some of the

9.3 Sheep in the Deverills - Wiltshire

9.4 English Woollen Fleece

breeding rams were purchased from Leominster in Herefordshire and Lindsey in Suffolk, both known for their fine wool.

The shearing of wool was an annual event and the influence of breeding, management and feeding could alter the unique characteristics. Each year, even within a single flock there were variations in the fleece quality, so no hard and fast rules could apply for grading wool. The process relied on the expertise of the wool merchants, pickers and sorters, The preparation and grading was an area in which the Cistercian monks excelled and their wool highly valued.

The sorting of sheared wool from large flocks was far more advantageous as greater quantities of uniform grades could be packed and sold. Depending on the condition of the fleece, once it was clipped, the pickers would remove the worst parts into separate baskets and the remainder would be rolled up for grading. A reasonable number of fleeces had to be accumulated before a judgement could be made on the overall sort and grade. The length and fineness of the staple determined the end purpose and those shorter than 2 inches were suitable for the woollen trade of this area. Several other traits were considered desirable, an outstanding property of wool was its affinity to dyestuffs so colour was important and the softness of the staple determined the feeling and handle of the cloth. Grading wool was a matter of good judgement and the experience to group together as much wool of a uniform standard as possible. Once the wool was classified into the different sorts from the best super to the worst inferior locks it was carefully packed in sacks of 364lbs and identified with the origin and grade. Canvas sarplers were made up of two and a half sacks which were loaded onto pack horses and

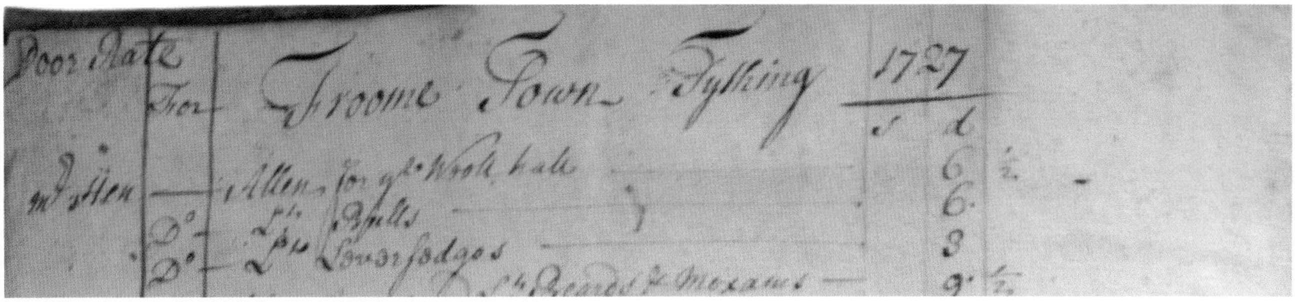

9.5 1727 Wool Hall Rate

transported to markets and ports for sale. The wool merchants reputation relied on careful sorting, it was far more difficult for the broggers who dealt in small quantities. They sometimes collected single fleeces so it was easier to mix many different sorts together which could result in the loss of sales from a poor quality wool which would not manufacture into a good cloth.

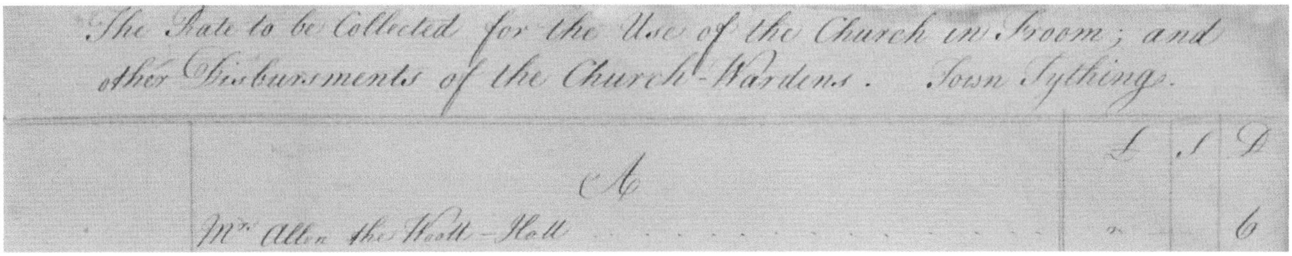
The Rate to be Collected for the Use of the Church in Froome; and other Disbursments of the Church-Wardens. Town Tything.

	£	s	D
A			
Mr. Allen the Woolt-Hall			6

9.6 1778 Wool Hall Rate

England with a predominantly agricultural economy until the mid 14th century was an exporter of raw materials and an importer of finished goods. Cloth production had centred around Ghent and Ypres in Flanders by the 12th century but growing demand required new sources of wool. Flemish knights and their followers who had been rewarded with land in England for their part in the conquest probably recognised the value of the native sheep. While it is unknown exactly when English wool started to be exported, trade was handled by foreign merchants, termed 'aliens' in the 12th century as English merchant capitalism had yet to be established. Flemish merchants travelled to and from the Low Countries to purchase wool.

The Italian merchants as well as buying, extended credit, provided capital and safe shipping routes for goods. They bought wool clips in advance

9.7 Memorial Brass of Sheep and Woolsack, Northleach - Gloucestershire

sometimes by paying the monasteries ten to twenty years ahead. To transact their business and to benefit from royal privileges foreigners established merchant guilds in English towns. One group with members from what are now fifteen different Belgian and German towns, led by Bruges established the 'Hanse' in London in 1266. The merchants negotiated the rights to free trade for their citizens, financial advantages and tax concessions from the King to promote their business interests. Politics revolved around the Crown's need for money, as commerce expanded in importance in both domestic and export trade, it was increasingly legislated and influenced by English and foreign merchants. Trade on a cash basis was comparatively limited, the export system was a chain of transactions over a period of months or even years, and credit in some form was a commercial necessity. Merchants often bought from wool samples and accepted delivery later, they sold at one fair and received payment at another. Their promissory notes were transferable in lieu of, or as part payment for goods. Their word was their bond both for themselves and on behalf of other less wealthy merchants.

England held the commercial advantage for several hundred years as the manufacture of luxury cloth in Flanders and Italy could not have expanded without English wool. Governments, influenced by merchants, designated particular towns on trade routes as preferred locations for all business transactions of specific commodities. The staple, as it was known, conferred considerable rights to the merchants and towns in the form of licenses, tolls and fines in exchange for payments to the crown. The designation was often contested and the staple was moved to serve divergent political and financial interests.

The raw material valued throughout Europe was symbolised by the woolsack in the House of Lords. The early years of the reign of Edward

III were a time of free trade and low taxation. At its peak, in the 14th century up to 45,000 sacks of wool were exported annually. To expedite business, a group of English merchants was granted a charter in 1319 to form the Company of Merchants of the Staple which established a compulsory English Staple abroad to control the export of wool and centralise the collection of taxes. The Merchant Staplers were bound to a membership of the Company and shipped their wool primarily to the Staple town of Calais where their wares were under the protection of English garrisons. The Staplers who travelled regularly to and from the continent competed for trade with members of the Hanse and a rivalry with the cloth merchants escalated as competition for markets expanded. Wool merchants,who were not members of the company, hoped that by encouraging the establishment of an English Staple in places like Bristol instead, it would reduce the cost of entry into the business, giving them more control and forcing foreign buyers to come to them. This was achieved for a few years in 1326 when it was decreed that no alien was to buy wool, hides, wool-fells or tin except at certain specified towns in England, Wales and Ireland. English merchants were not allowed to carry goods for sale for 15 days until they had fairly offered them for sale at one of the staples.[2]

9.8 Dunkirk Mill Token - 'Success to the Staple of England'

By the second half of the 14th century two thirds of the export trade was in the hands of the English Merchant Staplers through the Staple port of Calais. Medieval kings lacked feudal income, they needed strong foreign alliances and money to finance wars. Wool was the largest source of revenue and as a diplomatic tool its trade was encouraged and suppressed to influence favoured allegiances. In 1336, with war pending, the king temporarily banned the export of wool, which brought about swift economic retaliation. Subsequent policies attempted unsuccessfully to reconcile the competing demands of the king, the English and foreign merchants, the financiers, the wool growers and the dealers. The on-going disruption of the wool trade and its high taxation nurtured the development of the domestic cloth manufacture and the

9.9 Merchant Vessel - Greenway Chapel
St Peter's Church - Tiverton

selling of fine quality cloth became more profitable than exporting wool. The two trades ran concurrently, one steadily increasing while the other slowly declined.

The rise of the English cloth industry provided a domestic outlet for wool. Somerset, with both marshland and uplands, was ideal for sustaining large flocks. In 1178, Henry II had founded the Carthusian priory at Witham near Frome which by the 13th century was known as a wool selling monastery listed in the exchequer's price schedules.[3] Wool and cloth fairs were held annually, with the Pensford market and the George Inn at Norton St Philip serving the local area. Unlike Gloucestershire, Somerset had none of the great woolmen, but as the cloth industry expanded, merchants in Frome and the surrounding villages traded in wool to supply the domestic demand.

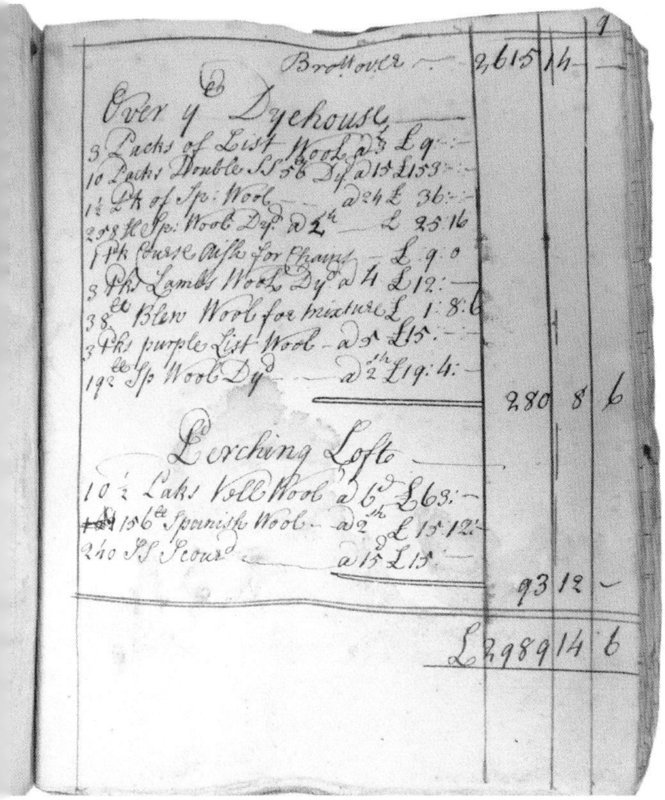

Brt over — 2,615 14 —

Over ye Dyehouse

3 Packs of List Wool @ 3 £ 9: —

10 Packs Double SS 56 Dy @ 15 £ 153: —

1½ Pk of Sp: Wool — @ 24 £ 36: —

298 lb Sp: Wool Dyd @ 2 £ 25 16

1 Pk Course ... for ... — £ 9 0

3 Pks Lambs Wool Dyd @ 4 £ 12: —

38 lb Blew Wool for mixture £ 1 8 6

3 Pks purple List Wool — @ 5 £ 15: —

192 lb Sp Wool Dyd — @ 2 £ 19: 4: —

280 8 6

Lorching Lofts

10½ Paks Voll Wool @ 6 £ 63: —

156 lb Spanish Wool — @ 2 £ 15 12

240 SS Scour — @ 15 £ 15: —

93 12 —

£ 2989 14 6

9.10 1734 E Halliday Inventory

Then as now, disputes arose from delays in delivery and damaged goods. The Law Merchant, a set of commercial laws and a code of best practice, was established to facilitate swift and informal resolution of disagreements according to plain justice and good faith. Transactional trade on credit made it very difficult to manage cash flow and many merchants were declared bankrupt. The recovery of debt was through the courts and as the king's authority extended, more complicated legal systems were established. Tolls and fines, usually constituted at the time of charters for fairs and markets, were collected by the bailiffs or the Lord's steward. The resolution of incidents such as fraud, forgery of bonds, assault and theft, were administered in courts of the Staple or Piepowder courts which held jurisdiction over the markets and fairs.

9.11 Wool Hall - Beckington

During the 15th century, there were decades of economic contractions and expansions. Early in the century, the demesne landholders rented their land to tenant farmers and the organisation of the wool collection came increasingly into the hands of the middlemen wool merchants dealing with the monopoly of the Merchant Staplers in Calais. The Cotswolds, in particular, were an important centre for the export of wool. The fleeces were stored in large wool houses and granges erected on the estates and as a non-perishable commodity it could be transported and consolidated in large warehouses in the ports of London, Bristol, Southampton and Calais. The substantial domestic purchases of the clothiers may have been stored in wool halls, possibly attached to dwellings and the wool from small holdings and independent cloth workers was kept dry in their wool lofts.

There is no evidence that the warehouse type building on Cork Street known as 'The Coach House' [4] constructed around the mid to late 17th century, was a domestic

9.12 The Coach House - Frome

dwelling, it may have been a Wool Hall. The imposing west facade was perhaps built as a reminder of the clothier's status in the town and to impress visiting merchants with whom they conducted business. The interior was simple but practical. It may have served as an office and storage for the Merchant (Marchant) family who lived opposite in Hall House which was built or remodelled around the same time or the Whitchurch family of wealthy drapers and mercers. The layout of the hipped roof building suggests that the ground floor may have been divided into a secure counting house as original bars still remain on one window and an adjacent scale or storage room for chains of warp and weft wools. Windows on the first floor would have enabled workers to read the marks on heavy wool sacks stored in the loft above before lowering them through the internal trap door to be weighed and distributed to the scourers, spinners and weavers. In the mid 18th century it was purchased by Thomas Bunn when it may have been converted to stables.[5]

9.13 Coach House - Wool Loft, Frome

Until the 1500s both wool and cloth were extensively traded overseas but as protectionist policies were introduced, the sale of wool declined in foreign markets and demand for the production of English cloth increased. When the French reclaimed Calais in 1558, the influence of the wool merchants diminished significantly as restrictive legislation led to the collapse of the Staple monopoly for export. Their livelihood threatened, members of the Company of the Staple petitioned for the sole rights to deal and market the raw wool for the home market. This struggle resulted in years of conflict with the broggers, the unlicensed wool dealers who extended credit to the small producers, the clothiers who negotiated their own deals with the farmers for wool best suited to their cloth production and the Merchant Venturers exporting cloth overseas.

[1] http://www.british-history.ac.uk/report.aspx?compid=102807

[2] The Staple Court Books of Bristol

[3] Munro 1978: Vol 9 Textile History 119

[4] Courtesy Julian Watson current owner of the property

[5] Selwood and Duncan, Measured Surveys Interpretation of Standing Structure 29 April 1998.

Utensils in Trade &c.

In the Shear Shop.

26 Pair of Shears
Pr. of Shear Boards and Trestle.
3 Cots of Leads
Scrave
Form.
Pr. of Perches
Oil kettle & do. small.
Rough Board
2 Oil brushes
3 Pr. of Hook stocks and Bols.
20 Handles.
4 Picking do.

In the Scribbling Shop.

4 Scribbling Horses
15 Pr. of Old Scribbling Cards
Pair of New ones.
7 Wool Baskets
2 Tucking do.
2 Pens for keeping Wool in
8 Shelves.
Iron beam and Scales
Smaller do. —
12 Lead Weights
10 Brass do. —

Outer Room.

3 Tilts
Long Board & Trestle.
Oval board.
Pair of Perches
Shelf
Cooler.

Cloth Room.

Stands of Cloth Tack
Square Table
Joint Stool
Oak Chest of Drawers. (The Widow's)
5 Cloth Wrappers.
1 Oak Chest. — (The Widow's)
Cloth box
Saddle and Bridle
3 doz. new Press Papers.
6 Tences
1 Sign Board
Fender, Tongs, Fire shovel and Brush & Fender

3 3

Cloth Room continued

Pattern Stamp.
Lead Weight
Folding Rod.
Close stool × (The Widow's)
Portmanteau.
Deal Box × (The Widow's)
2 Hat Boxes × (do. —)
3 Baskets with Linen.
20 Bundles of Twine.
5 Sheets.
2 Bolster drawers.
Counterpane
Remnant of Holland
Blanket
Sheet
Pr. of Green Window curtains
2 Sheets.
Bolster Cloth
Napkin
3 Table Cloths.
Diaper do.
Table Cloth
Napkin
Towel.

Picking Loft.

Basket
2 Picking Hurdles.
Beating Hurdle
Pr. of Steps.
4 Bundles of List.
Net Box.

Willey Loft.

Willey
Hand Willey
2 large Baskets.
Small do.
Long sweeping Brush.
Frame of Table Board.
Old Cupboard / Oak.
About 3 pack of Teazles.
Hand Brush.

In Garden.

2 Stages of Handles.
2 Water Tubs and 2 Stone Balls.

CHAPTER 10

MAKING CLOTH

An inventory of the Estate & Effects of the late Mr Amos Jenkins of Frome Selwood in the County of Somerset, cloth maker deceased.

Taken the 7th day of May 1789 by A. Crocker

The prehistoric Glastonbury Lake settlement was established around 250 BCE on the Somerset Levels, but abandoned in favour of higher grounds by 50 CE. Amongst the finds of a large collection of wooden items, there were sixty-three pieces of frame-work, parts of looms or other apparatus for making textiles, some dark colouring matter and fragments of woven woollen material. Amid the hundreds of bone and antler objects, there were more than eighty weaving combs, triangular loom weights and spindle whorls.[1] It would seem that Julius Caesar was misinformed

10.1 1789 A Jenkins Inventory

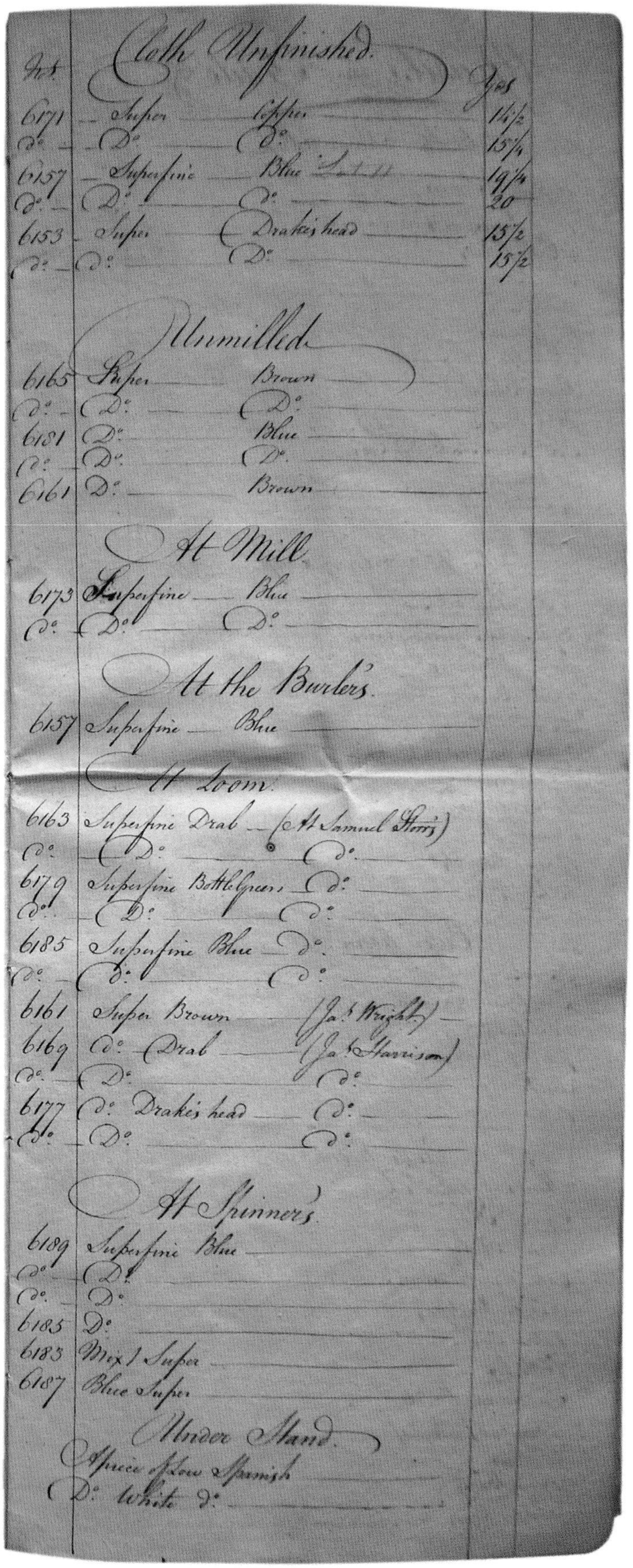
Cloth Unfinished.

No. | Yds
6171 Super Copper 14½
Do. Do. Do. 15¼
6157 Superfine Blue 19¼
Do. Do. Do. 20
6153 Super Drake's head 15½
Do. Do. Do. 15½

Unmilled
6165 Super Brown
Do. Do. Do.
6181 Do. Blue
Do. Do. Do.
6161 Do. Brown

At Mill.
6173 Superfine Blue
Do. Do. Do.

At the Burlers.
6157 Superfine Blue

At Loom.
6163 Superfine Drab (At Samuel Storrs)
Do. Do. Do.
6179 Superfine Bottlegreen Do.
Do. Do. Do.
6185 Superfine Blue Do.
Do. Do. Do.
6161 Super Brown (Jas Wright)
6169 Do. Drab (Jas Harrison)
Do. Do. Do.
6177 Do. Drake's head Do.
Do. Do. Do.

At Spinners
6189 Superfine Blue
Do. Do.
Do. Do.
6185 Do.
6183 Mix'd Super
6187 Blue Super

Under Stand.
A piece of Low Spanish
Do. White Do.

10.2 1789 A Jenkins Inventory

during the Roman occupation, when he was told that, except near the straits of Dover, the ancient Britons dressed in skins, knew nothing of agriculture and lived on meat and milk. Long before then, even the remoter and less civilised tribes were cultivating the soil and wearing woollen and linen clothes.[2]

Cloth is created by the interweaving of warp and weft yarns made from twisted fibres. In Europe, the process is depicted in Roman archaeology, Viking excavations and medieval paintings. Until the Saxon period, the occupation of wool combing, spinning and weaving was women's work which was done at home or in the company of a larger social group. A good cloth is produced from quality raw materials, the right tools for the trade and the skill of the workers. Over the centuries, innovations in all three brought about changes, and by the late Middle Ages, the introduction and improvement of hand tools and mill technology gave rise to this area's woollen cloth.

The West Country broadcloth, historically made of wool in

plain weave, was the generic name for a wide milled material of assorted grades. By the 18th century it required as many as twenty nine processes to manufacture. Sheep were washed and shorn in late spring and the wool was roughly sorted into three grades, good, medium and coarse. From the 15th century, it was graded more carefully by the wool staplers into ten or twelve different sorts which was reflected in the names of some woollen cloths of the 18th century: *'picklock'* the finest wool, *'prime'* which was not quite as good, *'choice'* where the staple was slightly coarser, *'super'* similar to choice, *'head'* the best of the inferior sorts, *'downrights'* from the lowest part of the ribs, *'seconds'* the best bits from the throat and breast, *'abb'* inferior to the seconds, *'livery'* the skirtings and edgings, *'short coarse'* and *'breech'* wool[3]. It was inspected and packed in sacks of 364 lbs, labelled with the grade of wool and the owner's mark. The canvas sacks were sewn up and carted to the ports or stored in tithe barns, wool halls and lofts.

While the sheep may have been washed prior to shearing, the better wool was scoured again in a lukewarm liquor composed of three parts 'fair' water (water mixed with bran, left to settle and then decanted), and one of urine, which loosened and dissolved the sheep's natural lanolin. It was then drained, put in wicker baskets and washed in the running water of a river then laid out to dry in the shade or the drying sheds. When dry, it was spread on wooden planks raised on hurdles and beaten with rods to remove any residual dust and filth then picked over by hand. The more it was beaten and cleared of bits, the softer it became and the better it could be spun. The initial preparation of scoured long staple fleece was to untangle and straighten the fibres on the great combs. By the 13th century wool cards with rows of long metal teeth attached to leather and mounted on wooden posts were invented and it became a man's job, that of woolcomber to heat the comb in a furnace and draw it through the wool to align and separate the long fibres from the short.

Dyeing wool has already been discussed (See Chapter 8), so the clean or dyed locks were next opened by rough carding on a twilly or willey, also known as a devil box. This was a piece of curved wood covered in metal spikes attached to a frame that could be swung back and forth over a tray

10.3 Devil Box

where the wool was placed by the handful. Once opened the wool was put on a clean floor and oiled with imported olive oil ready for the spinner. Coarser wool could be spun 'in the grease' when the wool was left unwashed, or sometimes it was washed and oiled with rancid butter.

Short fibres were carded by the spinners to form rolags, using hand held wooden carders with rows of short wire teeth. The process of combing long fibres and carding short ones prepared wool suitable for the lighter worsteds and the heavier woollen cloths which were then spun into yarn. The word yarn possibly derives from the Anglo-Saxon word '*gearn*'. Coincidentally, in the 1700s, it was thought that the River Frome had its principal source in Gearnfelle or Yarnfield Common,[4] a small settlement at the time of Domesday with six households and 124 sheep. Perhaps they were occupied in spinning yarns, however the word also means proximity to a river.

For centuries, spinning was done with a drop spindle which is just a stick with a notch at one end and a fitted disc shaped weight or whorl at the other. The combed wool was wrapped around a distaff and the carded rolag was held in the hand, both were drawn out and fastened to a previously spun thread attached to the spindle and twirled to transfer a twist to the fibres creating the thread. This method was cheap, easy to carry around and was in common use commercially until the 15th century and it is still popular today. By simply adjusting the amount and direction of twist a stronger thread could be spun for the warp and a softer one for the weft.

The making of commercial cloth required large

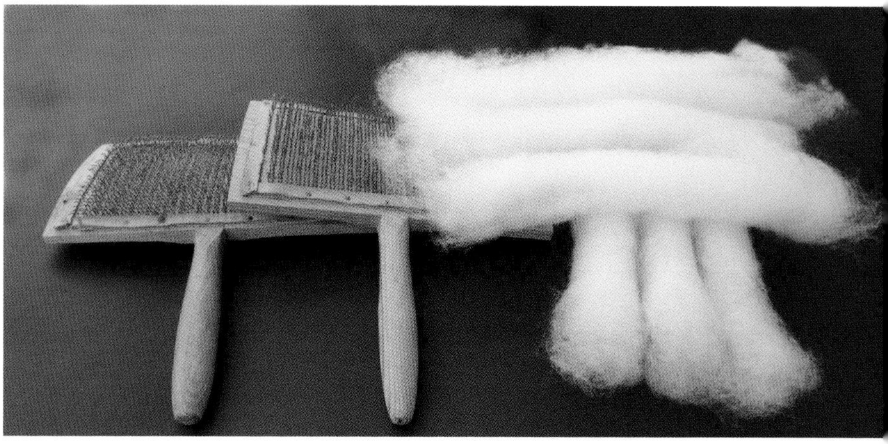

10.4 Carders & Rolags

amounts of handspun yarn, which was provided by the work of six to ten spinners who supplied each weaver. The wool was weighed by the clothier and put out to spinsters. The quality of spinning was important as a uniform cloth required an even yarn. Each spinner needed to draw a similar thickness of wool and spin a regular twist but spinning was not an apprenticed trade. It was a poorly paid occupation, fitted in by women and unskilled children around other household chores, and was quickly put aside for any better paid work, especially during harvest time. *On the 28th, September 1763 '...Sorry to hear spinning is so dear, but I hope it will be better after the harvest'. James Elderton*

10.5 Drop Spindle

Overseers of some parishes also considered it suitable work for the poor. A crossed out note from Rack and Collinson's research for the History of the County of Somerset mentions the destitute of Berkley, less than three miles from Frome, which suggests that *'...The poor are chiefly employed in husbandry, weaving and spinning for the clothing manufactory.*[5]'

The great wheel came into use in the 13th century but thread spun in this way did not produce as tight or as fine a yarn as the drop spindle but it was faster for the production of commercial cloth. Warp yarns were mostly spun using a drop spindle to produce a hard, strong yarn with a clockwise twist. The weft threads were softer and more loosely spun on the great wheel with an anti-clockwise twist. This combination of yarns made for a durable cloth that could withstand the friction of the loom beater and the hard pounding action of the fulling stocks, but as increasing production was paramount both yarns were often spun on the great wheel leading to breakages in the weaving and thin patches would show up in the fulling. With the introduction of the treadle wheel, good quality warp and weft yarns could be spun. These were wound on a clock reel into skeins of 320 yards to each pound of wool. The finished skeins were returned to the clothier with perhaps just a little extra wool missing.

The yarn then went to the warper, where it was measured out on a purpose made board and looped into chains; the board was later replaced by a twisting mill. The number and thickness of the warp and weft threads spread over a given length and width determined the grade of the cloth. Creating the warp was done by going backwards and forwards over a peg board to the required length of the cloth, each assemblage of 36 threads was called a handful, forty of these were required to complete a bundle. Locally, the warps, weighing about 60 lbs, were called 'chains' and the weft weighing about 40 lbs were called 'abbs'. These, along with the list wool for the selvedges would be collected by the weavers.

Evidence suggests that early cloth weaving was done on a vertical wooden frame loom with a fixed top and bottom cross beam. The warp threads were tied to the top beam and the bottom ends fastened in bunches to clay or stone loom weights which kept the threads parallel and provided an even tension while weaving. Weft yarn was passed over and under each warp thread to create a plain weave and beaten upward with a weaving sword. Alternating the process by going over and under several threads could change the weave patterns and varying the tension on the warp weights could produce a finer or looser cloth. The vertical loom for weaving household cloth was still in general use in Anglo-Saxon England and was either set upright in the ground or leant against a wall outside the home or in a weaving shed. The top beam was replaced by one that rotated so the cloth could be rolled as it was woven producing a longer yardage. The use of this type of loom to make household cloth may have continued for years, with any extra taken to market.

Weaving was a common place activity, and early in

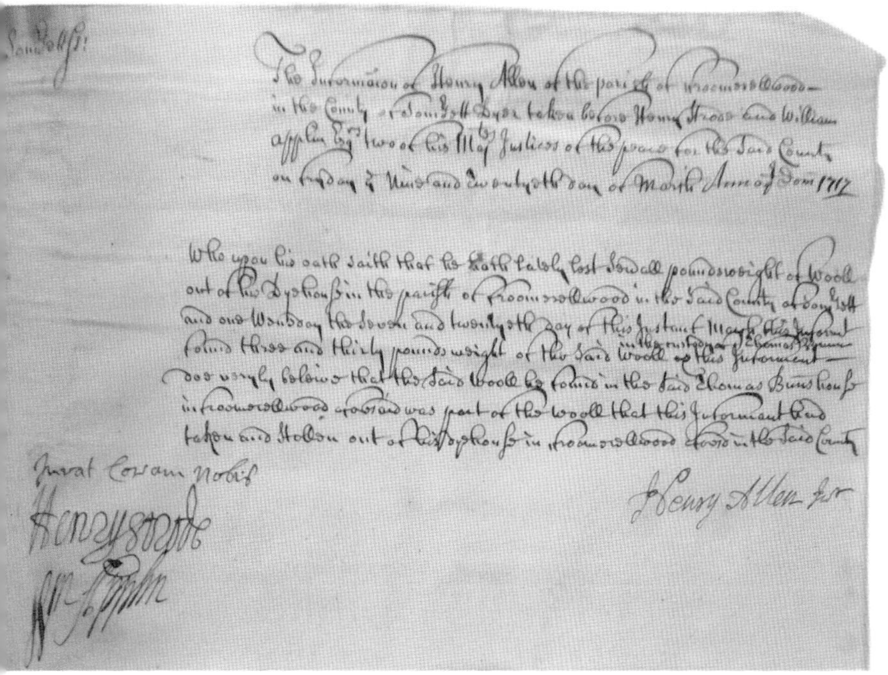

Somersetts:

The Information of Henry Allen of the parish of Froomeselwood in the County of Somersett Dyer taken before Henry [illegible] and William Applin Esqrs two of his Majs Justices of the peace for the said County on Friday the Nine and twentyeth day of March Anno Dom 1717

Who upon his oath saith that he hath lately lost Severall pounds weight of Wooll out of his Dyehouse in the parish of Froomeselwood in the said County of Somersett and on Wednsday the seven and twentyeth day of this Instant March this Informant found three and thirty pounds weight of the said Wooll in the custody of Thomas [illegible] and this Informant doe verily believe that the said Wooll he found in the said Thomas [illegible] house in Froomeselwood aforesaid was part of the Wooll that this Informant had taken and stolen out of his Dyehouse in Froomeselwood aforesaid in the said County

Jurat Coram nobis

Henry Allen Jur

Henry [illegible]

Wm Applin

10.6 1717 - Thirty Three pounds of Wool Stolen from Henry Allen's Dyehouse

the 11th century the horizontal floor loom with a rolling back beam was brought to continental Europe from Asia and by the 12th century pedals were attached to the heddle shafts. These looms were adopted in England around the 1300s making weaving considerably faster but it was still only possible to produce cloth that was as wide as the reach of the weaver passing the shuttle from one side to the other. It may have been at this stage that men started weaving because longer and heavier bolts of cloth could be woven as a commercial product.

Weavers had been using the double beam vertical chalon loom commercially to produce wide cloths for bed hangings. The 14th century brought further improvements, in addition to the chalon loom and the narrow horizontal loom sometimes called a kersey loom[6], there was the broad horizontal or broadcloth loom for weaving woollen cloth. These may have simply evolved from combining chalon looms, that could be used by two weavers with narrow horizontal looms with treadles and a rolling beam to produce a broad loom.

Weavers erected looms in their cottages, or they may have had several in adjoining worksheds. These large wooden structures occupied almost all the space of first floors, front rooms or attics; and three casement windows or more provided the maximum daylight in which to work.

Broadlooms were 6ft high, and about 9ft wide allowing two people to sit on the integral bench to throw the shuttle back and forth. The loom for woollens required two frames with string heddles and two treadles to lower alternative sets of threads to create a shed for the shuttle. Narrow looms to weave twill patterns required four heddle frames and four treadles to lower two frames at a time.

10.7 Weaver's Cottage Gentle Street - Frome

10.8 Modified Broadloom Adapted with a Flying Shuttle

The weaver coated the warp with a sizing of animal glue and water to smooth and bind the short fibres so they could withstand the constant friction of the beater. The warp chains were then rolled upon the back beam. Cross rods or lease sticks were put between the threads of the warp to regulate their separation. Each strand was passed through the eye of a heddle and then the reed before being tied to the front beam. This was a long process as an average broadcloth had between 1700 and 1900 warp threads depending on the grade of cloth. Young children sat and wound the weft wool on pirns or bobbins that were inserted into the shuttles, and the older ones assisted the weaver in throwing it back and forth across the double width of the broadloom. Each pick or row of weft wool was packed tightly by beating the reed against the fell of the cloth. These processes were subject to fraud, fewer warp threads could be put on the beam, the weft might not be packed quite so tightly, extra waste thrums could be gleaned by cutting the cloth a little short. All these materials could be re-used by the weaver to make

10.9 Foot Treadles

10.10 Warp Bundles Wound on Back Beam

10.11 Four Heddle Frames

a bit more money and similar instructions could be suggested by the clothier to maximise profit.

When the cloth was cut from the loom and returned to the clothier, it was taken to the burling shed where women under the supervision of the master burler, would pick out any remaining pieces of vegetable matter, using small tweezer like tools called spiling irons. It was hung over perches for inspection, the loose ends were sewn in and small flaws were rectified after which it was sent to the fulling mill. The cloth was scoured of oil and size added during the spinning and weaving processes. Before the fulling mill, this had been done in a trough filled with water and urine by a 'walker' or 'tucker' stomping on the cloth with his feet but by the 14th century, it was done by the fuller in a mill with fullers earth and urine. This first washing was the final process for worsted cloth, which were then dried and sold. For finishing broadcloths a second pass in the fulling mill stocks for up to 18 hours was required to matt and felt the fibres together which made it shrink and thicken so it became hard wearing and suitable for outerwear. The second fulling was the milling of the woollen cloth which used soap made with olive oil and relied on heat and friction produced by the action of the stocks to felt the cloth which could be shrunk by as much as two thirds in length and half in width. Milling was not a continuous process and the cloth had to be taken out at intervals by the mill men to be stretched between the lists and pulled square to see if it was shrinking evenly.[7] Once taken from the mill, the wet cloth was hung along its selvedge edges '*on tenter hooks*' either outside in the rack

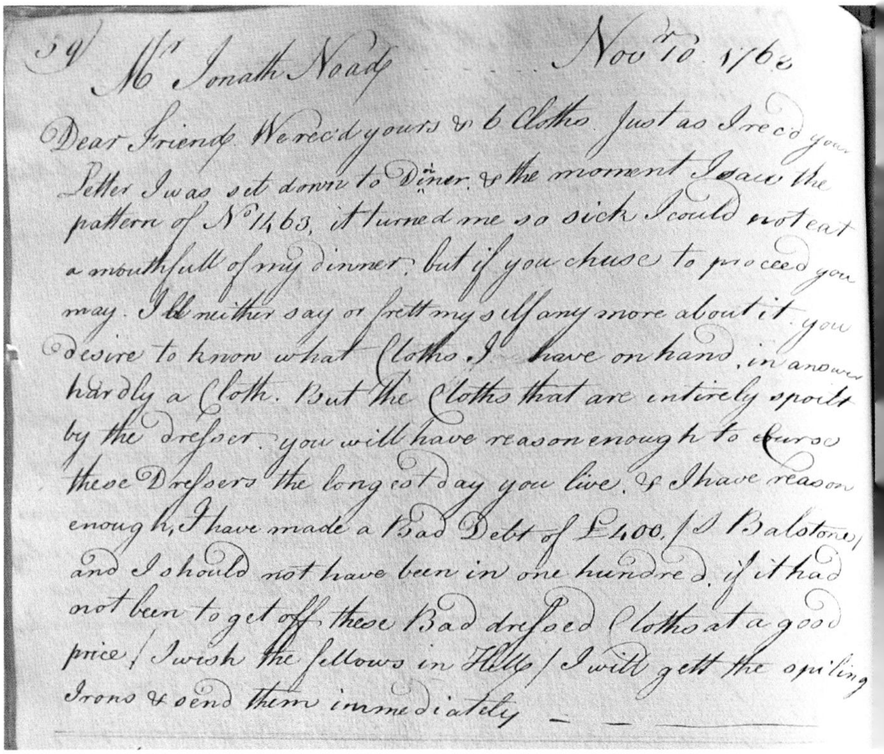
59 Mr Jonath Noad ... Novr 10. 1768
Dear Friend We recd yours & 6 Cloths Just as I recd your Letter I was set down to Diner & the moment I saw the pattern of No 1463, it turned me so sick I could not eat a mouthfull of my dinner, but if you chuse to proceed you may. I'll neither say or frett my self any more about it. you desire to know what Cloths I have on hand, in answer hardly a Cloth. But the Cloths that are entirely spoilt by the dresser. you will have reason enough to curse these Dressers the longest day you live. & I have reason enough, I have made a Bad Debt of £400. [illegible] and I should not have been in one hundred. if it had not been to get off these Bad dressed Cloths at a good price / I wish the fellows in Hell / I will gett the spiling Irons & send them immediately —

10.12 Elderton Letter Mentioning Spiling Irons

fields or in open sided barns where the material was stretched to the correct length and width stipulated by laws passed as early as the 11th century. One revision of 1483 attempted to prevent various fraudulent methods of making woollen cloth, especially that of stretching.

> *'...Tenters shall not be kept within doors, but alone in open places. Broad Cloths, shall be in length 24 yards and one inch in length and two yards or at least 7 quarters between the lists. Half clothe 12 yards long and not to exceed 16 yards; same width; streits 12 yards long, breadth one yard within the lists; kerseys 18 yards long and one yard and a nail between the lists.'*

Later laws also stipulated the weights of cloth. After brief periods of enforcement, these acts were quietly disregarded until once again faults became too glaring to overlook.[8]

10.13 Pair of Fullling Stocks

Good quality broad cloth was finished by the cloth workers. Raising or rowing the nap and shearing the cloth resulted in a very smooth finish. This required the nap of slightly damp broadcloth and the later medley cloth to be gently raised with teasels. *Dispascus Fullonum* is a type of thistle that was grown in the nearby fields of Frome and elsewhere in Somerset. The cloth would be hung over a beam and two men would gently brush the surface with the teasels set in wooden handles. Raising the nap, required hundreds of teasel heads, used ones were softer on the cloth for the first few passes and then new ones were used. The dried flower heads were set into wooden handles by a specialist teasel setter, where they acted as little velcro hooks catching and teasing the wool until an even haze of

10.14 Fuller's Teasel, *Dispascus Fullonum*

10.15 Teasels Set in a Stage Handle for a Gig Mill

fuzz covered the surface. As the teasels became clogged, children would sit and remove the wool fibres attached to the curled ends. Once clean, they were dried in a purpose built shed, called a handle house, with air vents so they could be re-used.

Raising the nap was followed by shearing which was carried out by highly skilled men, draping the cloth over a wooden horse, they rested their large shears across the surface. Then, closing the blade, the raised nap was cropped to leave a smooth surface with no long or loose fibres left to 'pill'. These last two stages could be repeated up to five times for the finest, silkiest finish. Finally the cloth was finished by the pressers carefully placing press papers between folds of the cloth and placing the bolt of material under heated plates in a large press, after which it was packed and carted to the factors in London for sale.

Over the centuries, the skilled cloth workers from the Low Countries and France, persecuted in their own countries, were given incentives to settle in England and with them came additional knowledge. These improved methods, tools and techniques were gradually disseminated across the country resulting in the production of a very valuable wool cloth for trading around the world. In later centuries came the introduction of machinery. The flying shuttle invented by John Kay in 1733 increased the speed of

10.16 Handle House near Shepton Mallet

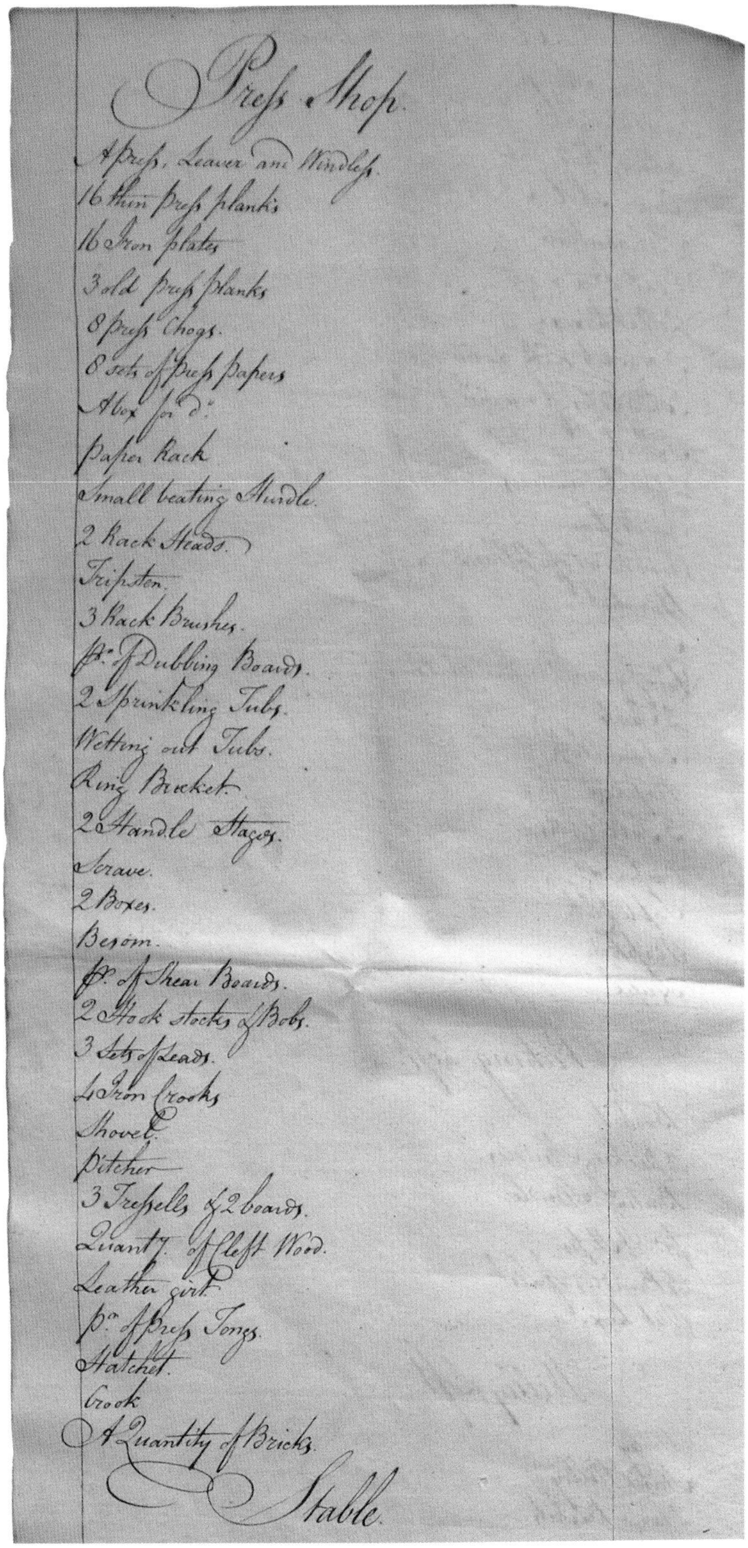
Press Shop

A Press, Leaver and Windless
16 thin Press planks
16 Iron plates
3 old Press planks
8 Press Chogs
8 sets of Press papers
A box for do
Paper Rack
Small beating Hurdle
2 Rack Heads
Tripston
3 Rack Brushes
Pr. of Dubbing Boards
2 Sprinkling Tubs
Wetting out Tubs
Ring Bucket
2 Handle Stages
Scrave
2 Boxes
Besom
Pr. of Shear Boards
2 Hook stocks & Bobs
3 Sets of Leads
4 Iron Crooks
Shovel
Pitcher
3 Tressells & 2 boards
Quanty. of Cleft Wood
Leather girt
Pr. of Press Tongs
Hatchet
Crook
A Quantity of Bricks

Stable

10.17 A Jenkins Inventory

weaving and reduced the cost by enabling a single weaver to produce broadcloth. The supply of yarn was then insufficient until the mechanisation of this process with the invention of the spinning jenny in 1764, which could wind eight spindles instead of just one. The teasel handles were eventually replaced in the late 18th century with the gig mill, a rotating drum covered in teasels. By 1794, the shear frame, a cropping machine and forerunner of the cylinder lawn mower, replaced two out of three shearmen's jobs and the remaining man's wages were considerably reduced as the work was less skilled. While all these innovations and others were eventually adopted by the manufacturers, rioting delayed their implementation in Wiltshire and Somerset until the 19th century.

[1] http://www.glastonburyantiquarians.org
[2] Collingwood, R & Myers, J 1937: 68
[3] Burnley 1969:85
[4] Collinson, J & Rack,E 1791: Vol1 xiv
[5] SHC A/AQP/12
[6] Blair, J & Ramsey, N 2001: 329
[7] Rogers, K 1976: 60
[8] Beck, W 1882: 71-72

We whose Names are hereunto subscribed Clothiers of the parish of Frome Selwood in the County of Somersett and places adjacent Do hereby Certify that John Smith of Frome Selwood aforesaid Clothier is a person of good Character and well and fitly qualified to execute the Office of one of the Inspectors or Measurers of Broad Cloth for the said County As Witness our hands the twenty third day of April 1745.

Jo: Jesser
Wm Humfry
James Collens
Wm Barton
John Sheppard
John Addams
Jno Olive
Stephen Addams
Jno Lacy
John Lydford
Willm Sheppard
John Smith
Richd Singer
Joseph Blunt
Robert Blunt
G: Davis
John Horton Junr
Jno Horton Senr

23 April 1745 We appoint John Smith of Frome to be an Inspector as above desired

James Chaffey Carigier

W Rowe

CHAPTER 11

THE CLOTH TRADE

The King and State began to grow sensible of the great gain the Netherlands got by English wool, the King, therefore, resolved, if possible, to reduce the trade to his own country, who as yet were ignorant of that art, as knowing no more what to do with their wool than the sheep that wear it. Their best cloathes being no better than friezes, such their coarseness for want of skill in the making'

Statute from the reign of Edward III (1327 - 1377)

By the end of the 3rd century, English cloth was exported and cloaks made of British wool became important articles of commerce. In the 4th century, there was an imperial weaving-mill at Winchester and the prices were fixed by Roman edict.[1] A letter written in 796 by Charlemagne to Offa of Mercia requested that the wool cloaks should be made as of old to the full length rather than the shorter ones.

11.2 3rd Century Carving of the Genii Cuculatti Wearing Cloaks - Hadrian's Wall

Luxurious fabrics from Asia were imported to Europe and the knowledge to make fine and coloured cloth spread further afield. The Mediterranean processes, inherited from ancient civilisations, and those from central and northern Europe, laid the foundations for the flourishing dyeing arts of the Middle Ages.[2]

Knowledge and skills spread to the wider population aided by monks, lay people working in the monasteries and foreign traders. Statutes and guild rules were enacted to regulate all aspects of production and sale. The Cloth Assize was first proclaimed in 1196:

> *'...woollen cloth, wherever it be made, shall be all of one breadth, two ells within the lists and of the same goodness in the middle as on the edges.[3]'*

This edict was reiterated in Magna Carta[4] and subsequently amended as different varieties of cloths were manufactured. While there was no indication of the size of the domestic market, for hundreds of years, the cloth woven in towns and rural households met the ordinary needs for clothing, bedding and the storage of goods.

As trade developed, sales were controlled within the towns walls, by the Merchant Guild associations formed predominantly by overseas merchants who negotiated privileges with the King and Council. Guilds enabled their members to trade more effectively by fixing prices, preventing outside competition and compelling out of town traders to sell their goods through affiliated merchants. Joining became more exclusive, freemen who produced cloth in the 13th century, formed Craft Guilds to represent their own interests, and subdivided into the specialist groups of weavers, dyers, shearers and fullers.

11.3 Charter of the Guild of the Fullers and Shearmen Clothworkers' Company - London

These associations, while similar to the Merchant Guilds, focused on fraternities of craftsmen engaged in the same occupation who joined together and paid subscriptions. Like the Merchant Guilds, they established themselves in London and large provincial towns to serve their members. They regulated and restricted their membership to ensure standards of quality and that best practices in the production of cloth were maintained. They also assisted their members in difficult times. The London Guilds of the Fullers and Shearmen, who finished woven cloth merged in 1528 to form the Clothworkers Company, which still exists today as a philanthropic and charitable foundation.

There were three stages to becoming a fully fledged member of a craft guild. The first stage, on payment of a fee, was an apprenticeship to a master which lasted up to 9 years, during which time an apprentice received board and lodging but no wages. Apprentices were not allowed to marry until they became journeymen in the second stage. They were paid artisans and could remain so for their working life. During this time, the craftsman was expected to make and submit his '*masterpiece*' to his chosen guild for evaluation. It was not until the third stage, if accepted as a fully paid member, that he could set up his own workshop and employ his own apprentices and journeymen. However, while the craft guilds regulated the specialist skills of production, the wholesale and overseas

11.4 Pepys Window in the Clothworkers' Hall - Clothworkers' Company - London

commerce of the cloth trade in the 13th century remained under the control of the Merchant Guilds.

The beginning of a manufacturing evolution started with the introduction of the fulling mill, the change from vertical to horizontal looms, the development of spinning wheels and then, in 1337 while his army was preparing to invade Flanders, King Edward III, passed an act which directed that:

'... no English wool should be exported and that none should wear any cloth for the future but such as was made in England. That all cloth workers should be received from any foreign parts and fit places and privileges assigned to them.[5]*'*

In the large towns, the mills that had harnessed the power of water to drive grinding stones did not have spare capacity for fulling mills. The growing cloth market encouraged entrepreneurial initiatives and offered people new opportunities to accumulate wealth and status. Social mobility introduced by earlier legislation allowed individuals to buy and sell land, and the increasing regulatory control by both guild associations may have led journeymen to settle in unchartered market towns such as Frome and more rural areas where they could set up their own workshops. There was plenty of scope on the rivers and the manor and monastery landholders were keen to increase potential income from their estates. In the wake of the plague of the late 1340s, more land was turned over to pasture for sheep, labour was scarce and people migrated in search of work. The town guilds which were firmly established and commercially influential, became increasingly protectionist. As the demand for cloth increased, the '*putting out*' system evolved from the traditional working practices. Experience and knowledge was provided by skilled workers excluded or disaffected by guild policies. Cloth production did not cease in towns but was more efficient and cost effective in rural localities where there was land for buildings, water was plentiful and labour was cheaper.

Producing cloth was not enough, the goods had to be sold and the export market offered huge potential. The restrictive ordinances of the urban cloth guilds forbade the town weavers and fullers from having their cloth finished in the country. They also refused to allow the sale of rural cloth in the town markets, but in a similar way in which the wool market evolved, export and wholesale cloth trade shifted to London. It was promoted by the new merchant class which included the wool staplers, the merchant venturers, the mercers and the drapers. The merchants dealt increasingly with middlemen who could provide large quantities of cloth, rather than travelling to each region to negotiate with individual weavers, dyers and fullers. The clothiers fulfilled this role. They had acquired investment capital from their trades; from inherited money; or, borrowed from peers with a promise of a share in the profit. Clothiers bought and stored wool and arranged for its distribution to spinners and weavers before collecting it for fulling and finishing. They also arranged for the collection and storage of cloth made by others until there was sufficient to be transported for sale.

English textiles were divided into three main categories each with different properties, the worsteds or says from combed wool, the woollens from carded wool and a combination of the two such as the serges. The wool in the Wiltshire and Somerset border area was best suited to the production of woollens such as broadcloths and kersies. Broadcloth, a warm, heavy and hard wearing woollen was most profitable to be sold undyed for finishing abroad. It would take a weaver and his assistant about two weeks to produce a cloth that conformed to the assize of 27 yards long and up to 75 inches wide. Kersie or kersey may have been a generic word to describe a type of material that was woven in many regions on a four shaft narrow loom, possibly originating in the village of Kersey[6] in Suffolk. Kersey cloth was an important innovation of the 13th century made from a large gauge yarn which was spun from inferior grades of carded wool and woven in a twill pattern. One definition suggests that kersies may have been dyed, and that they were fulled as much as a broadcloth. Another suggests that they were used for hose as the material was almost self-supporting. In 1262, its manufacture was recorded in Andover[7] because it included Spanish wool which was considered to be of such poor quality that it would sully the reputation of English cloth.

> *'...It was decreed by Henry II in 1248, that if any man made cloth of Spanish wool, mixed with English, the principal magistrate aught to burn it.[8]'*

The regions of production were not static, declining in some areas and expanding into others, but overall, the West Country woollen cloth trade extended from Gloucestershire to Devon and from Hampshire to Somerset. While household cloth was still woven in the home, the putting out system offered earnings and underpinned commercial production. The broad loom on which the cloth was woven was operated at a faster rate by two weavers and a hierarchy of wealthy principal clothiers transformed production. Producers varied in size from individual cloth makers to large scale suppliers subcontracting work to numerous weavers. While early on they may simply have bought the finished cloth from home weavers, as they earned capital they invested in raw materials managing the entire chain of production and paying for piecework. Those who could afford to, built workshops attached to their dwellings to accommodate looms for apprentices and the employment of journeymen. In the last five years of the 14th century, the four counties of Dorset, Somerset, Wiltshire, Hampshire and the town of Bristol produced nearly 54% of England's cloth.[9]

> *'...All merchants may safely and securely go away from England, come to England, stay in and go through England, by land or by water, for buying and selling under right and ancient customs and without any evil exactions, except in time of war if they are from the land at war with us. And if such persons are found in our land at the beginning of a war, they shall be arrested without injury to their bodies or goods until we or our chief justice can ascertain how the merchants of our land who may then*

be found in the land at war with us are to be treated. And if our men are to be safe, the others shall be safe in our land.[10]'

From the mid 1300s, West Country cloth was exported from Bristol to Gascony, Spain and Ireland. Southampton shipped cloth to Italy and the Low Countries and considerable overland trade connected the two ports. The increase in the variety of cloth manufacture and the introduction of the concept of fashion offered further opportunities for new products to be sold overseas. The export merchants unlike the Merchants of the Staple were not bound to one specific company; on application of licenses, they had the liberty to discover new markets and buyers for their goods.

The Guild of Merchant Venturers started as loosely knit regional groups of merchants engaged in the overseas trade of commodities other than raw wool.[11] Bristol organised its formal fellowship around the mid 15th century. These Adventurers, granted licenses and privileges by the King, sailed to Norway, Spain, Prussia and the Netherlands. Bristol's merchants traded almost exclusively with Gascony, their exports in the 1200s were insignificant, but their imports from Bordeaux were far more important and, after wine, woad was the most frequently mentioned. By 1350, no longer amenable for export to be handled by foreigners, English merchants now controlled the majority of their own maritime trade, building and investing in ships; negotiating their own deals; and, sending kinsmen to act as agents instead of relying on foreign factors.

Shipments were organised as joint ventures between wealthy merchants, clothiers and ship masters. Risk was minimised by sailing in fleets and dividing the goods across the cargoes of several ships. Roger de Walton, esquire of Frome Selwood and also a Walter Crace are mentioned in the Gascony Rolls of 1401 and may have participated in these ventures. Until 1453 when Gascony was no longer under English rule, even small traders and individual cloth makers shipped single broadcloths and in return imported wine and woad.

From the late 14th century, London was known for the trade of cloth, not for its manufacture. The export market presented an ideal outlet for the cloth of country clothiers but they competed directly with the London

11.5 Mark of Thomas Horton - Westwood

drapers who petitioned for the sole right to deal with the exporters. Disputes were settled when the government intervened and established Blackwell Hall in 1398 as the sole outlet for the rural clothiers wholesale and overseas trades. The building which adjoined the Guildhall, in Basinghall Street, was built on the foundations of an older hall and served as the place for inspecting, taxing, storing and selling cloth. The Hall was rebuilt in 1558[12] as a *'new, strong and beautiful storehouse'*; it was divided into separate rooms each known as a hall; Devonshire, Gloucestershire, Kentish, Somerset and others, there were also large warehouses and assigned spaces and standings for each type of material such as woollens, worsteds, and later the medleys and the Spanish.

> *'...if any citizen, freeman, or stranger, within the said city, put any broadcloth to sale within the city of London, before it was brought to Blackwell Hall to be viewed and searched, so that it might appear saleable, and that 1d might be paid for hallage of every cloth.*[13]'

Searchers and aulnagers were appointed to examine the quality, collect tax and seal the cloth to confirm payment before any transactions were undertaken. Your reputation was your mark. Wax seals were attached to ensure that it was *'up to the mark'* of the legislated assize and two hundred years later these were cast in lead from a stone mould. All cloth was supposed to be inspected and if found defective was confiscated and the clothier or merchant fined. At times, both of these were neglected as it was impossible to inspect every cloth and the collection of subsidies was more important than the quality of the goods. Some of the larger cloth producing towns claimed exemptions from compliance to these rules, as both imported and domestic cloth were made on different looms and varied considerably from the regulation measures.

11.6 Cloth Seal - 2.2cm Diameter

Seals were a clothier's brand, their hallmark of quality, they could be sold as good will with the business or inherited by relatives. They were attached at various stages of manufacture, single lobed ones with symbols of madder bags may have been attached by the dyers. Two lobed seals included merchant and clothier marks or initials, some identified the weight and type of cloth. These were fastened by folding and pressing a sort of rivet into the opposite half. A 1535 statute required

11.7 1627 Two Lobe Seal - 1.5cm Diameter

> *'...every Clothier within the Realm shall weave, or cause to be woven, his or their several Token or Mark in all and every cloth, Kersey and other Cloths, whatsoever they be, made and wrought to be uttered and sold.*[14]*'*

The weaving of different coloured wool in the selvedges denoted the type of cloth and possibly identified the weavers.

While the majority of clothiers were undoubtedly honest, the evidence for the time rests with court records, litigation and petitions that highlight crime and dishonest practices. In 1390, it was pointed out that some west country clothiers had not only endangered the reputations, but even the lives of the merchants who bought their cloth for export. Their deceitful means had brought dishonour on the English name abroad. Cloth was easily stretched beyond the regulation length, it was carefully folded to hide any defects and powdered chalk rubbed on the surface that concealed thin weaving. A length of bad cloth was attached to one of superior quality or a whole cheap cloth substituted for a fine one when purchased around dusk when the light was low. Forgeries of clothier and aulnager seals were also quite common as they were easily replicated or fraudulently purchased and attached to the cloth without having it examined. By the 17th century, a four lobed seal with a ring on one end and lead protrusion on the other replaced earlier ones. The one

11.8 Four Lobe Seal
6.5cm Long

shown dates to the early 18th century, it may have been an aulnager's tax seal and was probably mass produced, one lobe showing the head of King George I (1714 - 1727) and the other a lion rampant and 2 ½, which could have been the amount of taxation or duty. The aulnagers duties for the regulation of wool[15] were abolished in 1699, but cloth inspections continued through the 18th century.

By the 15th century, there was a growing importance in English society of merchants specialising in foreign commerce. English merchants selling English woollens were the most substantial men of affairs in the country in 1454, when Parliament declared

> *'...the making of cloth within all parts of the realm is the greatest occupation and living of the poor common of the land.[16]'*

In 1470, Somerset was still the second largest producer after Suffolk, with the West Country producing most of the white broadcloths. The rural middlemen clothiers acquired wealth and prominence and where previously the wool merchants had held considerable sway over policy, it was now the turn of the clothiers and the Merchant Venturers.

Foreign merchants had dominated English maritime trade, but by the early 1500s native merchants controlled most import and export commerce. They established London and regional associations of private individuals to spread the financial costs of overseas trading. Merchants like Thomas Kytson of London, John Smythe and John Whitson of Bristol bought large quantities of white broadcloth along with other goods and were prepared to underwrite the considerable risks in the hope of profits to be gained by exploiting existing markets and establishing new ones. In their endeavour to dominate the market, Merchant Venturers complained that the foreign merchants of the Hanse took away their trade. In response, the crown gave monopoly charters to many of these companies to limit competition and to help them become established.

The majority of Parliament's economic bills of the 16th century related to the cloth industry. Standards were restrictive as sorts and grades of cloth could vary considerably. The clothiers sought changes to the cloth statutes of 1552 which stated that broadcloth should measure 63in wide

11.9 Blackwell Hall in 1812

by 26 to 28 yards long after fulling and weigh 44lbs. Competition between the town merchants and country clothiers producing and selling cloth resulted in the successful petition by the merchants of the Weavers Acts in 1555 which aimed to encourage the industry in corporate and market towns. The country trade was restricted to where it had been in place for ten years, the length of apprenticeship was extended to seven years and they were prohibited from having more than one loom or of hiring out looms. Conflict was never far beneath the surface as wealthy merchants and clothiers continually exerted their influence to revise or repeal earlier statutes, to secure exemptions from regulations and to protect their own interests. Neither was Blackwell Hall exempt as new regulations and ordinances governed most business practices. Rules required anyone who was not a Freeman of the City of London, such as the country clothiers, to pay fees to store, display and sell their cloth at a standing in the Hall. A bell announced sale times which were held weekly between noon on Thursday and noon on Saturday, sales outside of these times were forbidden, any infringements were subject to fines and confiscation of merchandise. Agents or factors acted increasingly on behalf of the clothiers, a post often held by younger sons, nephews and other relatives who moved to London or travelled to foreign ports settling abroad to establish and support the family business venture.

Overseas commerce brought about the development of bills of exchange. Clothiers sold their goods via the factor accruing a financial surplus in London to pay bills, this system became essential for the transfer of taxation funds to central government. In spite of the legal efforts to confine the clothier's trade to Blackwell Hall, a lot was sold by private contract, and carted directly to the merchant's house avoiding both taxation and storage costs.

The white broadcloth market started to decline around the middle of the 16th century. Foreign economic policies, religious persecution and war had led to the collapse of old markets such as Antwerp, but the cloth trade as a whole was steadily bolstered by newly discovered foreign markets which required cloth suitable to their climates. Heavy broadcloth produced in the South West was easily sold in the colder countries, but in the warmer regions it vied with the lighter weight materials produced on the continent. In this country, competition came in the form of the 'new draperies' which were introduced by the refugee Walloon, Fleming and Huguenot weavers who had settled in Norwich around the 1560s and brought with them improved skills in production and manufacture. These lighter cloths were made from Spanish merino wool with a compact weave, a soft drape and weighing far less than the woollens of this area. Further rivalry came from the fashionable English materials, such as stuffs, bays, says and perpetuanas.

By the end of the century, additional regulations had been imposed on the sale of woollen cloth. The Merchant Venturers required export licenses for cloth above a certain value so instead, they promoted the sale of cheaper ones. In an attempt to break their hold on the export trade, William Cockayne, an Alderman of London, persuaded the government to pass a law in 1614 to prohibit the export of white cloth to Flanders and to bring the finishing and dressing of broadcloths to the London cloth workers. These policies had major repercussions along with earlier currency reform, foreign trade embargoes, the start of the Thirty Years War, economic and social changes all contributed to the eventual ruin of the market for the white cloth trade. English cloth workers emigrated to Holland, Hamburg and other parts of Europe, and many small towns including Frome suffered severe economic depression.

By the 18th century, the West Country putting out system was widespread and the general trend was moving towards the development of factory systems by the entrepreneurial clothiers with money to invest in the new technologies. Ancillary buildings such as weaving sheds, dyeing and finishing workshops and storage were erected to house the equipment and workers on a single site under the superintendence of foremen. The clothier's house which had been built near the mill to oversee production became the manager's and grander ones were constructed in more prominent locations befitting the owner's new wealth and status.

---

1 Collingwood, R & Myers, J 1937: 239
2 Brunello, F 1973: 116
3 Beck,W 1882: 68
4 Magna Carta 1215
5 Beck, W 1882: 69
6 Kerridge, E 1985: 5
7 Kerridge, E 1985: 5
8 Beck, W 1882: 68
9 Hare, J 2004
10 Magna Carta 1215
11 Carus-Wilson, E 1967: xxix
12 Stow, J 1603: 289
13 Statute 8&9 W.3.c.9.s.1
14 Henry VIII c12 c13
15 Smith, J 1647:-
16 Rotuli Parliamentorum, v, 274

CHAPTER 12

THE WHITE CLOTH TRADE

Bought of Leonard Shawler by the handes of William Baxter of Fromesellwood, 6th October 1536

Item: 15 Whites of his Best Mayking
Item: 10 Whites of his Second Mayking

Thomas Kytson Boke of Remembraunce

Perhaps one of the most important river valleys, situated south east of Bristol, was that of the Frome. The visitor who wanders along its deserted banks today would not at first think it was once one of the main industrial areas in England, but the evidence remains in the weirs and mill streams that were built to drive the undershot fulling mills until the late 18th century.[1]

12.1 1897 Frome Jubilee Procession - Two Shaft Narrow Loom possibly Adapted from a Broadloom

12.2 The Town Mill Wheel - Frome

A ban on the export of English wool in 1337 had considerably reduced the supply available to the Flemish merchants for their growing cloth market. In this area, the surplus wool was used to develop a new commodity, that of the white unfinished broadcloth, much of which was made in Frome. Many factors contributed to the development of this trade, not least the town and surrounding villages proximity to the overland trade route between the ports of Bristol and Southampton. Until 1350, West Country cloth production was primarily concentrated in Bristol, Bath and Wells. Of the monks at Bath Abbey, a writer mentions:

> *'...that the shuttle and the loom employed their attention about the middle of the 14th century and under their active auspices the weaving of woollen cloth which made its appearance in England about the year 1330, and received the sanction of an Act of Parliament in 1337 was introduced, established and brought to such perfection at Bath as rendered this city one of the most considerable in the West of England manufacture.[2]'*

Local cloth manufacture was becoming established, there was the fulling mill in Rodden in 1333 and one in Frome by 1349. The Wiltshire and Somerset downland sheep produced a medium grade wool that was well suited to weaving a good, thick cloth. The town merchants, notably John

12.3 1533 Official Copy of a Record of the Court of Common Pleas for Land, 40 Messuages, 4 Mills and 2 Dyehouses in the Manors of Flyntford and Rodden

Le Pew, John Le March and Stephen Wynslade traded considerable quantities of wool which supplied the rural producers with an eye on the foreign market. The few records of taxation and customs accounts indicate that there must have been many successful transactions, but other documents, witnessed by the authorities, attest to the default on payments.

The merchants dealing in the wool trade who were already established in Frome and its hinterland by the early 14th century, had the foresight and ambition to invest in cloth production for the domestic market and the nascent export trade. Landowners saw the potential for income with another manorial monopoly as broadcloth could not have been made as efficiently without the introduction of the fulling mill. In addition to new legislation, the consistently low price of wool from the 1380s helped the development of the English cloth industry and by the late 1300s it had reached to Frome.[3] A survey of the town in 1392 mentions the rack fields[4] for cloth tentering together with five fulling mills. The weavers of Stroud, Frome, Totnes and Exeter provided sheep farmers with local markets for wool and the availability of a rural workforce of tenant farm workers supported the region's textile industry.

There are three samples of fine early English broadcloth, although their provenance is unknown, fixed to a letter dated 1458, preserved in the archives of the Haute Garonne concerning a business transaction between two French merchants. The samples, attached to the document are fastened with blue string, are coloured *'light Bordeaux'* just under ¾ of an inch by 2 inches. Each was dyed with madder and traces of indigo, probably from woad.[5] These may have originally been undyed white cloths from this area.

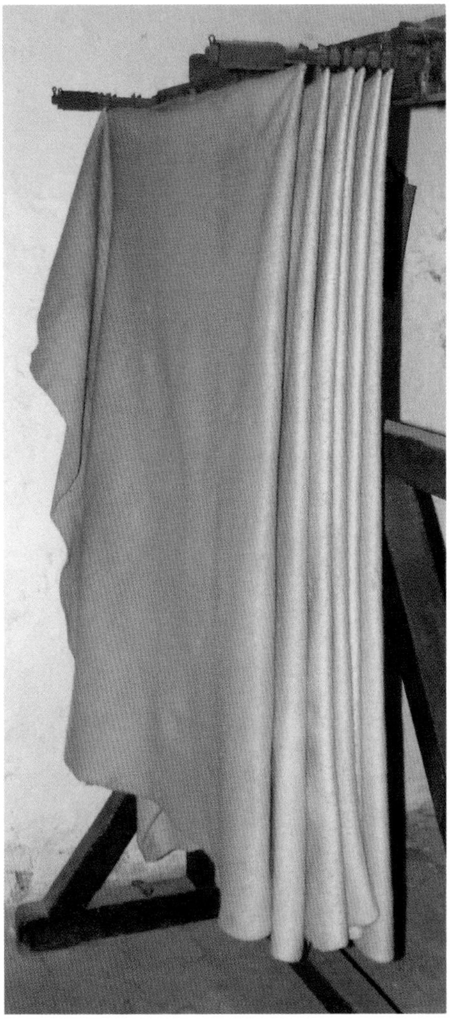

12.4 Undyed Broadcloth

Successful commercial products required the manufacture to be of a good standard and the marketing and distribution to be effective and reliable. The white undyed broadcloth was produced in large quantities in this area from the 14th until the 17th century. The trade had declined by the mid 1700s. The wool for its production was purchased from a wide area. John Le Pew and Richard Weston purchased a wool clip in 1341 and 1342 from the Deverill Manors which were part of the Glastonbury Abbey land holdings in Damerham[6]. The Glastonbury accounts were annotated in 1342-1344 that John Park stood surety for John le Pew when he bought more of the Deverill wool than he could afford, and he later defaulted on the payment.[7] In 1360, John le March owed £48 16s for wool bought from Walter de Frampton,[8] a Bristol merchant and others owed debts for wool purchased at the Bristol Staple. Perhaps, if business circumstances had been more favourable, Stephen Wynslade, Lord of Frome Manor may have been considered one of the great wool merchants. Instead in 1365, to settle his debts of more than £2000, his lands were seized by Edward Cheyne, the Sheriff of Somerset.

> *'...Stephen has at La Falaise (Vallis) a messuage and a garden worth 20s a year after expenses, 50 acres of arable in one close, 5 acres of arable in Langcroft, 66 acres of arable in the common West Field, 8 acres in the common Old Field, 13 acres in Inhouke in several, 34½ acres of meadow, mown in alternate years, 6½ acres of meadow in Langmede mowable in alternate years, 6½ acres of meadow in Inhouke, a close, 4 pastures, 300 acres of wood in Selwood Forest, the whole worth £16 10s. 7d.; annual rents worth £24; the pleas and perquisites of the court of the Hundred of Frome the profits of the market and fairs worth £20. Annual payments of £4 7s. Total nett annual value of the estate: £46 3s 7d.*[9]'

The cloth for the wholesale and retail domestic trade was sold at fairs and markets, but there is very little information other than the dates of Frome's charters. The town's annual fairs may have been as important as that of Pensford, which in 1395/6 was the largest cloth market in Somerset. Its clothiers were responsible for an average of 83 dozens, equivalent in length to half a broadcloth, a figure only surpassed by

12.5 The George Inn - Norton St Philip

Frome with 117.[10] The aulnage taxation accounts of the same years show that the combined area of Frome, Beckington, Rode and Mells produced 26.6% of the cloth by far the highest proportion for the county.[11] Despite some duplication and inaccuracy in these reports, by the end of the century, Somerset was still the most important cloth producing county.[12]

Annual fairs at the George Inn in Norton St Philip provided an outlet for locally produced broadcloth and dyed kersies. The inn was built by the Carthusian monks as a hostel for merchants travelling to the fairs, some of the oldest parts of the building date back to the late 14th century. In 1255 a charter was granted to the prior and convent of Henton for the right to hold a fair on the 30th April, and the 1st and 2nd of May. A revision in 1353 extended it to a five days with the 28th of April designated as a wholesale fair. From an inquiry in 1595, John Flower deposed that he had known:

> *'...Two wholesale fayers yerely to have ben kept at Philipps Norton...for the sale of lynnen and wollen clothe by the packe, fardell, ballett and other parcells with one three cleare dayes befor Philipp and Jacobes daye*

12.6 Courtyard of the George Inn

12.7 Gallery of the George Inn

and the other about a weeke after St Bartholomews day...[13]'

There were further discrepancies for the actual fair dates in the numerous almanacs that were published from the 1660s.

The 16th and 17th century Norton fairs were primarily for cloth and sheep. They were held in a field below the George called Fair Field. Trading was governed by statutes, after the dissolution, the rights to stallage, pickage, perquisites and profits previously collected by the monasteries, were farmed out in return for an annual rent. The holder of the fair rented the land on which it was held and was allowed to have access a few days either side for the erection and dismantling of standings, booths and pens for livestock. He held franchises to provide weighing beams and scales. Traders travelling long distances to the event could store cloth, for a fee, in the upper galleries of the George.[14] Another building, now the dining room was purpose built around 1457/8 for the storage of goods. The use of a hoist must have been necessary as Elizabethan statutes decreed that a fine broadcloth could weigh between 64 and 68lbs. Each cloth was folded into lengths just over five foot long and wrapped in packs of 10, the total weighing around 700lbs.

Bailiffs collected the tolls at the gate and the cloths could not be sold until the clothier had paid his tax and the aulnager had affixed his seal, but how many dyed kersies and white cloths from the local area were sold at these fairs is unknown. Buyers and sellers came from a wide catchment area, John Compton and others would have carried out their business at the Norton fairs and John Smythe, a Bristol export merchant attended regularly. In the early 18th century the fairs were managed by the Hardings who kept notebooks, most of which relate to the wholesale fair. There were two ledgers one held by young John Harding for the clothiers who sold the medleys, Spanish and other woollens, the other by his uncle Thomas for the broad clothiers who sold the traditional fine quality broadcloths. For the fairs held on 27th April, between 1708 and 1728 there were on average 184 clothiers whose stalls were arranged in eight ranks and 50 – 70 broad clothiers who occupied another three ranks.[15] Disputes arose in 1728 as some traders set up their stands in the street outside the allocated grounds and refused to pay the fees. Market bailiffs were summoned but the arguments escalated. In the following years trade rivalry contributed to considerable poaching of business and the fairs eventually declined around the 1760s.

12.8 1505 Brass Memorial John Compton and his wife St George's Church - Beckington

Frome was also well placed to supply the white cloth trade for export to foreign markets and much of it was carted to London's Blackwell Hall. There is evidence of the prosperity of a few town clothiers and also of their debts. In 1392 Henry Dunkerton, a merchant, had *'rekks'* (racks) for drying cloth *'next the churchyard on one side and on 18 acres of land once of Peuerell on the hill.*[16]*'* The will of John Cabell, by all accounts an affluent Frome gentleman, was proved in 1408, he left most of his possessions to his wife and two daughters Lucy and Dionysia. He also bequeathed '... *a blue gown furred to Sir John Grene, Chaplain.*[17]'

I have already mentioned the Craas family, Flemish or French immigrants; and, there may have been others whose names have long since been anglicised. While merchants had settled in the town and surrounding villages their dealings took them to London, Bristol, Salisbury, Southampton and abroad. A Venetian merchant John Manwyche, of Italian origin, living in London, bought 450 cloths from John Gawter of Beckington in 1442 for export to Venice; and probable re-export to the Middle East.[18] In 1437, Henry Wayfere son and heir of Robert Wafer of Rodden paid a £10 bond for three pieces of land to Thomas Herryes a Frome weaver.[19] This may have been for racks near to the Rodden fulling mill. John Wayffer, perhaps a relative, was mentioned in litigation as the third party involved in a debt recovery suit started in 1504 involving the Hanseatic merchants.

> *'...Piers Starke, a citizen and draper of London and Lutkyn Buryngm a merchant of Almain, abiding among the Esterlyngs in the Steel Yard failed to transfer a bond of John Wayffer, of Frome Selwood, tendered in part payment for cloth.[20]'*

It is not surprising that John Leyland on his visit to Frome in the 16th century mentions the '*...fayre stone howsys...*' that were built on the proceeds of the cloth trade. As well as importing woad and oil, the wealthy London Merchant Adventurer, Thomas Kytson dealt extensively in the white cloth trade. His 'Boke of Remembraunce' listing his accounts showed that his main supplier was John Clevelod and later John Gastard the Elder, both were from Beckington. In the 1530's he bought in excess of three thousand cloths from John Clevelod as well as purchasing from producers in Frome. John Thycke, Lewes Andley and Richard Cook could all supply him with cloth in packs of ten and probably supplied other merchants as well. Each had their own cloth marks but he only recorded those of new suppliers. In 1536, he purchased 15 whites of his best 'maykyng' at £28 the pack for a total of £42 and 10 whites of his second 'maykyng' at £24 10s from Leonard Shawler of Frome. The cloths supplied by Leonard were listed as '*under the hand of William Baxter*', suggesting that he was a clothier putting out work to several others. He also had a note

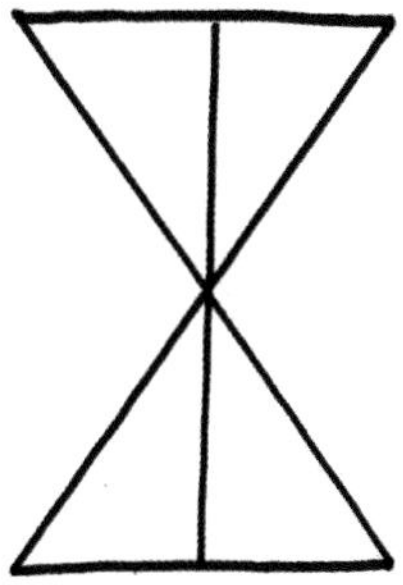

blew

12.9 Cloth Mark of Leonard Shawler

'...to deliver five more cloths of his best maykyng and a rebate for a fawtie clothe.[21]*'*

Thomas Kytson traded directly with his suppliers, paying for transactions in cash and extended credit at high interest rates. He bypassed Blackwell Hall arranging for the transport of goods directly to his warehouses and from there they were loaded in the cargoes of several ships and sent abroad to his factors at the four main annual cloth markets in Flanders. For the return voyages they organised the purchase of dyestuffs, oil and other goods.

John Clevelod may have been related to William Clevelod who held the lease of Stowford mill in 1500. When he died in 1537, John bequeathed a granary and a fulling mill in Beckington to his daughter Mary and also his cloth seal if his wife remarried, as Mary was to carry on the business. He left the execution of his will to be overseen by Thomas Kytson.

Other local families involved in the white cloth trade, have left their mark. In 1524 William Jordan of Keyford left *'to each weaver of mine 4d,*[22]*'* and in 1558, Richard Suddon of Tytherington bequeathed to his son Richard, amongst other things,

'...one kersey loom, a warping bar, a skyrne, a board and my silver buttins'. He also left *'...unto the almeshouse of Froome Selwoode 50 shillings to be paid to the use and behouse of the poore.*[23]*'*

The Webbs were amongst the most prosperous of the great clothier families.[24] Thomas Webb, a merchant of Beckington died in 1585. He once owned Clifford's mill and had bought property from John Compton's estate. His son Robert was clothier to Queen Elizabeth in 1596. Thomas Webbe, perhaps another son, was a fuller in Frome who leased a mill in 1594 from Edward Horton, Gent of Westward. The Horton family, originally from Lullington, were well known clothiers in Bradford on Avon and Trowbridge.

12.10 Cloth Mark of Thomas Webb

Thomas Yerbury, another Bradford on Avon clothier, stipulated in his will of 1611 that:

12.11 Westwood Manor - Remodelled by Thomas Horton

'...my wife shall use my cloth mark which now I use for as long as by the Judgement of my Overseers she shall continue her cloth making in that credit as now carrieth; and after her decease or discredit of the mark the same shall remain to my son Gyfford with an alteration to the first letter of his Christian name instead of the first letter of my name and also if my wife discontinue cloth making or discredit my mark then my

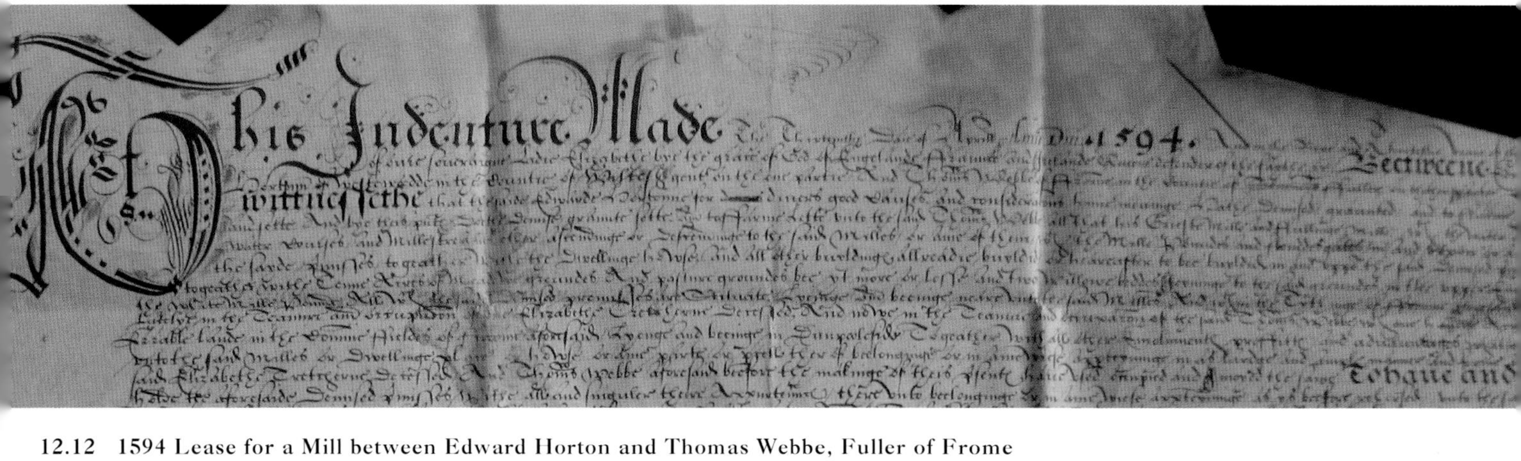

This Indenture Made ... 1594 ... Betweene

Witnesseth

To have and

12.12 1594 Lease for a Mill between Edward Horton and Thomas Webbe, Fuller of Frome

12.13 Elizabethan Cottages at Gorehedge

> *brother in law William Webb shall uphold my mark until my son William shall be of the age of 21.*[25]'

A fine balance was needed between the production and price of wool and the grain required to feed the growing population. On May 5, 1549 about 200 weavers, tinkers, and artisans from the area destroyed local enclosures.[26] At the time, Frome had a population of less than three thousand. The considerable number of weavers involved in the riot indicated that at least a third of the population was probably engaged in textile manufacture. A few years later in 1576, in response to the Weaver's Act, Peter Blackborough of Frome, described as a notorious mischief maker, denounced his fellow clothiers whom he believed were breaking the law imposed on the country clothiers that restricted the hiring of apprentices and looms.[27] The clothiers continuously submitted petitions and eventually the government could not risk the unemployment which would have followed and the clothiers of Somerset, Wiltshire and Gloucestershire were exempted.

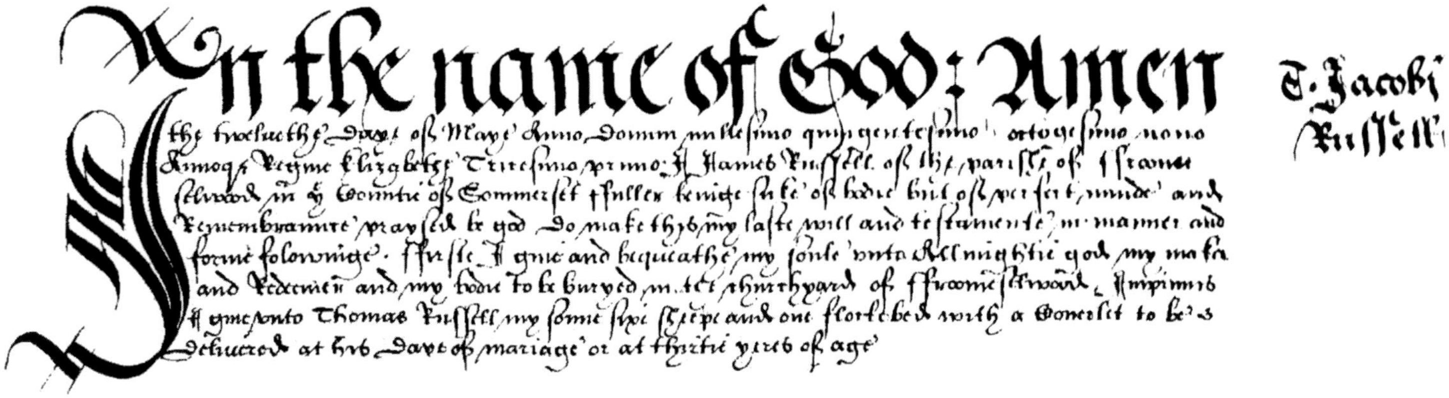
In the name of God: Amen
T. Jacobi Russell

12.13 1590 Will of Jacob Russell, Fuller of Frome, Bequeathed Sheep to his Children

The fortunes of this area were bound closely with the white undyed cloth trade, as the 'new draperies' became fashionable, the demand for West of England whites declined. The clothiers trade rivalry with the London Merchant Adventurers deepened and foreign competition brought about difficult times for Frome and the local area. In response to the crisis, the South West clothiers paid less to their weavers, spinners and shearers with predictable agitation, riots and grinding poverty.

[1] Ponting, K 1957: 26
[2] Beck, S 1882: 372
[3] www.sanhs.org/Documents/147/Hare of SANHS-147.pdf John Hare article on Pensford
[4] Rogers, K 1985: 18
[5] Harte, N & Ponting, K 1983: 123
[6] Farmer, D 1989; -
[7] Thirsk, J 1985: Vol 3 401
[8] TNA C241/144/134
[9] TNA C131/19/8
[10] Hare, J 2004: 174
[11] Hare, J 2004: 176
[12] Hare, J 2004: 173
[13] Brett, C 2002:-
[14] Pamphlet - The George Inn Norton St Phillip Devizes Wadworth 1999
[15] Brett, C 1999: 176
[16] McGarvie, M 2003: 54
[17] Weaver, F.W. 1905: 34
[18] Hicks, M 2015: Ch 7
[19] SHC T\PH\pls/1/17
[20] TNA C/1/357/65
[21] Brett, C 1999: 42
[22] TNA Prob 11/21/476
[23] TNA Prob 11/73/393
[24] McGarvie, M Pamphlet on Beckington Church
[25] TNA Prob 11/119/427
[26] Wood, A 2007: 58
www.history of parliament on-line.org/vol/1558 -1603/member/moore-jaspe

CHAPTER 13

THE FINE CLOTH TRADE

'... glad to know what blues you have under hand. I wish you had never made a medley. I wish you had continued in the Blue Trade entirely and made about six cloths per week, we always had a sure trade. Pray make one hundred good blues immediately or we shall lose our Blue Trade'

Mr Jonathan Noad - February 1765

The impact of the Cockayne bill had long term catastrophic consequences for the South West white trade. While it did not affect the ability of the clothiers to have cloth manufactured, the merchants export trade agreements with the Low Countries had collapsed. The new draperies were increasingly fashionable as they offered an alternative to the locally made woollens but a general economic depression continued throughout the first quarter of the 17th century. The vicar of Frome sent a petition on behalf of the inhabitants of the parish to the King and Council

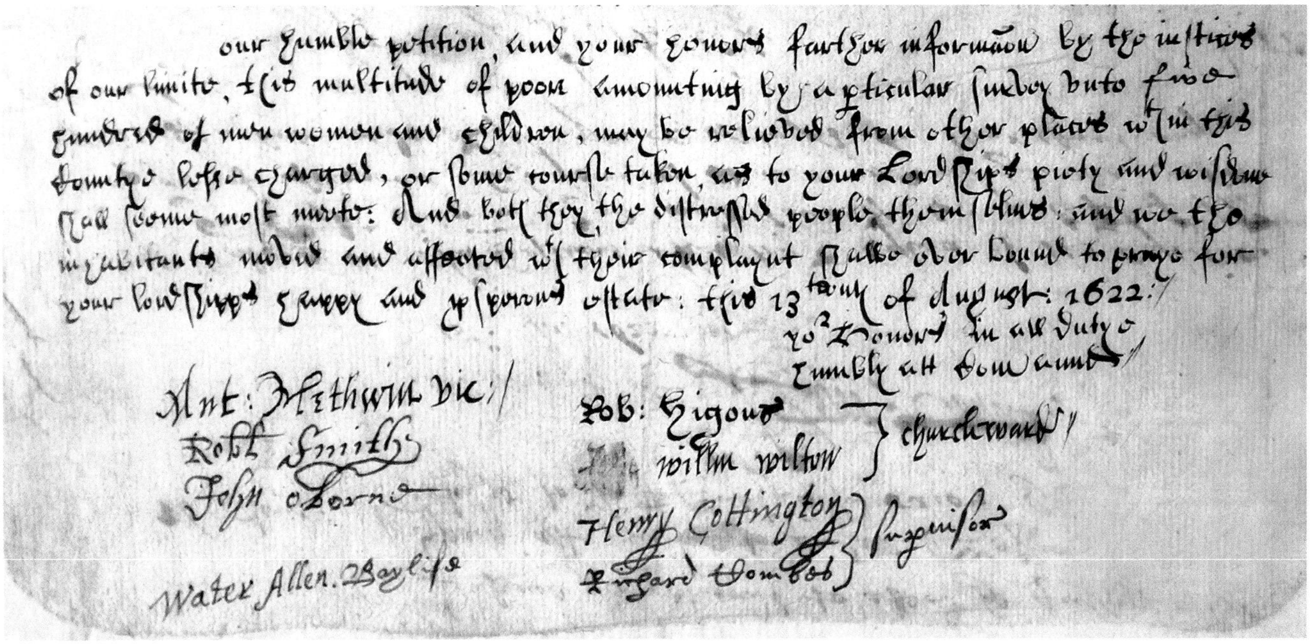
our humble petition, and your honors further informacon by the instance
of our Vicar, this multitude of poor amounting by a pticular survey unto five
hundreds of men women and children, may be relieved from other places wthin this
Countye before charged, or some course taken, as to your Lordships piety and wisdome
shall seeme most meete: And both they the distressed people themselves and we the
inhabitants moved and affected wth their complaynt shalbe ever bound to praye for
your Lordships honor and prosperous estate: this 13th day of August: 1622.
Yor honors in all dutye
humbly att Comaundt
Ant: Methwin vic:
Robt Smithe
John Osborne
Water Allen. Baylife
Rob: Higons
willm Wilton } Churchwards
Henry Cottington
Richard Thombes } Supervisor

13.2 1622 Petition from the Vicar of Frome

concerning the number of poor in the parish due to the decline of the clothing trade.[1]

An incident reported in the Taunton Quarter Sessions of 1612/3:

> '*...On July 12th last past a fire had happined in the house of one Joan Wilcox, widow and Thomas Wilcox of Barkley, Broodweaver, burning down the dwelling house and houses of the said Thomas and also the shop and working houses and therein also burned three broadweavers lomes and one kersey lome...Doe nowe therefore desire your Charitable Relief and Benevolence for the better helping of the said Joan and Thomas.*[2]'

Thomas had fallen and was injured while rescuing his broadcloths. A relief payment of £5.00 was approved.

New materials were desperately needed to revive the local industry, but how to compete in the development of different sorts of cloth, the discovery of new markets and the renewal of trade agreements? With the collapse of the white trade, all cloth for export now had to be dyed and finished, and the local clothiers were not about to lose work to the London guild of clothworkers. The coloured cloth trade arose in part

13.3 S. Rawlings & Son Ltd - Frome

from the availability of a good Spanish merino wool and improvements in the making of hand tools which refined its production. This was not the introduction of machinery but the small modifications in carding, spinning and finishing methods as all cloth was made entirely by hand. By the mid 17th century, Frome had become an important centre for the manufacture of woollen cards which gave employment to hundreds of workers. Samuel Rawlings established his carding firm which later diversified into leather belt manufacture and continued in production until 1972. As part of the 1897 royal jubilee celebrations in Frome, the firm sponsored parade floats depicting scenes of handweaving as it was a hundred years previously as well as the newest mechanical innovations of the period.

Over the centuries, industrial espionage had revealed competitive trade secrets, skilled men had found work further afield while some younger ones were apprenticed abroad, and many returned with new ideas, materials and working methods. In the mid 1500s, Benedict Webb of Kingswood, formerly in Wiltshire now part of Gloucestershire, had been apprenticed to a French merchant.

13.4 1897 Jubilee Procession - Pirn Winding

On his return around 1580, he introduced an alternative cloth to the Taunton weavers which was later produced in Shepton Mallet and Frome. The '*Spanish Cloth*' was predominantly woven from English mixed with Spanish merino wool which competed favourably with the lighter weight ones of East Anglia. This new trade may have contributed to the wealth of Robert Smith, the Frome clothier who died in 1625 who bequeathed:

> *'...to every one of my weavers twelve pence apiece and to every one of my spinners six pence apiece.*[3]'

The 1600s were a period of experimentation, the introduction of untried dyes shipped from the New World and elsewhere provided the clothiers and dyers with challenges and opportunities. Animal husbandry had influenced the balance of meat and wool production. Sheep on the pastures grew a moderately fine fleece, the wool of those in enclosures was coarser leaving an insufficient supply of good English wool to meet the demand for this area's cloth industry. The clothiers had to find other sources. Spain was producing a high quality, short staple, soft merino wool that could be spun into a very fine gauge yarn. From the 1630s onwards, the large scale buying of Spanish wool was organised by the collaboration of Spanish and English merchants resident in Bilbao.[4]

Considerable working capital was provided by the Blackwell Hall factors who supported the Spanish traders skilled in sorting and assessing the wool quality which was sold for profit to the clothiers. Wool was also available from the fellmongers of Bermondsey, it was bought by the London factors from the wool staplers at Southwark and carted on the return journeys by carriers who had transported the cloth to Blackwell Hall. Frome had its own fellmongers, one was rated for a tenement on the bridge which had cellars and stone vessels from where it would have been easy to dispose of the waste.

Washing bridges were also erected along the river, Mary Halliday mentions that one of hers was thatch covered and destroyed when her property was burgled. The yarn merchants bought Lincoln wool which was mixed with Spanish then spun and sold at local markets and there were many small independent suppliers. This may not have been used much in this area unless it was dyed in the skein or the woven cloth dyed in the say. Several entries in the letter books of James Elderton entreated his clothiers:

> *'... Pray for God's sake if you buy your wool at Bristol, do pray buy the best, for if the wool is coarse, cloth will never handle fine or look well or sell for the best price.' Feb 2nd 1764.*[5]

Frequent skirmishes during the Civil War had prevented the South West clothiers transporting their cloths to London for export, however the manufacture of 'Spanish Cloth' had succeeded in spreading to the local area and by 1650 the towns of Bradford on Avon, Frome and Trowbridge were the main centres for the new industry. In the 1630s, John Ashe of Freshford had invited Dutch artisans to settle in the area so they could teach their improved methods of spinning and carding. He then introduced a second generation of cloth made entirely from Spanish wool which was carefully pressed to give it a sheen. He commented that

> *'...the art of spinning was so much improved within these past 40 years that one pound of wool makes twice as much cloth as it did before the Civil War.*[6]*'*

Some of the lighter weight broadcloths were still sold white and undressed but most were now *'dyed in the wool'*. The famous West of England medley was one of the most successful of the woollens. This type of cloth, favoured from the 15th to the 19th centuries had two definitions. The early one

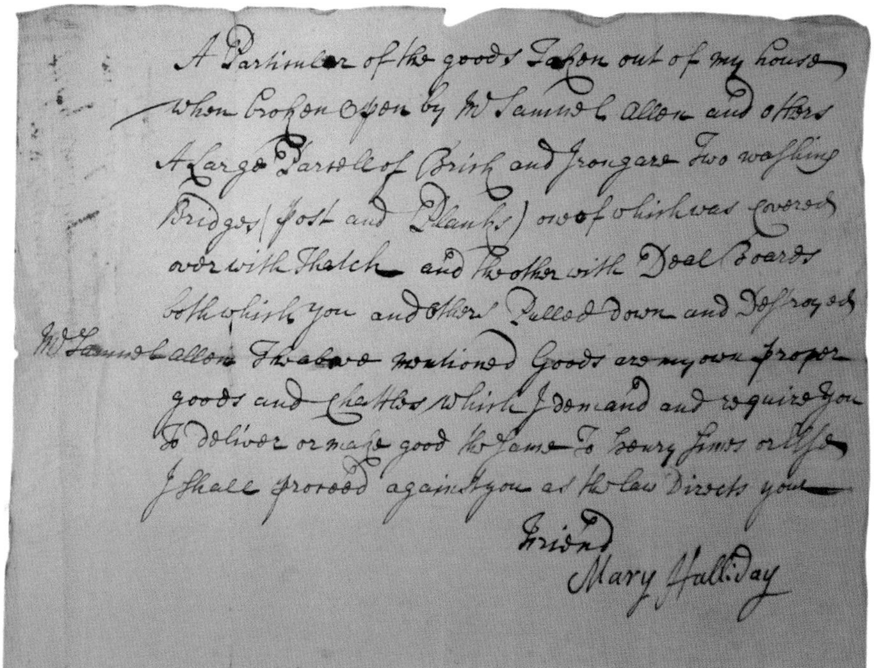
A Particular of the goods taken out of my house
When broken open by Mr Samuel Allen and others
A Large Parcell of Brick and Irongare Two washing
Bridges (Post and Planks) one of which was covered
over with Thatch and the other with Deal Boards
both which you and others Pulled down and Destroyed
Mr Samuel Allen The above mentioned Goods are my own proper
goods and Chattles which I demand and require you
To deliver or make good the Same To [illegible] Times or else
I shall proceed against you as the law Directs your
Friend
Mary Halliday

13.5 M Halliday Letter Concerning the Destruction of Washing Bridges

described it as any cloth made of mixed fibres and the other from the 17th century:

> '...*Medley is a cloth of mingled colours introduced around 1614 which ascribes its invention to the following; The States General of the United Netherlands having issued a placart, prohibiting the importation of any English woollen cloth that was dyed in the cloth, because it prevented their further manufacturing of our cloths by dyeing and dressing them as formerly, upon pain of confiscation of the goods and of 25 guilders per cloth besides. Whereupon the English clothier's ingeniously discovered the art of making of mixtures dyed in the wool rather than lose all the advantages of dyeing and dressing. This has ever since got the appellation of Medley cloth.*[7]'

13.6 Coloured Selvedge Cloth Fulled until the Plain Weave Obscured

At the time, its manufacture required two weavers and one spooler, two breakers, six spinners, one fuller and burler, one shearman, one parter and picker.[8] A common coarse medley cloth of 32 yards would take about ninety pounds of wool and once the first cloth was woven all other work overlapped reducing the total time of production from two months for the first cloth to three weeks for all subsequent ones. The best medleys were woven from a Spanish wool weft and an English wool warp[9] and commanded a good price. When thoroughly dyed in the wool, spun, and woven (a ratio of 40 warp threads per inch to 60 weft picks) the finished broadcloth was an attractively coloured medley with distinctive narrow selvedges.[10]

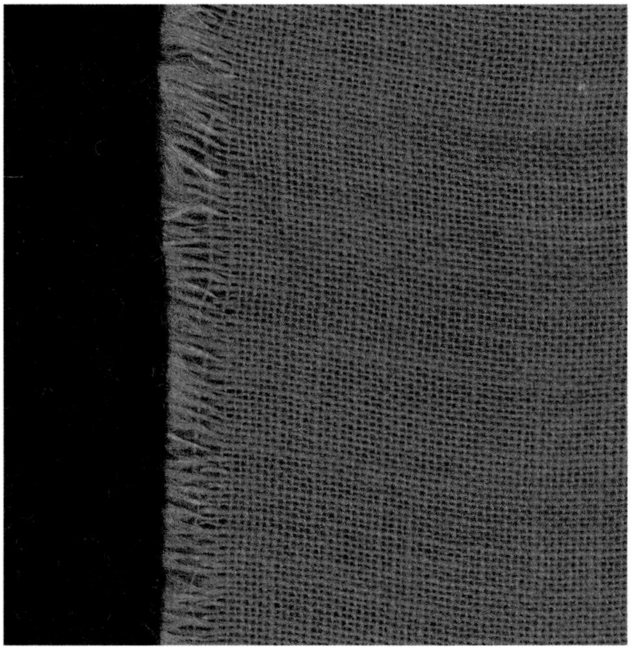

13.7 Cloth Dyed in the Say

From the mid 1660s onwards, against a backdrop of economic upheaval and food shortages, the government policies of the

Restoration once again encouraged woollen manufacture. In an attempt to protect the woollen trade, Charles II brought in the 'Burial in Woollen Acts of 1667' which lasted for more than a hundred years. The dead were to be buried in pure English woollen shrouds with a sworn affidavit marked in the parish records.

13.8 Scribbled Wool for Medley Cloth

In 1674, William Brewer of Lullington contributed to the knowledge of dyeing and finishing cloth, when he employed thirty two Dutch workers to teach the art of dressing Spanish cloth in the Netherlands fashion. His alternative to dyeing in the wool was '*dyeing in the say*' when the cloth was first taken from the loom. It was washed just enough to remove the oils and size used in spinning and weaving before being dyed. The practice of say dyeing was viewed with suspicion as it was suggested that it was a poor imitation of a '*dyed in the wool*' as the dye did not fully penetrate the fibres but sat on the surface of the cloth. However, imitations were cheaper to manufacture and purchase. The Brewers later moved to Trowbridge where they developed a very successful cloth business. A few chose a more fraudulent approach to earning a living as described in a case presided over by George Horner, J.P. in 1697;

> *'...Evidence given by Stephen Meade of Calne, Wiltshire, serge dresser, in which he states that Benjamin Fry of Frome came to work for him in Calne and when Meade said that he wanted money to buy seals, Fry taught him how to use a hole in a chalk stone to make impressions. Fry also offered to teach him to make counterfeit coins.'*

Despite trade disruptions, many Frome clothiers became affluent, Robert Smith the Younger built on his father's legacy of land and wealth. His inventory of 1661 included broadcloth of both '*mixt*' makes and of white makes.

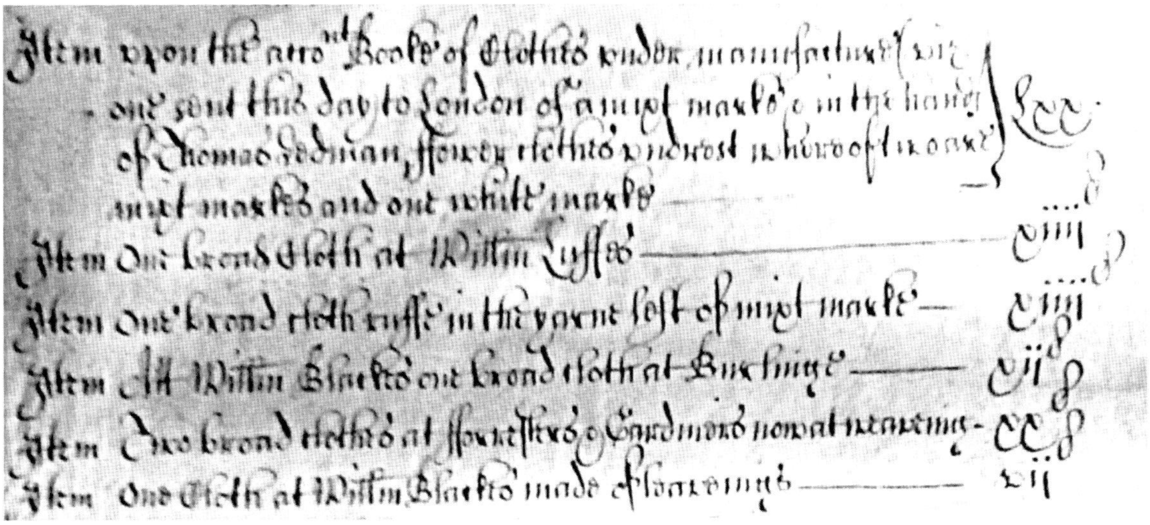

13.9 1661 Robert Smith Inventory

The cloth production in Frome and the surrounding area flourished until the mid 18th century. The manufacture of English cloth was now of as high a standard as that produced by the Dutch. John Coward of Frome went to Italy in the early 1700s to share his own knowledge and introduced the true making of an English cloth *'al vero uso Inglese'* into Piedmont and the French started producing *'Draps de Londres.*[11]' The last decades of the century, while still profitable, fluctuated between periods of high and low demand as competition was never far behind.

According to Collinson, by 1740 about 160,000 yards of cloth were made each year in Frome and the surrounding area, which required 1450 packs of wool.[12] The improved methods of scribbling, carding, spinning and finishing of English and Spanish wools produced a highly esteemed West Country woollen cloth of various grades from lightweight to heavy overcoating. These included the *'Best Superfine'* using the finest grades of wool, the *'Superfine'*, the *'Best Super'*, the *'Super'*, the beaver cloth which was milled to such an extent that it was almost waterproof. There were also the fine and low Spanish cloths and many coarse ones. Lower grade woollens such as the '*Second*s' were used for liveries, some of those, made from wool, included the *'whipcords'* which were hard twisted twills for uniforms along with the finely napped twill dress fabrics with a smooth finish.

13.10 A Jenkins Inventory

An Inventory

Of the Estate & Effects of the late Mr. Amos Jenkins,
Of Frome Selwood in the County of Somerset, deceased.
Taken the 7th day of May 1789, by

A. Crocker

Cash in house and Wearing Apparel.

One Tenement or Dwelling house, in Button Street with outhouses and a Garden adjoining —

2 pieces of Pasture land.

Messuage or Dwelling house in Trooper street.

Kitchen grate, Ash pit grate, Fire pan poker & tongs incl. of the Widow

~~[illegible]~~

~~[illegible]~~ See further on

Cloth,

In the Cloth chamber

Nos.		Yards
6131	Superfine	28
6133	Do.	14¼
3534	Do.	1¼
3190	Do.	6¼
6095	Do.	13¼
6095	Do. do.	3½
6089	Super.	1½
	Do. Sand Coloured	1
4062	Do.	3¾
6119	Do.	9
3524	Do.	11½
3226	Do.	2½
	Do. Blue	½
3483	—	4½
	Do. —	2
3454	Do.	8
3290	Do.	2
3796	Do.	1¼
3555	Do.	1½
3453	Do.	1¼
	Do.	1½
	Do. do.	6 nails
3522	Yds.	18

Most of these materials were broadcloths, but some superfines may have been narrow ones such as the cassimere which was a lightweight woollen twill fabric produced in this area that had been patented in 1766 by Francis Yerbury of Bradford on Avon.

> *'...A new method of making thin superfine cloth for the summer season at home, and for warmer climates abroad, yet notwithstanding the thinness of its texture it is more durable than cloth of a greater substance made in the common way.*[13]'

The superfine cassimere in white and buff was used for military dress breeches and mixtures of greys and blues for pantaloons. Various drab shades were popular for civilian day wear, white and black for formal dress. The wool was either all Spanish or mixed with English, the thread was drawn out to a much finer yarn with both warp and weft twisted in the same direction, it was then woven with an evenly balanced number of warps to weft rows. The handle was soft and the finishing was '*...smartly grounded at the fulling by a quick motion*', but insufficient to obscure the weave. A slight nap could be raised followed by a shearing to give a clean finish. These cloths were produced in several weights and this patent gave the woollen cloth industry the basis for the greater expansion into different types of fabrics which have been made to the present day.[14] Their names may later have been changed to the meltons, doeskins and gabardines for the fashionable swallow tail coats and breeches.

13.11 Coloured Broadcloth

The 1793 Universal Directory suggested that in the early 1700s seven wagons at a time left Frome laden with bales of cloth for London's

Blackwell Hall. The clothiers of Mells and other nearby villages brought in their goods and from here they were dispatched to town. Each wagon carried 140 bolts of cloth valued at £14.00 the piece. Such a train carrying about £700,000 worth of cloth a year was no inconsiderable traffic.[15] According to Julia de Lacy Mann 'It is improbable but not inconceivable that 980 cloths may have been sent to London in one week in exceptionally busy times as cloths were saved up for fairs, but it is unlikely that the value of cloth made in Frome and the surrounding villages was more than that estimated for the whole of Gloucestershire.'[16] However inaccurate these figures may have been this extensive range of coloured cloths on the factor's market standing and in the shops must have been an enticing sight in London and European cities.

---

1 SHC Q/SR/43/165
2 SHC Q/SR/15/74/74
3 TNA PROB 11/146/165
4 http://www.lse.ac.uk/economichistory/pdf/wp7103.pdf
5 SHC DD\X\MSL/7
6 Textile industries since 1550 www. British-history.ac.uk/vch/wilts/vol4/pp148-182
7 Becks, W 1882: 218
8 Lipson, E 1921: 257
9 Kerridge, E 1985: 37
10 Kerridge, E 1985: 38
11 Kerridge, E 1985: 32
12 Collinson, J & Rack E 1791: 186
13 Sholto, P 1847: 142
14 Berrett, RL 2012: http://www.burnleyandtrowbridge.com/1766revolutiontoevolution.aspx
15 Barfoot, P 1793: -
16 de Lacy Mann, J 1971: 55

DD/X/MSL C/679a

[redacted] 7 PART 2 of 2

Bx 54

Letter-book (?of Messrs. Elderton and Hall, London), containing letters to clothiers in Somerset (Frome area), Wiltshire and Gloucestershire, concerning wool distributed and cloth received for sale, 1763-69.

CHAPTER 14

A FACTOR'S CORRESPONDENCE

> *'I received from you today one cloth which I think very good, but am surprised you don't make a little more cloth. What a pity it is such a young gentleman as you should not exert yourself and make more cloth, for if ever a person makes any figure in life it is when they are young, for the beginning of a man's life is his fortune.'*
>
> *Letter to Thomas Woodyear; June 16th, 1763*

From the late 14th century, the clothiers from small towns and rural areas brought their cloth to sell at Blackwell Hall. As the routes to the West Country were cut off from the capital during the civil war, the direct selling of cloth by the clothiers started to shift. The plague and the great fire of London followed and the clothiers stayed away from the market leaving an opportunity for the factors to secure possession of all the stalls, which the clothiers had formerly occupied. The factors now fulfilled the same role for the cloth trade as the merchant staplers and broggers had for the wool trade. They succeeded in becoming the intermediaries rather than working directly for the clothiers, and they imposed their own terms of business as they increasingly controlled the market. They obliged the small manufacturers to accept advances at interest, lengthy terms of credit from the merchants and part payment of their goods in exchange for Spanish wool from their preferred suppliers. For all these transactions they charged commissions and fees.

Working in the bustling rooms of the hall, the factors developed their own sales networks and invested their surplus capital in overseas ventures to import dyestuffs and wool. At the peak of the cloth trade in the 18th century, they dominated the selling process, they were brokers in the true sense of the word. They negotiated deals with merchants *'...a pipe of oyle, a chest of sope'*. They nurtured existing wholesale and overseas accounts, secured orders and developed new business. To serve their interests, both the factors and the clothiers protested the changes, this led to the implementation of new regulations at Blackwell Hall.

> *Be it enacted That from and after the First Day of May 1697 the Governors of Blackwell Hall and their Deputies shall strictly keep the sett Times and Rules for the exact keeping and Government of the publick Markett of Blackwell-Hall. The said Markett shall be held on every Thursday Friday and Saturday from 8:00am till Noon and from 2:00pm till 5:00pm. The Hours for the begining & ending of the Marketts shall be knowne by the ringing of the Markett Bell [1]...A table 30 yards in length, with an inch to each shall be provided in Blackwell-Hall, for measuring medly broadcloth. The buyer shall give notice to the seller when the cloth is to be wetted, and if he does not attend the buyer may proceed to prove the cloth, and the keeper of Blackwell Hall shall measure the same, and his certificate thereof shall be the rule of payment to the buyer, and a conviction of the party offending.[2]'*

A commentary in The Gentleman's Magazine in 1739 reflects the extent of the change:

> *'...The Blackwell Hall factor, originally but the servant of the maker, is now become his master, and not only his but the wool-merchant's and draper's too.[3]'*

Before the invention of copiers, most letters that were sent were transcribed to a ledger. The letter book of James Elderton dates from March 1763 until March 1769 and comprises almost three thousand letters of business correspondence with his cloth suppliers in Somerset, Wiltshire and Gloucestershire.[4] His surname is a familiar local name which was mentioned in the Whitchurch dye recipe books and the parish records. An entry in the letter book dated November 8th, 1764 mentioned that James had '*...never seen trade so bad in these past 30 years.*' By then, he was probably a man in his late forties or early fifties who often corresponded with the Cockells, clothiers of Chapmanslade, uncles Nicholas and James. He may have been the son of John Elderton, a goldsmith living in Frome, recorded in court papers in 1687 or the son of James Elderton, a signatory of the landholders petition preventing the selling of old cards in 1711. In that year, a baptism was recorded in St John's church for James Elderton. About the age of fourteen, his family would have apprenticed him to a factor in London's Blackwell Hall and later he established his own brokerage firm with Ambrose Hall '*...who does intirely the counting house Business' Jan 8th 1767.*

The book, about 6 x 8in is a standard plain cardboard covered ledger with legible entries written in oak gall ink, each one separated by a hand drawn line. The first few pages list the names of his suppliers with an index of page numbers and in the back of the book are twenty six addresses. This list is not inclusive of all the names mentioned in the book, there are references to wholesalers, drapers and agents trading on behalf of the East India Company. A few letters refer to Samuel Fludyer, another factor, whose father was a London clothier originally from Frome[5]. Samuel later served as Director of the Bank of England, MP for Chippenham and held the post of Lord Mayor of London for several terms. He was later reprehended for his involvement in the scarlet cloth contraband to the detriment of the East India Company.

This remaining ledger from his co-partnership with Ambrose Hall, would have been one of many that underpinned their cloth business. Most letters concerned the cloth trade but a few touched on the more unusual purchases of buying and selling precious gold and silver, buying lottery tickets costing more than £11 each and the purchase of spiling irons and other sundry goods for manufacture. For his relatives and friends he bought silk, tulips and provided ingredients and instructions for making ink, and on one occasion he mentions horses as well. In return, they sent him occasional gifts of hares and salmon for which they were praised highly and thanked profusely.

Other ledgers would have held the correspondence with his customers, drapers like Mr Bodicoate, '*...I wish we could come to perfection on these light colours they are sent out, I will let you know what your draper says of them.*' Letters to the merchants of the East India Company for dyestuffs and suppliers for Spanish wool, correspondence for Italian orders and dealings with insurance brokers. In his letters to the clothiers he included their accounts, and also mentions *'dye as under'* presumably a separate order book, enclosed with the supplies, was sent back and forth to the clothiers. However, like overhearing an intriguing conversation, these letters provide his version of the story, the other side is left to the reader's imagination. He met with clothiers in London and offered lodgings at his house, as he writes:

> *Mr Edmund Eyres '...Should be extremely glad to see you in Town, as one hour's chat is worth a sheet of paper in writing', April 21st 1768.*

On more than one occasion, he travelled to the country to meet his uncles and to discuss matters in more detail.

> *'... Mr Elderton plans to be in Beckington in a fortnight ... Don't make any settlement with anyone else before you see him'.*

In the 18th century, men and occasionally women, formed simple partnerships or were sole traders. Limited companies were not common until the 1800s, and unlike today's company names, businesses were identified as *'The House of Noad'*, or *'The House of Naish'* or 'Read & Co' referring to sons or nephews. The only comparable businesses to retain this tradition is that of haute couture *'The House of Dior'* or *'The House of Worth'*. The family name was their reputation and their brand and the good mark of the clothier was his livelihood.

July 5th 1764, Read & Co '...The brown seems not quite as good as usual therefore be cautious, don't fall from your mark as at present you have got a very good name.' Sept 22nd 1763, Mr Naish & Tree '...The complaints I had of your two cloths last week is too disagreeable to mention... it is not well scribbled as it is full of white nubs, it is not well wove, it is not struck up well in the loomb it stretches like a stocking ...but must leave all this to Mr Naish's superior judgement. When once a man's mark has lost its name it is a hard matter to retrieve it again, pray for God's sake make your cloths better so as I may get them into esteem'. NB no man ever got a fortune by making bad cloths but a great many have by making good!'

James Elderton appears to have been very forthright in his views, even arrogant, but as the years of letters unfolded, I found myself becoming more sympathetic to his concerns as each week, a continuous refrain of complaints was written. James's experience of the cloth trade was well grounded and knowledgeable, he understood all the processes of production and freely offered support and advice.

April 16th 1767, Mr William Tree '...Your supers are the same width as liveries coarse and bad ... your cloths have of late been very thin, thready and burley and narrow therefore we think it incumbent upon us to acquaint you that without more care in these particulars the consequence must be a stock of cloth which will be very disagreeable. '...From good wool you may have good spinning and that will make good cloth, ...Three colours very motley suppose you never cleaned the scribbling horse, there seems to be black hair scribbled with them. ...It needs to be well set in the loom, it is too thin, put a higher hundred in them'.

Good cloth required a high number of warp threads but corners were cut by using less which affected the handle and wear. James also suggested boiling a purple cloth in vinegar to bring out the colour but despite admonitions, his advice was seldom heeded.

August 7th 1766 '...You desired me to be quite candid in regard to your cloths. Your cloth is dyed as different from the pattern as black and white! In a letter to his uncle Nicholas '...say nothing about no 11889 it will not do, you might as well have dyed them with brick dust, I don't believe they was dyed with anything much better,... no 11895 too dark by fifty shades, these are not times to Play with Trade, for I verily believe the Almighty has set a curse on this year...'

93 Messrs Read & Wilkins March 15. 1764

Gentn We shall be glad to know when we may expect any Cloth up and beg you to forward all Cloths as soon as Convenient

Mr Jonath Noad March 15. 1764

Dear Friend, We recd yours & one Cloth should be glad you would dye the black Grays as soon as possible. but dye 12 ps — I have ordered some blues of that very dark Colour. but should be glad you would dye some the colour of the Drabs. If you look back in the Pattern book of the year 1762, and see what a parcel of blues you sent me at the end of the year. If I had a hundred ps the Colour of No 1288 I could sell them directly; Dye 4 ps to No 1504 full as light & clear. I am sorry to find you cant get your Clo burled, but if you cant get a cloth burled in a month Hardy should not dress a Cloth as to Mr Jno Walker. I have desired him never to send me anymore of his dressing. If he does I will Immediately send it him done again. I would not have a Cloth of his dressing. — — — —

NB should be glad to know what has passed concerning what we talked off in Town — — — —

Messrs Naish & Tree March 15. 1764

We recd yours & 3 Cloths, I am weary of making Complaints No 2136 as bad a Cloth as ever I saw, a thin thready Cloth and not so much dressing as a livery. I sent for your Bro again to day. and I will assure you he did not seem a little uneasy. you are ruining your selves as fast as possible. but you are to do as you please. If you would make your Cloths a little stouter they then would bare the dressing better. and as I said before I am quite tired of finding fault —

NB should be glad to know what is become of No 2103. 2107 & 2122 &

Mr Geo Walker March 15. 1764

Sir We recd yours & have sent you 5 Baggs of wool would have you dye once more to the Pattern. And If that will not do will not trouble our selves about It — — — — —

Mr John Huntley March 18. 1764

Sir We rec'd yours & 6 Cloths should be glad to know what sort of cloth you Intend to make for the future. Let it be what ever sort I hope it will be quite the Thing & prime of the sort for I asure you unless It is It will not sell. for I forsee a great deal of bad Cloth will be made and I never saw Trade so bad in my Life at this time of the year I dare say you dont think what I say to be True but I promise you it is fact. I should be glad you would make one or two sorts of Cloth not make to many sorts. & what ever It is let it be quite prime. you say these Clos rec'd to day are quite the thing should be glad to know If you examined the light Colour or not I wish you would not attempt superfines but If you are determin so to do I hope you will take care to let them be the best. I dont say this because I have no demand for that sort of Cloths but am Afraid of the Consequence, I should like you should make S fine medleys as well as anything but I must tell you unless they are quite another sort of Cloth from what we have rec'd lately It will not do. But as you are a Judge of your Own manufactry I leave it Intirely to you. Good Cloth will sell bad Cloth will not -- Your Bill shall have due honour. We rec'd a £50 Bill ----

---

Mr George Walker March 22. 1764

Sir We rec'd yours & 2 Cloths the Blue sent this day No 4093 is a very bad Cloth being very full of Nubs & bracks, a great many large ~~bracks~~ Shutes almost as bad as threw and full of Aqua Fortis spots and likewise a large Threw. in short it is a vile Cloth We Must beg you will be very Carefull to avoid Complaints which are very disagreable. In regard to Sr Samuel's Bill you may depend on our Assistance and in every thing that is in our power Your Bill shall have due honour. and the blocks we will send down to you the first Opportunity send Cloths as fast as Conven

---

Mr Thos Woodyear March 22. 1764

Sr We rec'd yours & one Cloth in the disposal of which you may depend on ~~y~~ our Utmost Care for your Advantage ----

In his letters to new suppliers James set out the details of his business terms and established their reputation and mark with the wholesale customers. He advanced an initial allowance towards the cost of wool and then placed orders for cloth of particular sorts and colours selected from pattern cards. '*...Dye as under no 102 and to make 2 or more pieces.*' Once the wool was dyed and blended by the scribblers, a wool batt was sent to confirm it was suitable. Judging from the letters, not all samples were approved. No financial advance over £100 was given without the matching value of an equivalent stock of cloth on hand in the hall and then the common rate of interest prevailed.

> *Mr John Walker '... I will engage you on the same terms as your brother provided the cloths are good and saleable, if it will suit to provide two cloths per week, one half the value of the cloth to be paid in ready money, the other half to be exchanged for wool, also an advance of £100 at any time without interest. For your cloths received today, your bills shall have due honour'.*

In the 18th century cloth was sold in London and at the provincial fairs. The West Country suppliers sent two or three cloths a week to Blackwell Hall via carriers like Clavey's of Frome who left from the Waggon & Horses yard, formerly Clavey's Barton in Blindhouse Lane and delivered the goods along with their bills of lading. March 23rd 1769, Mr William Tree '*...Yours we rece'd but no cloth which we are surprised at as we find it is entered on the bill of lading.*' In accordance with the Hall rules, James employed a presser who measured and checked the cloth on receipt and noted any faults.

> *Jonathan Noad, Feb 1764 '...I never settle a Cloth without Measuring it, the custom of the trade is to allow one yard after the cloth is dampt and I never allow any more unless some very material fault.'*

The clothiers accounts were sent out monthly, quarterly or twice yearly listing the inventory of cloth sold, out on approval, and the remaining stock. Any surplus stock was stored at the warehouse and a fee charged which also offered the opportunity for a new commission service. James assumed the clothier's 'resting' cloth which was warehoused at Blackwell Hall should be insured.

July 26th 1764 '....I suppose you think the profit is very large in the insurance but in that particular for once you are out as we seldom receive the money in less than three months after the time we insure to pay us for the risk, we have not above 1 ¼ percent. I don't mention this in regard to the value of the thing as I don't mind a rash bit but it shows the disposition of a man. There is an old saying 'Live and let Live' but I find that is not your way, you will know we do your business on lower terms than any other person...'

Once approved, they could draw one part in money against the balance. The other part was in wool as agreed in the terms of business. September 1762, *'...have paid out lately £3,000 for wool'*. The wool was carefully weighed with an allowance for tare and a 2 ½ percent commission was charged by the factor. There were several letters of complaint from the clothiers for the delivery of bad wool which were resolved by asking preferred suppliers to verify its condition.

'...What is rotten shall be allowed for if agreed with the merchant if an affidavit is sent. Please to let him know the number of the bag.'

The clothiers set their prices to reflect the costs for the grade of the different materials, each sort was sold within a narrow price range. Coarse cloth was sold between 3/- and 3/6 and the best Superfines which were produced in Gloucestershire, Wiltshire and Somerset sold between 16/- and 17/6 a yard but pricing was also the cause of many disputes.

1764, Jonathan Noad '...The principal clothiers are come to a determination to advance their cloth prices. The principal drapers are come to a determination not to give any advance, pray what must the poor factor do between you both? I will assure you that the principal houses are come to the resolution not to look at the letter of any clothier who do ask an advanced price or ever will buy another cloth of the mark. The clothiers have begun to raise their cloth too late in the year, the drapers are all well stocked...'

Occasionally, prices were raised by a manufacturer to provide a fair wage to the workers as factors had been accused of forcing down the price of cloth at the expense of good wages. *Feb 7th 1768 '... as to the poor I am sorry for them, but it is of no use to a man to make cloth if it cannot be sold'* was the response to his Uncle Nicholas who was concerned for the weavers who relied on him for their livelihood.

Once the price was agreed, the factor sold the cloth. James made the rounds of his buyers and left goods on approval for a few days before going back to arrange payment or have the cloth returned with a tirade of complaints. The manufacturers generally retorted that it was not possible to get cloth burled or dressed easily and to a good standard. Nevertheless, many cloths were well made and James mentioned that for a period of three months he had at least thirty five on hand from Jonathan Noad. He solicited bespoke orders from the London drapers.

> *Nov 1st 1764, Mr Moses Withey '... Send the batts as soon as dyed, pray make these cloths good as it is the first order I had of the gentleman and if made well I am promised the continuance of his orders. Pray once more let these cloths be good substance and good cloth.' April 27th 1767, Mr Robert Turner, '...have sent you a little order for 6 pieces. I shall want them in 2 months time hope you will not disappoint me'.*

He also sold directly to buyers from his market stall in Blackwell Hall. *Oct 4th 1764 '...and the standings begin to fill charmingly'.*

Then as now, fashion dictated the colours. The letters mention all shades of blues, coppers, cinnamons, and a few greens. Public mourning and state funerals increased the demand for greys and blacks.

> *April 12th, 1764 '...in regard to Mrs Noad changing her hat, Mrs Elderton would advise her to keep the white hat as Blue ones are quite out of date and look very old fashioned'.*

There were two main seasons for buying cloth, one in winter and the other in spring. Clothiers had their cloth dyed in colours that they thought suited the London markets but they were sharply reprimanded if they had not heeded the factor's advice.

> *March 1769, Mr Thomas Bythesea '...As to these Cursed new Colours the Lord knows what will come of them the Shops are full of new colours and most of them the fawn Blue...The Flame seems to hear the Bell. ...Yours we rec'd and one cloth I wish you could dispose of these colours in the country, they will never be sold in London. ...Pray forward all the Town Colours you*

have underhand. ...Don't hurry to make bad cloth as the winter is coming on and I would have you dye the Dark colours mostly and keep the light colours for the spring. ...and don't dye any more Middling Blues yet, I can't sell middling blues there is nothing but dark blues wanted. ...I should want a good many of your blues in the Spring, I should be glad if you would dye 50 pieces of fine colours different shades, some must be full as dark as no 1500'.

All samples made for export required the buyer's approval, and had to be woven and finished in time for the sailing dates of the merchant fleets. Mr William Turner '...*your mark is stamped for the East India Company*' and also Mr Nicholas Cockell '...*the Company have stampt your samples*'. But a factor's trade could be seriously affected by the whim of company agents who despite approving the clothier's mark did not buy cloth.

Aug 7th 1766, Mr Robert Turner '...We have Shocking news, the Company did not buy any medleys this year ... what will be the consequence for there is great quantities of cloth made for them. ...the reason of the Company not buying any more Medleys is they have such complaints of their being so spotty when they get abroad by their not being properly cleaned in the say.' and to Mr Moses Withey '...The East India Company does not buy only one hundred olives and cinnamons and this year not one single medley.'

To ensure a consistent level of stock, James corresponded weekly with about twenty suppliers, some were principal clothiers like his friend Jonathan Noad who sent him four to five cloths a week. Others, he described as little clothiers who produced cloth seasonally if it fit with their other work. He dealt in many sorts of cloth and had a small trade for the undyed whites. The coarse, the kerseys, the liveries, the coatings and the heavier winter drabs;

April 2nd 1767, Mr Nicholas Cockell '...Asunder is a little order for three cloths be sure the drab is very stout and the liveries very smart... very neat and exact to colours. ...I have sent you an order for two drabs and one kersey. ...Have received one cloth from Uncle James I want dark blues I never ordered these blues, can they be milled into drabs if so will send them down.

The supers; April 30th 1767, Mr Watts '...I once more say these things must be very neat the wool of the supers must be a prodigious deal better, higher hundred full 6½ quarters wide, stouter and a vast deal better dressed.' and the superfines; Mr Nicholas Cockell '... But now in regard to the mixtures I hope you have got a good wool and the supers must be as neat and as smart as a superfine pray do be particular'.

Naish & Tree were medley manufacturers, and James requested batts to be sent monthly and that at least four cloths should be produced weekly. Their partnership dissolved in 1765 but they both continued independently supplying cloth to Mr Elderton.

Feb 9th 1764 Dear Friend, '...should be glad to know when you chuse to proceed on the Medley and will send you some Patterns and be sure let your Medleys be quite the thing.'

Other trade mentioned in later years included the Spanishes;

Mr Baylis '...The Spanishes should be seven quarters wide yours to narrow...' and the new cassimeres woven from the best quality fine wool. May 26th, 1768, Mr Noad ' ...pray how goes on your Cassimeres I think something might be done in that what could you afford them at, I fancy there is a good Profit.'

And finally, there was an entry for the '*pompadour*' in 1769, which was a small patterned fine woollen twill.

From reading his letters, the mainstay of the company was the blue trade.

February 1765, Jonathan Noad '... glad to know what blues you have under hand. I wish you had never made a medley. I wish you had continued in the Blue Trade entirely and made about six cloths per week, we always had a sure trade. Pray make one hundred good blues immediately or we shall lose our Blue Trade.'

James and his partner Ambrose were rigorous and methodical in their business practices but the quality of the cloth was dependent on many factors. The prices of raw materials fluctuated widely over the six years. Feb 4th 1768 '*...Wool exceedingly dear. ...ready cash is so very scarce in town it is hard to be got*'. Indigo was expensive in 1763 but considered cheap a few years later. July 16th, 1767, Mr James Cockell, '*...the Indigo is sent as desired hope will please*'. Of considerable concern was the even dyeing and exact colour matching for his bespoke orders.

Feb 12th, 1767, Mr Robert Turner '...should be glad to know what you expect for these dark blues but surely not above 6/6 as they are not in any respect better than your 6/- cloths, and if you give 6d a pound for these dark blues but however your dyer is, he does not do you Justice, as it is I am very certain not above a 4d blue, for my part I see no reason such prises should be given for dying blew, as Indigo is at this and has been very cheap.'

July 16th 1767, Mr N Cockell '...Yours we rec'd and two cloths with £305~ Mr Banks of Frome will send you some wool to dye pray be exact as its for an order. The following letter; Joseph Banks '....these cloths on hand it is not at all like the colour, you can't think the disappointment besides your cloths are coarse and thready. ...I am quite tired of sending orders, however have sent you six pieces more. I want them as soon as possible and if they are not exact and good these shall be the last I ever will send. I must have them dyed at Chapmanslade as your dyer can't match the colour. ...I want the colours I write for, I could have sold at least 12 of your cloths if they had been the colour I ordered for example 11971 to light, 11962 not like the colour to dark, 11965 too dark nothing like the colour.'

May 28th 1767, Mr Watts '...the beauty of the colour is gone nothing like the batt its a nasty colour... this dyeing will ruin me and every maker I have. ...I am tired of writing about dyeing it makes me crasey, I never can have a pattern matched, I must loose all my trade. I don't want 9/- cloth I want 9/6d cloth and if you don't put better wool in them than the last they absolutely will not do.'

Throughout the six years of the ledger, he corresponded with his friend Jonathan Noad at Shawford, but there were times when the content of the letters must have strained their friendship. For the first eighteen months the letters are addressed as *'Dear Friend...last night I arrived safe in Town am much obliged to you for all Favours...*'

May 18th 1763, Dear Friend '...I rec'd yours and seven cloths which I believe are very good. You may depend on 5 baggs of wool being at Road next week, I shall see it loaded myself this evening...' and by June he had sent another ten bags of wool which seems to have started a quarrel. James complained bitterly about the quality of the cloth Jonathan was sending to London,

June 16th 1763 '...No man was ever used so ill as you are by a parcel of dressers, I declare that the cloths are entirely spoilt. I declare it makes me

tremble to think the prejudices these people do you will entirely ruin your mark and credit.....Send for them and read them the above.'

As the argument escalated; *June 30th 1763 '...Yours is rec'd and is now before me and I must inform you it has given me a great deal of uneasings after all the care that I always have taken in your business. You say you would not recommend to pay some regard to your interest which expression I think very ungenerous nay ungrateful there is no one man in this world who strived to oblige one person more...'*

Feb 23rd 1764 '...If I was not almost certain it was the dressing I should think you mixt your good wool the handle is so coarse'. '...You say you will pay a proper regard to my last, I hope you will, but not an improper one, and can't but say but the conclusion of your last few lines is rather ungratefull as I have always done all that lay in my power to serve Mr Noad but if your friendship is built on so ticklish a foundation as I fancy it must be by this, it is but of a short duration.'

Some issues were resolved, while others provoked further reproach and by August 1764 James writes:

'...the small quantity of cloth lately received makes us suppose you are going into some new Method of Trade, should be glad to know that particular as then can order things from other people accordingly...' Sept 13th 1764, Mr Noad '...I wish you success in your country trade, I hope it may answer your end.'

By October they seem to be back on good terms but the tone is more reserved.

'...Shall be extremely glad to see you in London and hope shall settle things to our mutual satisfaction, My house is your Home' and by April 1767 business had resumed '...We received yours and the cloths advised, shall be extremely glad to see you in London. If you have any more sky blues underhand desire you forward them as fast as possible.'

By the end of the letter book, while his partnership with Ambrose may have continued for several more years there is no further information in the archives. In 1768, James was asking his suppliers in Gloucestershire to recommend a superfine scarlet cloth maker who could produce around two hundred cloths per year as there was still a demand for the best superfines but as for the other trades, James was far more pessimistic.

> *March 23, 1769, Mr Robert Turner '...Yours we rec'd and 6 Cloths there is no Trade and I hope you will make but Little Cloth.'*
>
> *Mr Joseph Banks '... we may sell a few drabs but as yet there is none wanting'.*
>
> *Mr Nicholas Cockell '... I have only one thing to add I believe the coarse trade to be quite over and as to the Livery trade and what little there is... But pray do take my advice and Make very little Cloth I think trade is at an end Gloucestershire and Yorkshire are in far bad a situation...'*

---

1 www.british-history.ac.uk/ Statutes of the Realm Vol 7 page 199 - 200
2 Thomas Walter Williams; A compendium and comprehensive Law dictionary; elucidating the terms
3 The Gentleman's Magazine February 1739: 89
4 SHC DD\X\MSL/7
5 www.historyofparliamentonline.org

Plan of part of the Town of Frome prior to 1810.

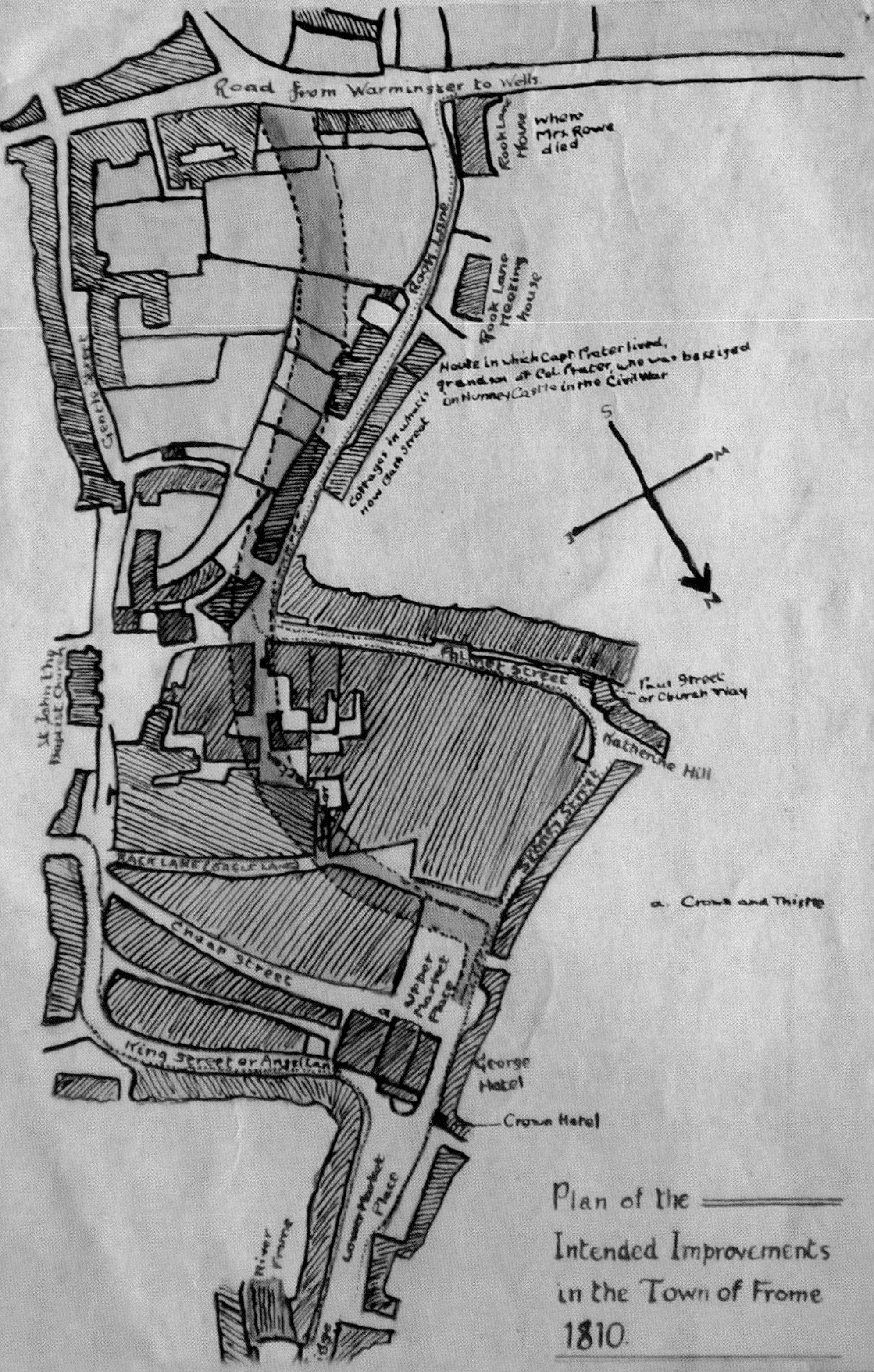

Plan of the

Intended Improvements

in the Town of Frome

1810.

L. F. J. NORVILLE 10/8/38.
(COPY)

CHAPTER 15

THE DECLINE OF TRADE

'...I took a post chaise in the afternoon of yesterday and went to Frome... This appears to be a sort of little Manchester. A very small Manchester indeed; for it does not contain above ten to twelve thousand people, but it has all the flash of a Manchester....'

William Cobbett, 1825 Rural Rides

The Cloth Trade dominated English manufacture in the early 18th century. Daniel Defoe described it as:

> *'the richest and most valuable manufacture in the world. ...Nothing can answer all the ends of dress but good English broadcloth, fine camlets, druggets, serges and such like.[1]'*

15.1 Plan of the Cutting of Bath Street

These materials were all made from different grades of mixed English and Spanish wools, some with a close sett and finely spun yarn others more loosely woven giving a softer drape. The array of colours indicated that the methods of the 18th century dye recipe books were of a good standard and that workshops could produce evenly dyed wool. New sorts of cloth were introduced as domestic consumption increased, along with an export market for what must have seemed an insatiable demand. The immigration of skilled artisans from the Low Countries and the diligence of English workers had all contributed to technical improvements, new methods and products.

Factors and clothiers had to be mindful as their livelihood relied on retaining their good reputation. Throughout the century government statutes stipulated the length and weight of cloth in an effort to control fraud. Attempts had been made to modify the weight of common cloth by setting the warp and weft threads more widely apart while still using the accepted practice of a hard warp yarn and very soft weft with an opposite twist however the resulting cloth was thready and less durable. Revised laws in 1727 appointed inspectors at local mills, instead of searchers at Blackwell Hall, which proved unpopular with the clothiers.

> *'..A petition submitted by John Phelps of Frome Selwood, clothier and clothworker, requesting that he should be appointed as one of the inspectors of fulling mills and racks in Somerset, 1736.*[2]*'*

Then as now, profit was important to maintain a competitive advantage. Corners were cut, cheaper dyes and wools were substituted and less experienced workers were employed all of which had

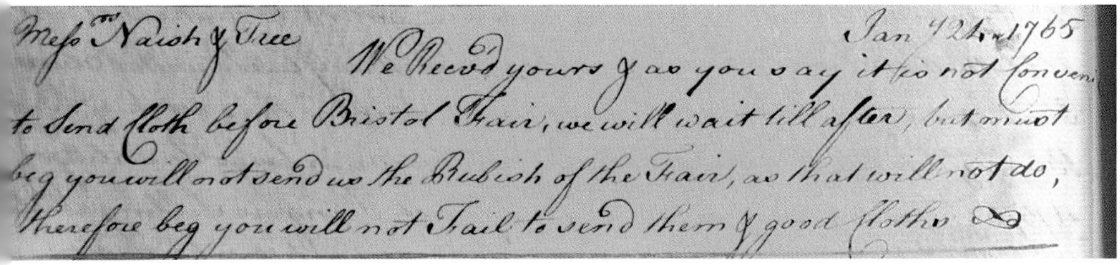
Messrs Naish & Tree Jan 12th 1765
We Rec'd yours & as you say it is not Conveni
to send Cloth before Bristol Fair, we will wait till after, but must
beg you will not send us the Rubish of the Fair, as that will not do,
therefore beg you will not Fail to send them & good Cloths &c

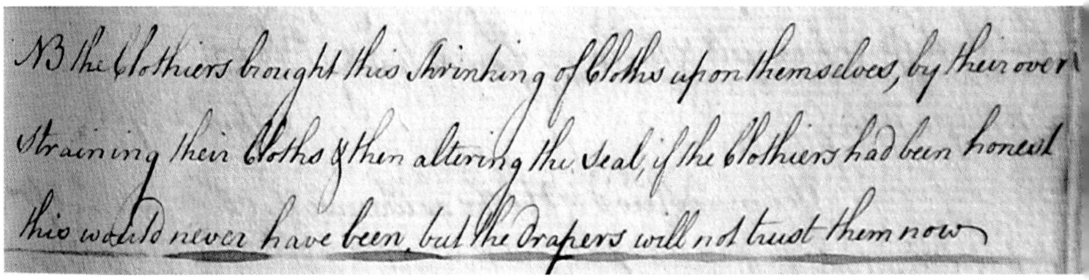
NB the Clothiers brought this Shrinking of Cloths upon themselves, by their over
straining their Cloths & then altering the Seal, if the Clothiers had been honest
this would never have been, but the Drapers will not trust them now

15.2 Elderton Letter Book

led to Mr Elderton's many complaints.

However, for long periods during the century, good commercial dyeing had ensured plenty of work especially as fashionable colours started to change with the seasons and the finished materials were eagerly awaited.

There was a downturn in trade in 1769 judging by the letters sent by James Elderton and there were glimmers of the decline to follow as Defoe commented

'...it is true, Europe take it by and large as we express it from end to end, does not produce a wool capable of making our fine broadcloths of Warminster, Trowbridge, Bradford and Froom. The quality of the Froom broadcloth was unmatched in Europe, but cloth of a lesser quality was found to be just as suitable for most purposes and regardless of the emphasis on trying to persuade consumers to purchase such a fine article, price and fashion were dictated purchases. First upon this unhappy falling into the French fashion of wearing stuffs instead of broadcloth, I mean for the mens wear, They brought their silk stuffs, Spanish druggets and light thin French serges into wear and fashion.

15.3 1790 Quilted Cottons for Petticoats

Following French fashion rather than setting English. A manufacture valuable in itself, infinitely profitable to the poor, pleasant to the rich, not too hot for the summer, not too cold for the winter, light enough for July, warm enough for December, better than even silk itself and yet ornamental and rich in its own lustre. Receptive of the brightest and deepest colours, gay enough for the bridegroom, solemn enough for the widow, rich enough for the coronation, grave enough for the deepest mourning.

15.4 19th Century Printed Cotton

One reason to be given for disliking it, the weakest of all reasons, the love of change and variety. , we cannot persuade ourselves to wear our own produce, to propagate our own industry, or employ our own people. Callico, chintz, silks, painted cottons. The hands that would have laboured could get no work, the trade sunk, the manufacturers starved, and the wool lay by in heaps unwrought and unsold to the general impoverishment of the people and the ruin of the manufacture itself.[3]'

Economic disruptions of trade over the course of the century were common but two comments are worth a mention. The papers of George Wansey, a clothier of Warminster are held in the Wiltshire archives.

'*...this book is designed to contain an account of my stock and all the yearly increases and decreases made thereof.*[4]'

15.5 19th Century Coarse Linen

Dated between Aug 27th 1751 to August 1759. The first entry comments on the change from the Julian to the Gregorian calendar.

'*... This day the old stile ceases and the new stile takes place. So that tomorrow which should have been the 5th is to be the 14th of September. That this month of September 1752 is the shortest month we have ever known. It containing no more than 19 days and but 2 Sundays.*'

The other, a major disaster that affected the export trade of many clothiers including George and his brother, who was an agent in Portugal;

'*..November 1st 1755, this day about ten o'clock in the morning, the City of Lisbon was intirely destroyed, & many thousands of inhabitants killed; by a most* *terrible earthquake, succeeded by a general conflagration. By which event I expect to be a great sufferer in my stock.'*

The competition to maintain a dominant position in the market meant that the manufacture of more goods for less money was relentless. The selection and sorts of material from other counties and abroad made it increasingly difficult to promote all except the finest quality south west woollens. The woven twills of fine yarn did not need to be fulled, and were thinner and lighter than broadcloth with a smooth finish well suited for export to warmer climates. Medium weight broadcloths were made into liveries, suiting and outerwear. Calicos and chintzes, both cotton prints, had been introduced to England in the 1690s and were replacing the fine light weight woollens. Striped, checked and plain Calamancoes, with soft glazed sheen, were made in Norwich from fine worsted wools which were ideal for petticoats, linings and work clothes. Camlets were woven in either plain or twill mixtures from wool, hair and silk suitable for tailored outfits. As well as being a coarse cloth, stuffs were the generic term for woven textiles of different grades and sorts such as druggets, serges, dozens, blankets and kerseys all of which competed for different sectors of the domestic and export markets.

During the 1700s, the West of England cloth industry was still organised on a putting out basis and financed by the middling clothiers. As the century progressed, weavers who had previously earned a living from their own looms now had to accept the factory system where they worked for the clothiers and the divide was so great that few could hope to make the transition from worker to master. The larger water powered mill buildings with adjacent dyehouses were enlarged to control more of the manufacturing operations and some were rebuilt when steam power became available. Industrialisation was gaining momentum and mechanical innovations were threatening livelihoods. The workers only recourse was to riot. In July 1776 a group of twelve clothiers attempted to introduce the spinning jenny into the workhouse at Shepton Mallet. The negotiated trial of the jennies did not meet with the approval of the neighbouring woollen workers who felt provoked by the clothiers:

15.6 Cart Entering Frome on Bath Street

'....A riotous mob of weavers, shearmen, etc collected from the towns of Warminster, Frome etc assembled together and proceeded to the town with the intention to destroy under cover of night a machine lately erected by the clothiers.[5]'

While the town's clothiers did not suffer from a lot of destruction, the local hand loom weavers and shearmen of Frome were well organised, and led or participated in riots in Bath, Bradford on Avon, Shepton Mallet and Trowbridge which was a contributing factor to the eventual decline of the woollen cloth trade.

> *'...On Thursday night last about 2 or 300 men with their faces blacked and armed with bludgeons entered the house of a Sheargrinder at Nunny (about 3 miles from Froome) and demolished about thirty pounds worth of shears belonging to the manufactory of Messrs Bamford Cook & Co of Twerton after committing this outrage the rioters assembled in another place to the amount of 8 or 900 and resolved to proceed to Twerton in order to hang up Bamford and two of his men to burn down his works and those of Culliford on the opposite side of the river...[6]'*

The cavalry were summoned and a request was made for troops to remain in the clothing towns of Frome, Bradford on Avon, Trowbridge and Beckington

'...as it will convince those deluded men of the impropriety of their conduct and impossibility of their succeeding in their intentions. Your Grace's most obedient ...Mr Bowen, Dec 20th 1797.[7]'

Around the 1800s a pamphlet had attributed the loss of trade of some of the West Country cloth trade to Yorkshire's cheaper cost of labour and necessaries of life and to the fact that;

'...Yorkshire manufacturers can with much greater facility introduce machinery than we can in the West of England. The opposition that we generally meet with in introducing machinery is so great that until the Yorkshire manufacturers have stolen the article away from us, we are almost afraid to introduce it.[8]'

In 1803, William Sheppard who owned the factory and mills at Spring Gardens, described the difficulties of introducing the gig mill to the government commissioners. The shearmen would not agree to its use and the firm had to accept orders for cloth to be delivered unfinished or send their cloth to Gloucestershire where some mill owners had been more successful at overcoming the opposition.

The Napoleonic war was Frome's last hurrah. Enlistment in the army depleted the workforce and Spanish wool was in short supply but the demand for material for military uniforms was considerable. In 1801 it was reported that 160 miles of cloth were made annually.[9] By 1805 the Sheppards firm was the only one in Frome making fine cloth and cassimeres to fulfil the orders but within fifteen years the cassimere trade had declined.

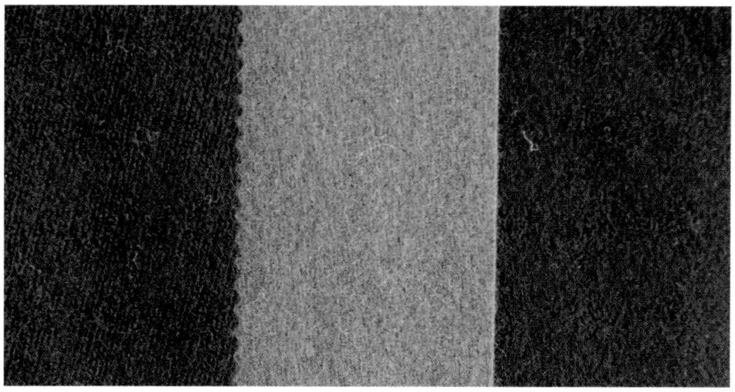

15.7 Cavalry Twill and Broadcloth

Saturday, September 2nd, 1825 what befell the workmen, spinners and weavers like Joseph Harrison, Joseph Wright and Samuel Storrs, who

LOT 6.

A VERY SPACIOUS

CLOTH FACTORY,

called or known by the name of *Heathers-Mill*, situated in the Parish of *Frome-Selwood, Somerset*, with A COTTAGE HOUSE and Half-an-Acre of LAND thereto adjoining. These Premises are admirably calculated for Trade, and abundantly supplied with Water; they are now occupied by Messrs. WILLIAM and JOHN ROSSITER, on Lease, at a clear Yearly Rental of £100.

15.8 1840 Public Auction

were mentioned in Amos Jenkins' inventory; they may have been amongst many of the families breaking stones as described by William Cobbett on his rural rides

'...I took a post chaise in the afternoon of yesterday and went to Frome, where I saw upon my entrance into the town, between two and three hundred weavers, men and boys, cracking stones, moving earth and doing other sorts of work, towards making a fine road into the town. I was, I must confess, glad to find proofs of the irretrievable decay of the place I remember how ready the manufacturers had been to call in the troops.

Let them, said I to myself, call the troops in now, to make their trade revive... let them now threaten their poor workmen with the gaol, when they dare to ask for the means of preventing starvation in

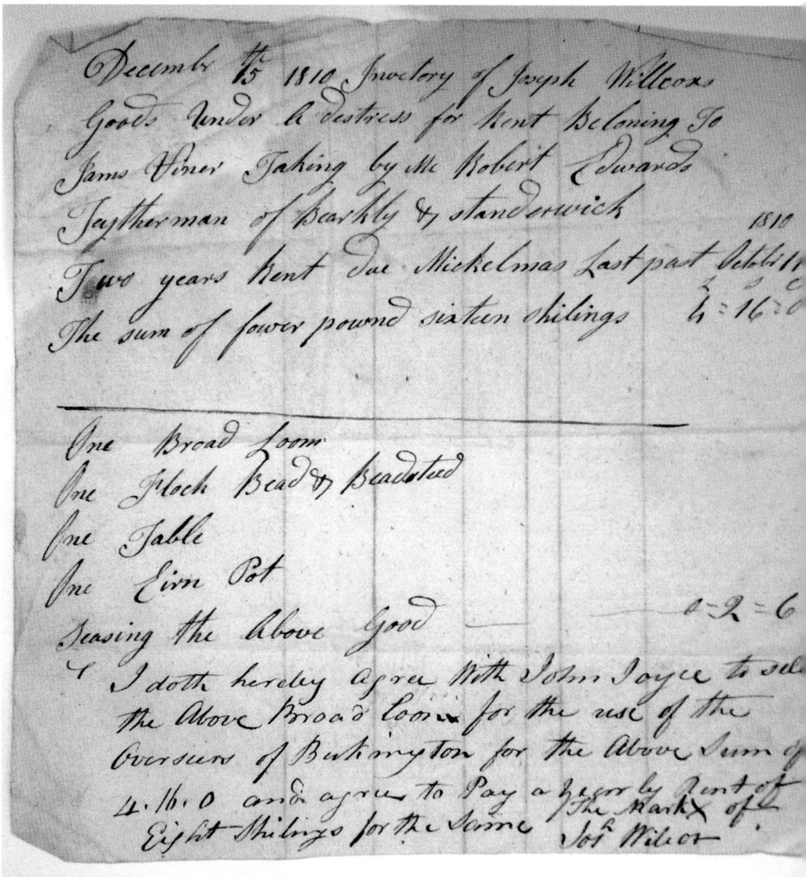
December 15th 1810 Inventory of Joseph Willcox
Goods Under a destress for Rent Belonging To
James Viner Taking by Mr Robert Edwards
Tythingman of Bearkly & standerwick 1810
Two years Rent due Mickelmas Last past Debt
The sum of fower pound sixteen shilings 4 : 16 : 0

One Broad Loom
One Flock Bead & Beadsted
One Table
One Eirn Pot
Seasing the Above Good 0 = 2 = 6
I doth hereby agree With John Joyce to sell the Above Broad Loom for the use of the Overseers of Bukington for the Above Sum of 4.16.0 and agree to Pay a Yearly Rent of Eight Shilings for the Same
The Mark X of Jos Wilcox

15.9 1810 Loom Seized by the Bailiffs for Unpaid Rent

their families.When I got to the inn, I sent my post chaise boy back to the road to tell one or two of the weavers to come to me at the inn.... I had a long talk with them, at Frome they are all upon a quarter work, it is the same at Bradford and Trowbridge.[10]'

From 1796 machinery for scribbling, carding, spinning and the fly-shuttle was adopted. This was not the end of the industry but a slow decline that led to the diversification of some companies like Rawlings and the closure of the dyeing businesses. There was a host of minor clothiers, whose firms continued until the Second World War but all had ceased trading by 1965 when Tucker's Mill closed.

'*...Their poor work people cannot be worse off than they long have been. The parish pay which they now get upon the roads is 2/6d a week for a man, 2/- for his wife and 1/3d for each child under eight years of age. These poor creatures at Frome have pawned all their best clothes, their blankets and sheets, their looms...and though this is a sort of manufacture that cannot very well come to a complete end still it has received a blow from which it cannot possibly recover.*[11]'

15.10 Sheppards Mill at Spring Gardens in a State of Disrepair

---

[1] Defoe, D 1728: 190
[2] SHC Q/SR/304/45/45-46
[3] Defoe, D 1727 :-
[4] WHSC 314/2/1
[5] Randall, A 1991: 72
[6] Randall, A 1991: 151
[7] TNA HO 42/41/6
[8] Lipson, E 1921: 252
[9] SHC DD\LW/134
[10] Cobbett, W 1924: 72
[11] Cobbett, W 1924: 72

BIBLIOGRAPHY

Abbreviations

AHR	Agricultural History Review
BAHS	British Agricultural History Society
BA	Bristol Archive
BBHA	Bristol Branch of the Historical Association
EHR	Economic History Review
FSLS	Frome Society for Local Study
HALS	Hampshire Archives & Local Studies
KSLHS	Keynsham and Saltford Local History Society
NA	National Archives
SALS	Somerset Archives & Local Studies
SANHS	Somerset Archaeological and Natural History Society
SPAB	Society for the Preservation of Ancient Buildings
WANHS	Wiltshire Archaeology and Natural History Society
WRS	Wiltshire Record Society
WSHC	Wiltshire & Swindon History Centre

Publications

Aldhelm de Laud, Virginity Sherbourne: C680

Aspin, Chris, The Woollen Industry, Oxford: Shire 2006

Baines, Patricia, Spinning Wheels – Spinners and Spinning, London: Batsford 1977

Baines, Patricia, Flax and Linen, Oxford: Shire 1985

Balfour-Paul, Jenny, Deeper than Indigo, Surbiton: Medina 2015

Balfour-Paul, Jenny, Indigo in the Arab World, Richmond: Curzon 1997

Balfour-Paul, Jenny: The British Museum Press 2011

Bancroft, Edward, Experimental Researches concerning the Philosophy of Permanent Colours, Philadelphia: Thomas Dobson 1814

Banessy, Sandrine, Le Pastel en Pays d'oc, France: Tourisme 2002

Bantock, Anton, Earlier Smyths, Bishopsworth:Malago 1982

Barber, Richard, Edward III and the Triumph of England, London: Penguin 2013

Barfoot, Peter The Universal British Directory London: 1793 Vol III

Barlow, F. , The Feudal Kingdom of England 1042 – 1216, London: Longman 1972

Bartlett, Robert, England under the Norman and Angevin Kings 1075-1225, Oxford: OUP 2000

Bath, Daphne, Longleat, London: The Longleat Estate 1967

Beck, S. William, The Draper's Dictionary, London: The Warehousemen & Draper's journal 1882

Beech, Franklin, The Dyeing of Woollen Cloth, London: Scot 1902

Belham, Peter, Villages of the Frome Area: A History, Frome: FSLS 1992

Belham, Peter, The Making of Frome,Frome: FSLS 1973

Bemiss, Elijah, The Dyer's Companion (Facsimile), New York: Dover 1806(1973)

Benson, Anna & Warburton, Neil, Looms and Weaving, Oxford: Shire 1990

Berg, Maxine, Luxury & Pleasure in Eighteenth Century Britain, Oxford: OUP 2005

Berrett, R.L. 2012 www.burnleyandtrowbridge.com /1766revolutiontoevolution.aspx

Berthollet, C.L. & A.B. (Translated by Ure, Andrew), Elements Of The Art of Dyeing and Bleaching, London: Thomas Tegg 1841

Berthollet, M (Translated by Hamilton,William), Elements Of The Art of Dyeing, London: J. Johnson 1791

Bettey, J.H., The Cultivation of Woad in the Salisbury Area during the late 16th C and 17th C, Textile History Vol. 9, 1978.

Bettey, J.H., Wiltshire Farming in the 17th Century, WRS Vol 5 2005

Billingsley, John, General View of the Agriculture in the County of Somerset , London: W. Smith 1794

Blackburn, Cally, Costume from 1500 to the present day, Norwich: Pitkin, 2003

Blair, John and Ramsay, Nigel (Eds), English Medieval Industries, London: Hambledon 2001

Blake, Robert By the Queene. A proclamation against the sowing of woad London; 1585

Bone, M.R., Notes & Queries for Somerset and Dorset XXXI– Bridport Textile Industry 1814-1945

de Bonnefons, Nicholas (Translated by John Evelin), The French Gardiner, London: B Took 1691

Braudel, Fernand, Civilization and Capitalism Vol 1 – 3, London: Fontana 1985

Braudel, Fernand, The Mediterranean and the Mediterranean World, London: Fontana 1981

Brett, Colin Thomas Kytson and Somerset Clothiers 1529 - 1539 SANHS:1999

Brett, Colin The Fairs of Norton St Phillip SANHS: 2002

Bridbury, A.R., Medieval Cloth Making, London: Heineman 1982

Brill, Edith, Cotswold Crafts, Newton Abbott: Batsford 1977

Bronson, J. and R., Early American Weaving and Dyeing, New York: Dover 1977

Browne, Charles, North Wansdyke Past & Present, Bristol: KSLHS 1994

Brunello, Franco, The Art of Dyeing, Vicenza: Neri Pozza 1973

Bryant, Arthur, The Age of Chivalry, London: Collins 1969

Burnley, James , The History of Wool and Wool Combing (Facsimile), New York: Kelley 1889(1969)

Burton, Anthony, Life in the Mill, Pitkin 2013

Cam, Helen M., The Hundred and the Hundred Rolls, London: Methuen 1930

Cameron, Nancy Foy, Woad – it's History, how to grow it, how it works, Atholl Browse 1998

Campbell, R., The London Tradesman, London: T. Gardner 1747

Cardon, Dominique, Dyes in History and Archaeology Vol 10 1992

Cardon, Dominique , The Dyer's Handbook: Memoirs of an 18th Century Master Colourist, Oxbow 2016

Carus-Wilson, E.M., The Merchant Adventurers of Bristol in the Fifteenth Century, Bristol: BBHA 1962

Carus-Wilson, E.M., Medieval Merchant Venturers, London

Cennini, Cennino d'Andrea, The Craftsman's Handbook New York: Dover 15th C (1954)

Chapman, Stanley (Ed), Devon Cloth Industry, Torquay: The Devonshire Press 1978

Chapon, Felicien, Nouveau Manuel Complet Du Fabricant De Bleus , Paris: Encyclopedique de Roret 1858

Cholmely, William, The Request and Suite of a True Hearted Englishman (Reprint), London: Camden Society 1553

Clapham, Sir John, A Concise Economic History of Britain, Cambridge: CUP 1951

Clarke, Leslie J., The Craftsman in Textiles, London: Bell 1968

Cobbett, William, Rural Rides, Everyman's Library 1820's (1924)

Collingwood,R.G. and Myers, J.N.L., Roman Britain and the English Settlements, Oxford: OUP 1963

Cooper, Thomas, A Practical Treatise on Dyeing, Philadelphia: Thomas Dobson 1815

Crump, Thomas, A Brief History of How the Industrial Revolution Changed the World, London: Robinson 2010

Culpeper, Nicholas, Complete Herbal, London: 1653

Cumming,V., Cunnington, C.W. and Cunnington, P.E., The Dictionary of Fashion History, Oxford: Berg 1976
Cunningham Phyllis, Eighteenth Century English Costume, London: Faber & Faber 2007
Dampier, Samuel , A letter to Mr Thomas Coad of Stoford
Darby, H. (Ed) , The Domesday Geography of South West England Cambridge:CUP 2009
Davenport, Elsie, Yarn Dyeing, London: Sylvan 1955
Davis, Mick & Pitt, Valerie, Historic Inns of Frome Bath: Akeman Press 2015
Davis, Thomas, General View of the Agriculture of the County of Wilts, London: 1794
Dean, Jenny, The Craft of Natural Dyeing, Search Press 1995
Dean, Jenny, Colours from Nature, Search Press 2009
Defoe, Daniel, A Journal of the Plague Year (Reprint), London: Cassell 1721(1909)
Defoe, Daniel , A Brief Deduction of the Original, Progress, and immense Greatness of the British Woollen Manufacture, with an enquiry whether it be not at present in a very Declining Condition. London 1727
Defoe, Daniel, A Plan of the English Commerce, London: Rivington 1728
Deloney, Thomas, The History of Thomas of Reading and other worthy clothiers of England (Facsimile)
Denvir, Bernard, The Eighteenth Century – Art Design and Society, London: Longman 1983
Domerham, Adam (Hearne,Thomas), Historia De Rebus Gestis Glastoniensibus, Oxford: 1727
Douglas, D.C. & Myers, A.R. (Eds), English Historical Documents 1327 - 1485, London: Eyre & Spottiswoode 1969
Downing, Sarah Jane, The English Pleasure Garden 1160 – 1860, Oxford: Shire 2011
Dunning, R.W., A History of Somerset, Bridgwater: Somerset County Library 1978
Dyer, Anne, Dyes from Natural Sources, London: Bell 1976
Dyer, Christopher, Everyday Life in Medieval England, London: Hambldon 1994
Dyer, Christopher, A Country Merchant 1495-1520, Oxford: OUP 2014
Edmonds, John, The History of Woad and the Medieval Woad Vat, Historic Dyes Series No 1 2006
Edmonds, John, The History and Practice of Eighteenth Century Dyeing, Little Chalfont : Edmonds 1999
Ellis, Asa The Country Dyer's Assistant Brookfield MA: Merriam 1798: Routledge 1908
Evans, Joan, Life In Medieval France, London: Phaidon 1996
Fauque, Claude, Les mots du textile, Paris: Francais Retrouvé 2013
Farmer, D.L., Two Wiltshire Manors and their Markets, AHR Vol. 37 BAHS 1989
Fella, Thomas, Divers Devices (Facsimile Edition) , Dorchester: Henry Ling 1622 (2012).
Fossier, Robert.(Ed), The Middle Ages 420 – 950, Cambridge:CUP 1997
Fossier, Robert.(Ed), The Middle Ages 950 – 1250, Cambridge: CUP 1997
Fossier, Robert.(Ed), The Middle Ages 1250 – 1520, Cambridge: CUP 1997
Freudenberger, Hermann, The Waldstein Woollen Mill: Noble Entrepreneurship in Eighteenth Century Bohemia, Boston,Mass: Harvard 1963
Gill, Derek and Buckley, John, Willow Vale Frome, Frome: FSLS 2010
Gill, Derek, Frome, Stroud: Alan Sutton 1995
Gill, Derek, The Sheppards and 18th Century Frome, Frome: FSLS 1982
Gill, Derek (Ed), Experiences of a 19th Century Gentleman, Frome: FSLS 2003
Gimpell, Jean, The Medieval Machine, London:Pimlico 1992
Giobert, Traite sur le Pastel, Paris: L'Imprimerie Impériale 1813
GomezSmart http://www.gomezsmart.myzen.co.uk/
Goodall, Rodney, The Industries of Frome, Frome: FSLS 2009
Goodall, Rodney, The Buildings of Frome, Frome:FSLS 2013
Goodwin, Jill, A Dyer's Manual, London: Pelham Books 1982
Grierson, Su, Dyeing and Dyestuffs, Oxford: Shire 1989
Hadfield, Miles, A History of British Gardening, Harmondsworth: Penguin 1985
Haigh, James, The Diers Assistant, Poughkeepsie: Paraclete Potter 1813
Hakluyt, Richard, Principal Navigations, London: Bishop 1552
Hallam, H.E. And Thirsk, Joan, The Agrarian History of England and Wales:, Volume 2, Volumes 1042-1350 Cambridge: CUP 1988
Halsey, Mike and Youngmark, Lore, Foundations of Weaving, David & Charles 1975
Hammond, J.L. And Hammond, Barbara, The Town Labourer, London: Longman 1995
Hare, John, Pensford and the Growth of the Cloth Industry in late Medieval Somerset, SANHS 2004
Harte, N.B. (Ed), Fabrics and Fashions – Studies - the Economic and Social History of Dress, Leeds: Pasold 1991
Harte, N.B. & Ponting, K.G. (Eds) Cloth & clothing in Medieval Europe Essays in Memory of E. Carus-Wilson Manchester: Manchester University Press 1983
Harte, N.B. and Ponting K.G.(Eds), Textile History and Economic History – Essays in Honour of Miss Julia de Lacy Mann Manchester: Manchester University Press 1973
Harvey, J.H., Notes & Queries for Somerset and Dorset XXXI– Templar Holdings in E Somerset, Bridport: 1981
Hearne, Thomas, The History and Antiquities of Glastonbury, Oxford: 1722
Hearne, Thomas, The Works of Thomas Hearne Vol I London: Samuel Bagster 1810
Helm, P.J., England Under the Yorkists and Tudors, London: Bell 1968
Hicks, Michael (Ed), English Inland Trade, Oxford: Oxbow 2015
Hofenk de Graaff, Judith H. et al., The Colourful Past , London: Archetype Publications 2004
Hopkins, David, The Art of the Dyer 1500-1700, Bristol: Stuart 2000
Hurry, Jamieson B., The Woad Plant, Oxford: Kelley 1930
Hurst, Derek, Sheep in the Cotswolds, Stroud: History Press 2014
Jacob, E.F., The Fifteenth Century 1399 - 1485, Oxford: OUP 1961
Jefferies, Richard, The Toilers of the Field (Reprint) London: Heritage 1892(1981)
Kay-Williams, Susan, The Story of Colour in Textiles, London: A.C. Black 2013
Kerridge, Eric, The Agricultural Revolution, Taylor & Francis 2005
Kerridge, Eric, Textile Manufactures in Early Modern England, Manchester: Manchester University Press 1985
Kohler, Eugen Medizinal-Pflanzen in naturgetreuen Abbildungen mit kurz erläuterndem Texte :Gera-Untermhaus :Fr.1883
Lane Powell,E.H., Damerham & Martin, Tisbury: Compton Press 1761
Lawrence, C.H., Medieval Monasticism, London: Longman 1984
Leadbetter, Eliza, Spinning and Spinning Wheels, Oxford:Shire 2009
Leech, Roger, Early Industrial Housing – The Trinity Area of Frome, HMSO 1981
Leland, John, The Itinerary of John Leland the Antiquary: In Nine Vols, London: Thomas Hearne 1770
Lennard, Reginald, Rural England 1086-1135, Oxford: OUP 1997
Lewis, Samuel, A Topographical Dictionary of England, London: Samuel Lewis 1831

Liles, J.N., The Art and Craft of Natural Dyeing, Knoxville: University of Tennessee 2010
Ling Roth, H., Studies in Primitive Looms, Halifax: King 1934
Lipson, E., The Economic History of England Vol 1, London: Black 1945
Lipson, E., The History of the Woollen and Worsted Industries, London: Black 1921
MacCaffrey, Wallace T., Exeter 1540-1640, Cambridge, Mass: Harvard 1975
Mairet, E., A Book on Vegetable Dyes, London HHW 1916
Manchester, William, A World Lit Only by Fire, London: Papermac 1996
Mancell, Peter C., Hakluyt's Promise: An Elizabethan's Obsession for an English America, Yale University Press 2010
de Lacy Mann, Julia (Ed), Wiltshire Textile Trades in the 18th Century, Hereford: WANHS 1964
de Lacy Mann, Julia, The Cloth Industry in the West of England from 1640 to 1880, Oxford: OUP 1971
Mantoux, Paul, The Industrial Revolution in the Eighteenth Century, London: University Press 1961
Mattson, Anne, Indigo in the Early Modern World, University of Minnesota 2008
McGarvie, Michael, The Book of Frome, Frome: FSLS 2013
McGarvie, Michael, Around Frome, Stroud: Chalford Publishing Co 1997
McGarvie, Michael, Argyll House , Frome: FSLS 1979
McGrath, Patrick, John Whitson and the Merchant Community of London, Bristol: BBHA 1970
McKinley, Catherine, Indigo, London: Bloomsbury 2011
Minchinton, Walter, The Port of Bristol in the Eighteenth Century, Bristol: BBHA 1962
Morris, Robert Textiles and Materials of the Common Man and Woman 1480-1580 Bristol: Stuart 2005
Mortimer, Ian, The Time Traveller's Guide to Medieval Britain, London: Vintage 2009
Mortimer, Ian, The Perfect King - the Life of Edward the III, London: Pimlico 2002
Mortimer, Thomas A general Commercial Dictionary: Comprehending Trade, Manufactures ... London: Longman 1819
Napier, James, A Manual of the Art of Dyeing, Glasgow: Richard Griffin & Co 1853
Nash, R.C., South Carolina indigo, European Textiles and the British Atlantic Economy in 18^{th}C, Economic History Review, 63, 2 pp 362-392 2010
Origo, Iris, The Merchant of Prato- Daily Life in a Medieval Italian City, London: Penguin 1992
Oulton, W.C., The Traveller's Guide, London: James Cundell 1805
Palmer, Marilyn and Neaverson, Peter, The Textile Industry of South West England, Stroud: Tempus 2005
Parker, J.H. British phaenogamous botany, Oxford: 1834
Parrish, John, Bath & West of England Society Letters and Papers on Agriculture, Planting, &c. Vol XII 1810
Parkinson, John, Theatrum Botanicum, London: Thos. Cotes 1640
Partridge, William, A Practical Treatise on Dying, New York: Walker (Pasold) 1823(1973)
Pastoureau, Michel, Blue – the History of a Colour, Princeton: Princeton University Press 2001
Payne, Robert, A breefe discription of the true and perfitt makinge of woade, 1568
Peachey, Stuart (Ed), Textiles and Materials of the Common Man and Woman 1580-1660, Bristol: Stuart 2001
Peachey, Stuart (Ed), Dyeing Clothes of the Common People in Elizabethan and Early Stuart England, Bristol: Stuart 2013
Peachey, Stuart & Hopkins, David, Dyeing the Clothing of the Common People 1480 – 1580, Bristol: Stuart 2003
Pelham, R.A., Fulling Mills – A study in the Application of Water Power to the Woollen Industry, Chichester: SPAB 1958
Percy, Sholto, Mechanics Magazine and Journal of Science, Art and Manufactures Vol 47, 1847
Pinkerton, John, A General Collection Of The Best And Most Interesting Voyages And Travels In All Parts Of The World Vol2, London: Longman 1808
Plowright, Charles, On the Archaeology of Woad The Journal of the Archaeological Association 1903
Ponting, K.G., Wool & Water, Bradford-on-Avon: Moonraker Press 1975
Ponting, K.G., The Woollen Industry of South West England, Bath: Adams & Dart 1971
Ponting, K.G., The Structure of the Wiltshire-Somerset Border Woollen Industry 1816 – 40, Harte, N.B. Ponting, K.G. Textile History and Economic History Manchester 1973
Ponting, K.G., Sheep of the World in Colour, Poole: Sackville Press 1980
Ponting, K.G., A Dictionary of Dyes and Dyeing, London: Bell Hyman 1980
Ponting, K.G., The West of England Cloth Industry, London: MacDonald 1957
Ponting, K.G., Logwood an Interesting Dye, JEEH 2:1 (Spring 1973)
Pope, Charles, A Practical Abridgement Of The Custom And Excise Laws, Relative To The Import, Export, And Coasting Trade, London: Robert Baldwin 1814
Postan, M.M., The Medieval Economy and Society, London: Pelican 1978
Power, E.., A Textile Community in the Industrial Revolution, London: Longman 1969
Press, Jonathan, The Merchant Seamen of Bristol 1747 – 1789, Bristol: BBHA 1976
Pressnell, L.G. (Ed), Studies in the Industrial Revolution, London: The Athlone Press 1960
Pryor, Francis, Britain in the Middle Ages, London: Harper 2006
Rabah, Saoud The Muslim Carpet: 2004
Ramsay, G.D., The Wiltshire Woollen Industry In The Sixteenth Century, London: Cass 1965
Rack, E. & Collinson J., The History and Antiquities of the County of Somerset, Bath: Crutwell 1791
Randall, Adrian, Before the Luddites, Cambridge: CUP 1991
Raymond, Stuart A., My Ancestor was an Apprentice, London: SGE 2010
Riding, Jacqueline, Mid-Georgian Britain, Oxford: Shire 2010
Ridley, Jasper, A Brief History of the Tudor Age, London: Robinson 2002
Roach, John, Social Reform in England – 1780-1880 London: Batsford 1978
Robinson, Stuart, A History of Dyed Textiles, London: Studio Vista 1969
Rogers, Ken, Warp and Weft, Buckingham: Barracuda 1986
Rogers, Ken, Wiltshire & Somerset Woollen Mills, Edington: Pasold 1976
Rowse, A.L., The England of Elizabeth,London: Papermac 1981
Sandon, Michael and Styles, John, Design & Decorative Arts – Tudor and Stuart Britain 1500 – 1714, London: V&A 2004
SANHS, Somerset Archaeology and Natural History Society Vols 133, 134, 141, 143, 144, 151
Saoud, Dr Rabah, The Muslim Carpet and the Origin of Carpeting, Manchester: FSTC 2004
Sawyer, P.H., From Roman Britain to Norman England, London: University Press 1978

Scott Thomson, G., Wool Merchants of the Fifteenth Century, London: Longman 1958
Seymour, Robert, A Survey of the Cities Of London and Westminster, London: J. Read 1735
Sherborne, J.W., The Port of Bristol in the Middle Ages, Bristol: BBHA 1965
Sholto, Percy Mechanics Magazine and Journal of Science, Art and Manufacture, London: 1847
Shorrocks, Derek (Ed), Visitation 1594 and Smalle Booke 1593-1595, SANHS
Smith, John, The Memoirs of Wool (2 Vols – Facsimile), London: Gregg 1747(1968)
Smythe, John (transcript Angus, J.), The Ledger of John Smythe, Bristol: BRS
Snodin, Michael and Styles, John, Design and the Decorative Arts Tudor and Stuart Britain 1500-1714, London: V&A Publications 2004
Stevens, C.B., Colour in Wool Fabrics, London: IWS 1957
Storey, Joyce, Dyes and Fabric, London: Thames & Hudson 1985
Stow, John, Survey of London London: 1603
Stuart, Denis, Manorial Records, Chichester: Phillimore 1992
Styles, John, Threads of Feeling – the London Foundling Hospital's Textile Tokens 1740-1770, London:London Foundling Museum 201
Styles, John, The Dress of the People, New Haven: Yale 2010
Styles, John, Spinners and the Law, Textile History Vol 44
Sutton, Denys, Westwood Manor, 1962
Swift, Katherine, The Morville Hours, London: Bloomsbury 2008
Tann, Jennifer, Gloucestershire Woollen Mills, Newton Abbott: David & Charles 1967
Tann, Jennifer, Wool & Water, Stroud: The History Press 2012
Tenen, I., This England 1485 – 1714, London: MacMillan 1962
The Lowell Offering, Mind amongst the Spindles, London: Charles Knight 1844
Thirsk, Joan, Alternative Agriculture, Oxford: OUP 1997
Thirsk, Joan (Ed), The Agrarian History of England and Wales: Vol 4, Cambridge: CUP 1985
Thompson, Daniel V., Materials and Techniques of Medieval Painting, New York: Dover 1956
Thrupp, Sylvia L., The Merchant Class of Medieval London, Michigan; The University of Michigan Press 1989
Thurstan, Violetta, The Use of Vegetable Dyes, Leicester: Dryad 1939
Trevelyan, G.M., English Social History, London:The Reprint Society 1948
Trowell, Samuel, A new treatise of Husbandry ..., London: James Hodges 1739
Tucker, Josiah, Instructions for Travellers, Dublin: William Watson 1758
Tucker,William, The Family Dyer and Scourer, London: Sherwood, Neely, and Jones 1818
Underdown, David, Somerset in the Civil War and Interregnum,Newton Abbott: David & Charles 1973
Ure, Andrew, A Dictionary of Arts, Manufacture & Mines, London: 1840
Ure, Andrew, The Philosophy of Manufactures, London:Charles Knight 1835
Van Houtte, J.A., An Economic History of the Low Countries, London: Weidenfeld & Nicholson 1977
Vanes, Jean, The Overseas Trade of Bristol, Bristol: BRS 1979
Vanes, Jean, The Port of Bristol in the Sixteenth Century, Bristol: BBHA 1977
Walker, David, Bristol in the Early Middle Ages, Bristol: BBHA 1971
Warner, Richard, The Topographical Works: Excursions from Bath, Bath: 1802
Weaver, F.W., Somerset Medieval Wills, SANHS 1905
Welsford, A.E. , John Greenaway 1460-1529, Tiverton: Longman 1984
West, John, Village Records, Chichester: Phillimore 1982
Weston, R., Tracts on Practical Agriculture and Gardening, London: S. Hooper 1773
Westerfield, Ray Bert, Middlemen in English Business, New Haven: Yale University Press 1915
White, Richard and McGarvie, Michael (Eds), Memoirs of a Victorian Farmer, Frome:FSLS 1990
Willett-Cunnington, C. And Cunnington, Phillis Handbook of English Costume in the Eighteenth Century, London: Faber & Faber 1964
Wills, Norman T., Woad in the Fens, Boston, Lincs: Ruskin 1979
Wilson, Charles, England's Apprenticeship 1603-1763, London: Longman 1966
Wingate, Edmund, An Exact Abridgement of all statutes in Force and use until 22nd of November in the Third Year of King James II, London 1687
Wood, Andy, The 1549 Rebellions and the Making of Early Modern England, Cambridge: CUP 2007
Wood, Margaret, The English Medieval House London: Studio Editions 1994
Wood, Michael, Domesday – A Search for the Roots of England, London: BBC 1986
Woods, William, England in the Age of Chaucer, St Albans: bca 1976
Wool Knowledge (Ed), Centuries of Achievement in Wool, London: Wool Knowledge
Worlidge, John, A Compleat System Of Husbandry and Gardening, London: J. Pickard 1716
Worst, Edward F., Dyes and Dyeing, California 1970
Young, Arthur, General View of the Agriculture of Lincolnshire London: Sherwood, Neely, and Jones 1813

~ Handlooms and Cloth Halls – Domestic Cloth Making in the South Pennines before 1780 Halifax: Pennine Heritage Network 1982
~ The Draper & Clothier London: Houlston & Wright 1860
~ A Narrative of a Tour into the West Country London: John Offor 1823(1973)
~ The Statutes at Large from the Third Year of the Reign of King George the Second ... Vol6 London: Mark Basket 1764
~ Encyclopedia Or, a Dictionary of Arts, Sciences, And Miscellaneous Literature Philadelphia: Thomas Dobson 1798
~ The Whole Art of Dying London: Pearson 1705
~ Frome Society Year Book Frome: FSLS
~ History of Froome Selwood with Notes on Neighbouring Villages Cuzner 1866
~ Dictionarium Rusticum London: 1726
~ The Statutes at Large from Magna Carta to the End of the reign of Henry the Sixth London: Mark Basket 1763
~ Letters and Papers on Agriculture, Planting &c. Bath: Bath & West Of England Society 1810
Pamphlet - Silk of Lyons
Pamphlet - The George Inn Norton St Philip Devizes Wadworth 1999
Pamphlet - The Worshipful Company of Weavers

ILLUSTRATION & PHOTO CREDITS

Bath In Time	Cover Image © Bath Central Library
TNA	Back Cover Image **C 104/221**
Chapter 1	
Enking, Leonora	8 © L. Enking
Frome Museum	3 © Frome Museum
HRO	13 - Jervoise of Herriard Collection
44M69/L30/76	
Lumsden, Anne Mieke	1 © A. M. Lumsden
SHC	15 - **DD\X\WS/5**, 16 - **DD\SAS/C909/32**
Stean, Jon	2, 4-6, 7 public domain, 9-12, 14 © J Stean
Chapter 2	
Frome Botanical Artists	4 - © Lynfa Cameron
Glastonbury Abbey	2 www.glastonburyabbey.com
Griffiths, Frantzine	14 © F. Griffiths
Stean, Jon	1,3, 5-13 © J. Stean
WSA	15 - **865/558**
Chapter 3	
Bath In Time	4-15, 19-33 © Bath Central Library
Frome Museum	3 © Frome Museum
SHC	17 - **DD\X\MSL/7**
SANHS	16 - **DD\SAS/C909/32**,
Stean, Jon	1, 2, 18 © J. Stean
Chapter 4	
Stean, Jon	2, 4 © J. Stean
TNA	1, 3, 5-29 - **C104/3**
Chapter 5	
Belham, Peter	2 © G. Hawkings
Frome Museum	9, 10, 13, © Frome Museum
FSLS	7, 15, 16 © FSLS
SANHS	3 - **DD\SAS\C795/FR/32**
SHC	8 - **DD\LW/4**, 11 - **MAP\DD\X/FMM**, 12 - **DD\X\MSL/7**, 17 - **A\CFH/4/2/155**
Somerset Rivers	14 (Telisford Mill) © Somerset Rivers
Stean, Jon	1, 4-7, 14 © J. Stean
Chapter 6	
Buckley, John	5, 11 (Photos), 14 © J. Buckley
Frome Museum	2, 3, 11 (Map), 12, 15, © Frome Museum
Hedges, John	1© J. Hedges
Stean, Jon	4, 13, 16 © J. Stean
Undated postcard	12 with kind permission Lenny
WSA	10 - **628/16/14**
TNA	6-9 - **C 104/221**
Chapter 7	
John Bright Collection	8, 9 www.thejohnbrightcollection.co.uk Property of Cosprop (London, UK) Project funded by the Heritage Lottery www.hlf.org.uk/our-projects/john-bright-historic-costume-collection-revealed
Frome Museum	4, 6, 7, 10-12 © Frome Museum
SHC	1, 16 - **D\P\fr.jo/13/1/1**, 19 - **DD\LW/7**, 20 - **D\P\fr.jo/13/1/1** , 21 - **DD\LW\7**
Stean, Jon	3, 5, 12, 17, 18 © J. Stean
TNA	2 - **Prob 11/91/271**, 13, 14, 15 - **C 104/221**
Chapter 8	
BHL	4 - British Phaenogamous Botany,
Frome Museum	16 © Frome Museum
SANHS	15 - **DD\SAS/C909/32**
Stean, Jon	2, 3, 7, 8, 11, 12, 13, 14 © J Stean
Stean, Jon	5 with kind permission St George's church, Beckington
Chapter 8 (Cont)	
TNA	1, 10 - **PC1/37/111**
Wellcome Images	6 (CC- creativecommons.org/licenses/by/4.0/)
Alex Madden	9 © A. Madden
Chapter 9	
SHC	5 - **DD\LW/4**, 6 - **D\P\fr.jo/13/1/1**
Stean, Jon	1-4, 7-9, 11 © J. Stean
Stean, Jon	11 with kind permission Warren Jones
TNA	10 - **C 104/221**
Watson, Julian	12, 13 © J Watson
Chapter 10	
Frome Museum	7, 15 © Frome Museum
SANHS	1, 2, 17 - **DD\SAS/S416/7**
SHC	6 - **Q/SR/28015**, 12 - **DD\X\MSL/7**
Stean, Jon	4, 5, 13, 14, 16 © J. Stean
Stean, Jon	3, 8 - 11 with kind permission Philip Butler Helmshore Mill
Chapter 11	
Bishop, Mike	2 © M. C. Bishop
British Library	9 public domain British Library's Collection
The Clothworkers' Company	3, 4 © The Clothworkers' Company
SHC	1 - **Q/SR/313/11-12**
Stean, Jon	6 - 8 © J. Stean
Bradford on Avon	5
Chapter 12	
Frome Museum	2, 13 © Frome Museum
Pitt-Rivers Museum	1 © Pitt-Rivers Museum
SANHS	3 - **DD\SAS/C795/FR/2**
Stean, Jon	4-7, 9 © J. Stean 11- samples supplied by A W Hainsworth
Stean, Jon	8, 10 with kind permission St George's church, Beckington
Stean, Jon	11 with kind permission Emily Azis
TNA	14 - **Prob 11/75/403**
WSA	12 - **212B/7463**
Chapter 13	
Pitt-Rivers Museum	4 © Pitt-Rivers Museum
SANHS	10 **DD\SAS/S416/7**, 9 **DD\SAS/S2062**
SHC	2 - **Q/SR/43/165**
Stean, Jon	1, 3, 6-8, 11 © J. Stean
TNA	5 - **C 104/221**
Chapter 14	
SHC	1 - 3 - **DD\X\MSL/7**
Chapter 15	
Frome Museum	1, 6, 10 © Frome Museum
SHC	9 **D\P\bec/23/4**
Stean, Jon	2-5, 7 © J. Stean 11- samples supplied by A W Hainsworth
WSA	8 - **628/16/9**

Abbreviations

BHL	Bio Diversity Heritage Library
HRO	Hampshire Record Office
SANHS	Somerset Archaelogical and Natural History Society
SHC	Somerset Heritage Centre
TNA	The National Archives
WSA	Wiltshire and Swindon Archives

GLOSSARY

Abb	Synonym for Weft and /or rough wool from the inferior parts of the fleece
Agranat	French term for couched woad (see couching below)
Alum	Potassium Aluminium Sulphate used as a mordant
Aulnage, aulnager	The official supervision of the taxation and quality of woollen cloth
Barwood	Tree from Central West Africa which produces a fugitive red dye
Batt	Sample of wool taken from the dye batch to show the initial colour
Bays (baize)	A coarse felt-like woollen material
Bottoming	Dyeing with a base colour (see ground)
Bray , braying	Process used for cleansing cloth after dyeing
Brazil, brazill	Wood from Brazil that yields a red dye
Broadcloth	Dense plain woven cloth made of wool, heavily fulled, hard wearing and weather-resistant
Brogger	Middleman who bought and sold wool from the small producers
Burler, burling	To remove knots, knibs, linnets & spiles from woven cloth
Camlets	An imitation of a camel hair woven cloth
Camwood	See Barwood
Carders, carding	A process that disentangles, cleans and mixes the fibres before spinning
Cassimere	A worsted wool cloth made of a twill weave
Chain	Standard bundles of warp yarns
Chalon loom	Medieval two beam vertical loom used by makers of hangings, rugs, and coverlets
Chipped	Preparation of the dyewoods by rasping or in the grinding mill
Cloth Assize	Standard measurements for cloth set by statute
Cochineal	A crimson dye made from the bodies of scale insects found in Central and South America
Combing	The process of preparing fibre for spinning (see carding)
Compting house	Place where a firm carries out its accounting operations
Copperas	Ferrous Sulphate - it is a reducing agent also known as green vitriol
Cropp Mather	Grade of madder usually the best probably from the Dutch - Krappe madder
Couching	Controlling fermentation process of wetting and turning dried woad balls to extract indigo pre cursors
Drug house	A separate store for the dye materials ensuring that these are kept away from damp and other causes of decay
Dyed in the say	Where cloth is dyed as it is cut from the loom before being fulled
Dyed in the wool	Where wool is dyed before being spun into yarn
Dyewoods	A wood from which colouring matter is extracted for dyeing
Factor	A person who receives and sells goods on commission. The factors in Blackwell Hall were agents who charged a fee to handle the cloth trade
Fast	A dyed object that will not lose its colour in light or by washing
Fell, fellmonger	Dealer in sheepskins
Fermentation process	Mixing proportions of ingredients to produce bacterial activity
Flannels	A cloth made using short staple carded wool
Florry	When ready to work, the surface of a blue vat has oxidised indigo pigment referred to as 'florry'
Fugitive	Term used to describe dyes that are not colourfast or are prone to fading
Fulling	Process that cleans a cloth by eliminating oils and size and shrinks it to a thick felted cloth
Fustick (fustic)	A bright yellow dye that is very colourfast when used with mordants. Old Fustic comes from Maclura Tinctoria found in Southern and Central America. Young Fustic comes from Rhus Cotinus found in Southern Europe and Asia
Grain	See kermes
Green vitriol	See copperas
Grist mill	A mill that grinds grain into flour
Ground	Ground is a base of blue before overdyeing with another colour (see bottoming)
Heartwoods	Core of a tree that may contain dyestuffs
Heddles	Part of a loom which separates the warp threads for the passage of the weft thread
Hogaster	A young sheep between 9 and 18 months
Indigofera	Indigofera is a large genus of over 750 species of flowering plants belonging to the family Fabaceae. They are widely distributed throughout the tropical and subtropical regions of the world
Journeyman	Day labourer from the French for day rate,
Kermes	A red/scarlet dye produced from the dried bodies of female scale insects found in Europe (see grain)
Kersey	A type of cloth woven on a narrow loom
Kersey loom	Narrow horizontal loom
Leys	Growing of crops and grass in rotation
Liberty	A district within a county - may cover multiple parishes
Logwood	Species of flowering tree native to Mexico and Northern Central America also known as peachwood or campeachey. Produces a fast black when used with copperas

Madder, Mather	Red dye made from the root of the plant Rubia Tinctoria
Manorial demesnes	The portion of land allocated to a feudal landlord for his own use
Manufactory	A place of manufacture noting that the size of early manufactories could be little more than an outbuilding
Medley	Cloth made of wool dyed and blended before being spun
Meltons	Fulled cloth made of wool woven in a twill pattern
Mordant	Substance used to set dyes also called a dye fixative
Mull Mather	Lower grade of madder
New draperies	Light weight worsted material introduced in the 16th century
Noils	The short fibre left over from combing wool
Oil	This was generally olive oil (aka Gallipoli oil) that was used to make scribbling wool easier to work
Overcoatings	A heavy outerwear cloth
Peachwood	See logwood
Perpetuanas	Durable wool serge cloth
Piepowder	Medieval Court that sat during Public Markets or Fairs to resolve disputes
Pirn	A weavers bobbin
Domesday Plough	The taxable amount of land that can be ploughed by a team of eight oxen
Pressers	After shearing, the cloth was passed to pressers to finish the cloth using heated plates
Protein fibres	Fibres obtained from animals and insects
Provisioniato	Italian word for a supplier or supplying agent
Raising the nap	Process whereby the surface of a cloth was brushed using fullers' teasels to enable the cloth to be sheared
Reducing agent	A reducing agent is an element or compound that loses an electron to another chemical in a redox chemical reaction. Since the reducing agent is losing electrons, it is said to have been oxidized.
Rolag	A prepared roll of fibre used to spin woollen yarn
Sadden	To dull a colour
Sanderswood, Sandalwood	A hard wood tree that is used to produce a red dye
Sarplers	A quantity of wool defined as 80 tod where a tod is 28lbs
Scouring	The washing of wool with soap or stale urine (Sig)
Scribbling	A process that opens the locks of fleece and blends colours before carding
Selvedge	Self finished edge or list of a fabric that keeps the edges from fraying
Shearing cloth	Skilled process that uses a heavy (30lbs), large set of shears to cut the surface of the cloth
Shed	Raising and lowering a set of warp threads In order to pass through a shuttle wound with the weft threads
Shumach, sumach	A red-purple dyestuff derived from the bark of plants of the genus Rhus
Sig, sigg	Urine left to age to release ammonia used in the weaving and dyeing industries
Size	Weak solution of glue used to strengthen the warp threads
Sorter, sorting	The quality of each fleece varies. The sorter or picker assesses the quality separates it into different classes
Spanish	A type of cloth made from Spanish wool mixed with other wool
Stapler	Large scale wool merchant appointed by royal authority as part of a licensed monopoly
Stuffs	A type of coarse thickly woven cloth - originally all wool, later wool and linen
Suitings	A length of cloth suitable for a set of men's clothing or women's riding habit
Sumptuary Laws	Laws made for the purpose of restraining luxury or extravagance, particularly against inordinate expenditures in the matter of apparel, food, furniture, etc.
Tare	Allowance for canvas packaging when a sack of wool is weighed and transported
Tentering, tenterhooks	Lengths of wet cloth would be hooked on nails to a rail and stretched while drying
Thrums	Short pieces of waste warp yarn left over from the weaving process
Tucking	See fulling
Vat	An indigo or purple dye extraction process. A vessel for containing a dye liquor
Venturers	A group of entrepreneurs who came together to undertake or underwrite risky or hazardous business projects
Warp	The set of lengthwise threads of a cloth (see chain)
Watchet	A variant of blue used in the description of the colour of cloth
Weft	The thread or threads drawn through the warp (see abb)
Wether	Castrated male sheep
Wets	Bundles of wet wool (240lbs when dry)
Woadwaxen	Also known as dyer's greenweed, a plant that yields a yellow dye
Woaded	Wool dyed with a blue ground

INDEX

C

D

E

F

G

H

M

N

O

P

Q

R

S

T

U

V

Y

Z